FOOD ARTISANS
OF
ALBERTA

YOUR TRAIL GUIDE OF OUR LOCALLY
TO THE BEST   CRAFTED FARE

KAREN ANDERSON &
MATILDE SANCHEZ-TURRI

TOUCHWOOD EDITIONS

Edited by Kate Kennedy
Designed by Colin Parks
Cover images: Neil Zeller (top); Edmonton Tourism (lower left); Karen Anderson (centre and lower right)
Photograph, pages 2–3: Photo by Paul Zizka, courtesy of Banff Lake Louise Tourism

LIBRARY AND ARCHIVES CANADA CATALOGUING IN PUBLICATION

Anderson, Karen (Karen Joy), author

Food artisans of Alberta : your trail guide to the best of our locally crafted fare / Karen Anderson, Matilde Sanchez-Turri.

Includes index.

Issued in print and electronic formats.

ISBN 9781771512466 (softcover).

1. Local foods, Alberta. 2. Food industry and trade, Alberta. I. Sanchez, Turri, Matilde, author II. Title.

TX360.C32A5 2018   641.30097123   C2017-906559-9   C2017-906560-2

We acknowledge the financial support of the Government of Canada through the Canada Book Fund, and the province of British Columbia through the Book Publishing Tax Credit.

Canadä

The interior pages of this book have been printed on 100% post-consumer recycled paper, processed chlorine free, and printed with vegetable-based inks.

Printed in Canada at Friesens

22 21 20 19 18   1 2 3 4 5

For the generous, fiercely intelligent, and
selfless souls we encountered in our travels
through Alberta's food community

CONTENTS

INTRODUCTION

When it comes to experiencing all our province has to offer, our friends at Travel Alberta adopted the tag line "Remember to Breathe." It speaks to the inherent beauty of this naturally endowed place and how gobsmacked we all are when we have the chance to stop and take it all in.

Alberta's terrain starts as solid rock at the peaks of the Rockies and softens into hills and windswept prairie grasslands with hoodoos and coulees distinguishing the Badlands in the east. Stunning by day, Alberta's northern dark sky preserves shimmer and bounce with the cosmic magnificence of the aurora borealis. In the south, the deep black velvet of the night invites us into the Milky Way's starry embrace.

Mighty rivers like the Athabasca and Peace, the North and South Saskatchewan, the Oldman, the Bow, the Slave, and the Milk run to the Arctic, to Hudson Bay and to the Gulf of Mexico from our pristine glacier-fed lakes. There are five national parks and over 250 provincial parks that protect our wildlife and conserve the otherwise quickly diminishing wilderness on earth.

We've only just started to honour and access the wisdom of the Aboriginal people of Treaties Six, Seven, and Eight—in truth and reconciliation. Their cultures hold the inherent knowledge it took to thrive here for tens of thousands of years as the first people. Those of the subarctic lived on boreal foraged plants, moose, and caribou through all seasons, along with ice fishing in the winters. The people of the Great Plains were one with the bison, which they called their "staff of life." In the central aspen-filled parklands, the people hunted and foraged. From Aboriginal people to homesteaders and immigrants from the world over, the food of today's Alberta is emerging as one of the world's most authentic tastes of place.

As food lovers, our motto is "Remember to eat." It's a tongue-in-cheek nod to our friends in tourism. Joking aside, our focus reflects an emerging sector called food travel. Food and travel are as inseparable as food and existence. We like the World Food Travel Association's inclusive definition of a food traveller as "someone who would travel across town or around the globe to try something new." If you are holding this book, you are most likely one of us.

Because food is so primal and travelling in our province is so enjoyable, we want to help you find food that's authentically Albertan so that, whether you live here or are just visiting, you'll be able to enjoy great taste memories. We know our food will reinforce the imprint of this place and transform your experience here. We also want you to connect with and support the people who grow Alberta's food consciously, ethically, and with a level of skill and care that is uniquely theirs.

That's why we were willing to tackle this book.

Matilde and I started building and leading daylong adventures and delicious farm tours with our mentor and chef friend, dee Hobsbawn-Smith, back in the late '90s. We worked with Calgary's *City Palate* magazine to take busloads of people on "Foodie Tootles" through Southern Alberta. We did it so that city folk could meet farm folk and understand what it takes to grow food in this province. There were always epiphanies for our guests.

Making connections always matters. The simple act of meeting together in a field to hear stories of the challenges farmers face and the fortitude it takes to overcome them is transformative. Making meals of the food we gathered along a tasting trail of three to four farms in a day renewed our fellow city dwellers' commitment to eat differently.

When we ran the Tootles, they typically sold out within moments of being announced; there was nothing else like them. Now, there are over 100 farms you can visit on Alberta Open Farm Days each August and dozens of long-table feasts held in the fertile black fields of our farmlands throughout the growing season.

In a way, this book feels like a snapshot of what amounted to our biggest Foodie Tootle ever. Matilde and I divided to conquer the province in the summer of 2017. Matilde mainly covered Calgary and the south. I mainly tackled everything north of Calgary.

Alberta is 661,848 square kilometres. It's roughly the size of Texas— or France, Belgium, and the Netherlands all together. We learned so much about our homeland and are excited to share it with you.

The land in Southern Alberta is dry prairie in the east. It's part of an area known as Palliser's Triangle. In the mid-1800s, surveyor John Palliser looked at the land and declared it a semi-arid steppe unsuitable for agriculture. Later, it was found to be suitable for growing wheat. Today, it is extensively irrigated and productive in certain regions with a high concentration of commercial greenhouses producing vegetable crops mainly for domestic consumption.

Central Alberta's topography varies greatly. There are native prairie grasslands in the designated "Special Areas." These areas were literally dust bowls in the drought of the 1930s. Parkland regions of the lower boreal forest pop up throughout the area.

Once you are north of Edmonton, the land alternates between prairie and boreal forests of mixed black and white spruce, aspens, poplars, white birch, and lodgepole pine. Lakes, swamps, and sloughs left behind by glaciers connect like dots in between. The west of the province rises through foothills to those tireless guardians we call the Rockies all along the border we share with British Columbia.

Alberta has a greatly varied landscape, but when we poll people as to what is the food that comes from this place, the response is unanimous: beef is the refrain most commonly heard. It's true, Alberta is famous for its beef, but this book will take you beyond beef to discover a more complete bounty of the food offerings available here.

In 2015, the Alberta Culinary Tourism Alliance (ACTA), in conjunction with Cook It Raw, named beef, bison, canola, honey, Red Fife wheat, root vegetables, and saskatoon berries as Alberta's seven signature foods. With the global influences of our diverse population, you'll be surprised how these ingredients are transformed and how our cuisine continues to evolve. This book will broaden the work of our friends at ACTA, and continue the conversation they began in defining the unique culinary offerings within our province.

Still, going back to that beef, you'll never hear any Albertan dis it. We're very proud that Alberta beef really does taste better than any other in the world. A "steak out" here can involve slicing into the salty lemon gremolata of a Bistecca alla Fiorentina or letting the juices of a classic flame-broiled Triple-A Angus dribble off your lips while sipping a delectable wine or craft beer with it.

We savour the tenderness that comes from the difference in marbling achieved with barley- or grass-finished animals and we have the opportunity to learn at a taste-bud level the difference 28 days of dry or wet aging can make. Ranchers like Trail's End Beef's Rachel and Tyler Herbert (see page 284) in Nanton are steering away from industrial feedlot beef, leaving their cattle to graze the grasslands on their sprawling ranch from birth to plate. Rachel's great-grandfather was one of Alberta's original cowboys in a time before there were fences and she's ranching much like he did 150 years ago.

While Alberta's beef is beyond belief, we'd like you to savour the rest of our story too. A 2017 *New York Times* article cited recent archeological research from the University of Alberta confirming bison have roamed Alberta for 120,000 years. They represent the indigenous taste of Alberta along with elk and deer. These native species are recognized for their health benefits for humans and the wildlife and grasses they help regenerate when left to roam the land. They are a keystone conservation species and are regaining their primacy in the Alberta food landscape.

Canola was naturally selected here to become a flavourful and healthy cooking oil. Alberta is the world's fifth-largest honey producer with over 40 million pounds of honey harvested annually. Red Fife wheat was first grown in Ontario and was distributed across Canada. It proved vital in sustaining our pioneers because it was one of the first varieties of wheat that would grow here. Root vegetables are sweeter here because sugars are formed in the roots during our cool nights. Saskatoon berries are indigenous and, along with the bison, were a key source of food for Aboriginal people. They are still a perennial favourite for people of the Prairies.

Rocky Mountain and Prairie regional cuisines that celebrate our local signature foods have slowly gained prominence over the last 25 years. The chef community here has depth, character, and a spirit for collaboration. Organizations like Slow Food International have forged bonds between chefs and farmers to ensure the sustainability of local ingredients and their producers.

There are dozens of year-round farmers' markets around Alberta and while rural farmers' numbers are on the decline, the urban agriculture revolution has arrived with Small Plot INtensive (SPIN) farmers making a living growing food on borrowed patches in people's backyards throughout our cities. A group called YYC Growers and Distributors have joined with their rural colleagues to collaboratively market their farms in a food hub consortium.

The Red Fife wheat that kept early pioneers alive has made a comeback along with other heritage varietals. Our wheat is used in crazy-good bakeries that take days to make sourdough breads, use only real butter and organic flours, and still crack every egg by hand.

Our plentiful grains are also used in craft beer making and the distillation of fine spirits, like those of Eau Claire Distillery (see page 254), which is putting tiny Turner Valley on the map. Along with honey meaderies and fruit wineries, there are many lively watering holes to quench a food traveller's thirst. We think Alberta will become a beer and spirits tourism destination, just like the Okanagan and Niagara are for wines.

Albertans also have a fondness for the exotic. Calgary's Choklat (see page 179) and Edmonton's Jacek Chocolate (see page 72) are two of only a handful of bean-to-bar chocolate makers in the country. Alberta has percolated oodles of third-wave coffee houses with baristas hand pouring coffee like born-again Seattleites. Phil & Sebastian Coffee

Roasters (see page 154) are leading a fourth wave of single-origin coffee roasters who are partners in and microfinanciers of boutique coffee farms throughout the coffee-growing regions of the world. They recently bought their own coffee plantation as well.

While Alberta is an outdoor enthusiast's paradise, two-thirds of travellers choose their destination based on the food offerings and events they'll enjoy when they arrive. As fellow food travellers, we welcome you. We wrote this book to help you explore Alberta's culinary landscape and give you an authentic taste of Alberta, no matter where your adventures take you in the province. We're excited to introduce you to the people who are shaping the future of our food system and are making our culinary scene another great reason to visit our province.

HOW THIS BOOK IS ORGANIZED

After driving Alberta from Peace Country in the north to the International Peace Park near Waterton in the south—and everywhere in between—we can tell you there's a lot of ground to cover. We've divided the province into six sections, very similar to what our colleagues in tourism do, so that you can use this book as a companion to their publications to plan your food travel.

Each area—Northern, Edmonton, Central, Calgary, the Rockies and Southern Alberta—has unique flavours for you to discover.

The Northern section of the book is pretty much anything north of Edmonton. Driving across Peace River Country in the summer, it feels like your car is a ship lost in a sea of golden canola fields. But a few hours straight north of Edmonton, and you are on the cusp of the northern boreal forest. Here, the people enjoy storied rivers like the mighty Athabasca and large lakes like Lesser Slave and Lac La Biche. Cold Lake and the northeast Lakeland region is filled with rolling hills and dells that reveal the province's francophone history in towns like St. Paul and its Ukrainian heritage in Vegreville.

Edmonton is the provincial capital and a city of festivals. A deep river valley divides it north and south, and fertile farms fight for a future within its boundaries. Cultures mix and young chefs reclaim and celebrate their food heritages while also championing our farmers.

Central Alberta is everything between Edmonton and Calgary—for the purposes of this book. This is the historic and still most plentiful growing area in the province, and that is reflected in the sheer number of artisans in this section of the book. A four-lane highway known as the QE2 divides it east and west. The shelterbelts of trees that line the route are treasured legacies that keep farmhouses from being deluged with dust and snow. So much dust rolled through the semi-arid Special Areas of East Central Alberta during the Great Depression of the '30s, there are still sand dunes in some pockets of land here.

Calgary's skyline defines its downtown core but a necklace of livable, walkable, food-centric neighbourhoods surrounds it. Each has its own vibe, from party-central 17 Avenue in the Southwest to historic Inglewood in the Southeast, groovy Kensington in the Northwest and re-emerging Bridgeland in the Northeast. With each bust of the oil and gas markets, the maverick entrepreneurial spirit rises and the city diversifies a little more—bracing and recovering—as it always does.

The Rockies tower to the west—beacons of tourism that pull 5 million visitors each year to the Bow River Valley that carves its way through them. Chefs from the world over have come to work here and never left. Backcountry hiking and skiing, world-class downhill ski resorts, fishing and floating on rivers—this is a playground for humans and a refuge for wildlife.

Southern Alberta's Crowsnest Pass Highway meanders from the mining towns of Coleman and Blairmore to Lethbridge. The latter has a history of World War Two Japanese internment camps but now celebrates that culture with the Nikka Yuko Japanese Garden— one of Canada's top 10 garden attractions. Irrigation and long, hot summers make this a prime food-growing region for Alberta, and from Lethbridge to Medicine Hat, the area is dotted with hothouses. Locals here forage for rare pincushion cactus berries along with the common saskatoon berries. Looping back to Calgary, you'll pass through parks filled with fossils and the Badlands filled with hoodoos and coulees.

In each section of this book, foodstuffs and where to find them will be arranged in alphabetical order with artisan products; baked goods, tea, and coffee; lists of farmers' markets; foraged foods; fruits and vegetables; grains, seeds, and pulses; meat, poultry, and pork; and cooking schools and specialty foods all highlighted. You'll find eateries featured in association with chefs and restaurateurs. Many of our favourite watering holes are featured and they include fruit wine makers, meaderies, distilleries, and breweries.

ALBERTA'S TERROIR

What is the terroir or the taste of this place? As a very young province in a very young country, we're still working that out. We've got some clues and are starting to pay attention to how the land expresses its characteristics in the taste of the drinks and food grown here. We're paying even more attention to the wild foods nature shares in abundance. Those foods represent our real terroir. We don't have many answers just yet. Mostly, we've got a long list of questions, but we are excited by the possibilities and the quality harvested by the explorers on this path.

The time is right for the culinary knowledge of Aboriginal people to be recognized beyond bannock, pemmican, saskatoon berries, and bison. Preservation of the wood and plains bison will be crucial. Letting them feed strictly on the native grasslands they help preserve certainly provides a distinct flavour and taste of the land. Growers who try to rush them by feeding them grains are missing the point of the meat's true flavour and health benefits.

Though honeybees are not indigenous to Alberta, they—mostly—thrive here. We can see the development of honey sommeliers who are versed in the difference in tastes of honey from bees foraging on nectar and pollen close to a fireweed or buckwheat patch versus those foraging on clover or alfalfa. Pairing honey with beverages and food will soon be a thing.

We know our root vegetables taste sweeter because of our soils and climate. Can we also taste a difference between corn varietals grown in Taber versus the Kohut corn grown in Didsbury? These are fun things for our taste buds to explore.

Another facet to explore is the foods grown here because of immigrant influxes. From the former Chinese railway workers to early Ukrainians, Eastern Europeans, Scandinavians, and Hutterites to the interned Japanese and post–World War Two Italians to the '70s influxes of East African Ismaili Muslims to today's Pakistani and Punjabi Indians, Syrian refugees, Vietnamese, and Filipinos—each group adds to the diversity of our collective cuisine as they add to our population.

We are also fascinated with the terroir of our grains as they are expressed in glasses of craft beer and fine distillation spirits. While we don't grow grapes yet, our honey and prairie-hardy fruits, in the hands of the world's finest mead and fruit wine makers, are starting to win international competitions. Spending time with the food artisans of Alberta has given us more clues to our terroir as each of them has led us further down the taste-of-place rabbit hole.

MEASUREMENTS USED IN THE PROFILES

We went with whatever our subjects used. In true Canadian style, it's a mishmash of metric and imperial.

WHO MADE IT INTO THE BOOK AND WHY? AND WHAT'S A FOOD ARTISAN, ANYWAY?

This book represents a curated look at the province, and we chose who was included with certain biases for sure. Farmers and ranchers received top priority. They risk the most and are virtually invisible to our predominantly urban populations. It's time to bring them into the light.

The average age of a farmer in Alberta is close to 60. If the average age of people in an industry is over 30, it is considered a dying industry. When it came to food artisans, we sought out elders who've been successful at sustaining their land and at mentoring others to do the same. We include youthful farmers with bright ideas on how to successfully make it back to a life on the land.

We've always been biased toward food producers whose methods regenerate and build soil health and those are the sorts of producers you'll find here. One thing is certain, if we don't have farmers and healthy soil, there'll be no food, let alone artisans.

For other artisans, we were looking for people who made things with their hands. They might specialize in hunting, fishing, baking, making, brewing, distilling, aging, foraging, or even importing—in the case of chocolate, tea, and coffee—but all the artisans included make or allow us to make something delicious. They elevate our food scene and Alberta's reputation as a place to enjoy food. They increase the value in living or visiting here.

Confucius said, "The only way is to have many ways." As we highlight the many ways of being a food artisan here, we use a lot of quotes from our subjects to bring you into their world so you may value their contribution to our lives.

This book is a snapshot of Alberta's culinary landscape in the summer of 2017. If we didn't have a full-stop deadline, we could've kept going for a lifetime. Both the people's passion for what they do and our passion for them would have fuelled that.

While there is nothing definitive about our list of food artisans, we think you'll find this book fascinating and useful. If you have the chance to meet any of these people, we know from first-hand experience that they will connect you from one to the other. That's a food community. That's the start of a caring food culture. That is what we want Alberta to be known for.

—*Karen Anderson*

Facing page: photo by Neil Zeller Photography

NORTHERN ALBERTA

For the purposes of this book, Northern Alberta includes everything north of Edmonton. We realize, if you look at a map of Alberta, that most of the food businesses we write about in this section are technically still in Central Alberta but, since not much grows north of Peace Country in the west and Lakeland Country in the east, we'll focus here on the northern piece of Central Alberta.

As far as being able to grow food, it's very challenging in this region, and yet people of the north need to eat too. The food artisans here go to great lengths to provide nourishment that would otherwise only come from afar. Fortunately, what the north suffers with frigid winters, they make up for with warm summers filled with 20 hours of daylight.

You can visit many of the artisans in person, but some of them only have a wholesale business and aren't open to the public. Make sure to check out the artisans' website for more details on where to buy their products.

Travel Tips

➤ Check out the Honey Festival in Falher, Alberta, each June.

➤ Looking for a taste-filled road trip? Download the Alberta Culinary Tourism Alliance's *Raw Trails North: Alberta Aboriginal and Early Settler Culinary Trail from Edmonton to Lac La Biche* at albertaculinary.com for a DIY way to tasteful travel.

Previous spread: photo by Karen Anderson
Facing page: photo by Karen Anderson

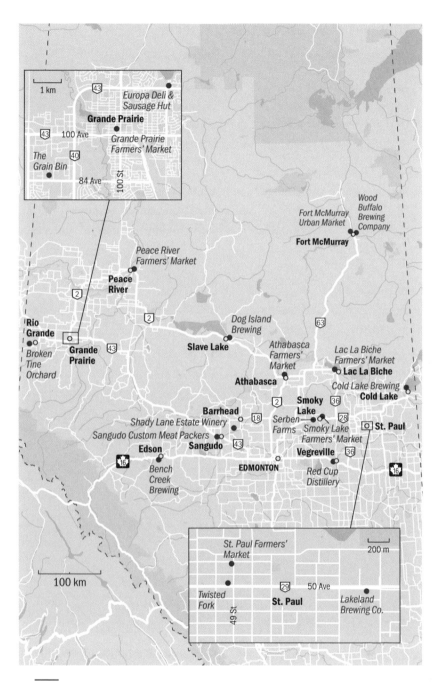

Note: Only artisans and producers who welcome visitors on site are shown on this map.

FOOD ARTISANS OF NORTHERN ALBERTA

Athabasca Farmers' Market 42

Bench Creek Brewing 43

Broken Tine Orchard 32

The Cheesiry 28

Cold Lake Brewing and Distilling 43

Dog Island Brewing 43

Europa Deli and Sausage Hut 27

First Nature Farms 36

Fort McMurray Urban Market 42

The Grain Bin 43

Grande Prairie Farmers' Market 42

Hog Wild Specialties 37

The Homestead Farm 34

Lac La Biche Farmers' Market 42

Lakeland Brewing Company 43

Lakeland Wild Rice 35

Meadow Creek Farms 38

Nature's Way Farm 39

Peace River Farmers' Market 42

Debra Poulin 30

Red Cup Distillery 31

Red Willow Gardens 33

Sangudo Custom Meat Packers 40

Serben Farms 41

Shady Lane Estate Winery 44

Smoky Lake Farmers' Market 42

St. Paul Farmers' Market 42

Twisted Fork 30

Winding Road Artisan Cheese 29

Wolfe Peace River Honey 26

Wood Buffalo Brewing Company 44

Wolfe Peace River Honey | Guy | peaceriverhoney.co

Gilbert and Sharon Wolfe. Photo by Jodi Sware, A Thousand Words Photography.

Gilbert and Sharon Wolfe have Canada's largest organic apiary and produce a million pounds of certified non-GMO honey annually. Gilbert convinced his father to buy him 50 hives when he turned 16. Anyone who keeps bees will tell you that if you have some, you'll always want more.

The Wolfe family now keeps 7,000 hives. That's about a half billion bees—a good thing when it takes 12 bees their life-span to produce a teaspoon of honey. The beehives summer in Peace Country and winter near much milder Abbotsford, BC.

Sharon contributes much to the success of the operation by rearing the apiary's own queen bees. Daughter Paige says, "It's a hot, humid workroom and she can only last one hour at a time. It takes a lot of patience and Mom is really good at it." Having healthy Alberta-raised queens contributes to the amount of honey produced because thriving queens lay lots of eggs, which in turn means lots of worker bees constantly hatching and going out to collect pollen and nectar.

Between the queens laying great brood and the worker bees having easy access to alfalfa and red clover, it's not uncommon for the Wolfes' hives to produce 150 pounds of creamy white honey per year. In 1988, each hive yielded a whopping 400 pounds. The average in Alberta in 2016 was 125 pounds, while globally most hives produce about 40–100 pounds per year.

Peace River is the honey capital of Canada because of the abundant forage and long days of sunshine afforded by the area's northern latitude. Amid widespread colony collapse disorder, it's uplifting to see the Wolfe family's success. Paige, who will run the family's international marketing when she finishes her business degree at the University of Alberta in the spring of 2018, says, "My dad won't be happy until he has helped change the world. He's convinced being organic and working with nature is the only way to save the bees." The Wolfes' sweet success speaks for itself.

Europa Deli and Sausage Hut | 9131 Crystal Lake Drive, Grande Prairie
780-532-9292 | facebook.com/EuropaDeli2017

Leslow Zep (left) and Srijohn Mandal at Europa Deli and Sausage Hut. Photo by Karen Anderson.

Leslow Zep's father was a sausage maker in Poland. Zep grew up under a Communist regime there and though he was relatively well off, two things spurred him to immigrate to Canada. On a vacation in Yugoslavia, he went to a grocery store and was dumbfounded by the abundance. In Poland, supplies often ran out before his family's monthly ration could be utilized. He did not want that for his son. Then, while watching the Calgary '88 Olympics on television he had another awakening. "I was struck by how happy people in Canada looked—especially the older people. Old people in Poland seemed so beaten down and grouchy. I decided I had to find a way to get to Canada so that I didn't end up that way."

Arriving in Grande Prairie in 1990, after three years in refugee camps in Turkey, he worked two jobs, learned English, got his high school diploma and retrained to work in the oilfield. With his wife, Anna, he opened Anna's Pizza in Beaverlodge in 1997 and after selling it in 2006, spent the next few years gaining the expertise he needed to open Europa.

"My father always said simple is best. We add salt, pepper, and garlic but it's not what you add, it's how you prepare it. There are no shortcuts. I'm an old-school butcher who practises nose-to-tail respect for the whole animal." The shop is whistle clean, there's a smoker in the back, a wall of walk-in fridges and display cases piled high with precisely cut meats and a plethora of sausages and salami. Dry goods from Poland, Hungary, and Italy are arranged attractively.

Zep has worked hard to bring a bit of his Polish heritage to Canada. Zep's son has a lucrative career as a mechanic, and his successor in the business is Sri Lankan native Srijohn Mandal. Through his own dreams Zep is shaping the dreams of another immigrant. After taking a photograph of Zep and Mandal side by side, I buy a big coil of kielbasa and leave with a smile nearly as wide.

The Cheesiry | Kitscoty | 780-522-8784 | thecheesiry.com

Rhonda Zuk Headon in the pastures of the Cheesiry. Photo by Karen Anderson.

Between 2010 and 2015, Rhonda Zuk Headon had between 100 and 140 East Friesian sheep on her family's farm in the rolling hills of Kitscoty near Lloydminster. "I've got six-year-old twins so I decided to stop the full production and retail wholesale business a few years ago, but I'm still making cheese seasonally and I still love it."

Zuk Headon is a former agronomist who realized at age 30 that her work—which involved prescribing a lot of synthetic fertilizer—was too far from her personal organic credo. So, she quit.

On a tour of Italy, she fell in love with pecorino sheep's cheese at an organic farm in Pienza. She did a two-month cheesemaking apprenticeship there as a wwoof (World Wide Opportunities on Organic Farms) volunteer.

Shortly after her return to Alberta she married into a family with a large cattle and chicken operation. She tried to get dairy quota for cows and failed but the inspector suggested sheep or goat milking instead. She built her own processing facility on the farm and now makes cheese when the ewes lamb and produce milk from May to October. Because she is down to fewer than a dozen sheep now, and they only make an average of 1.5 litres per day, she also uses Jersey milk from a neighbour to broaden her offerings.

"I have a wonderful recipe book for small-batch cheesemaking. I leave everything in a fridge in the barn and people pay on an honour system." Will she have more sheep? "Making cheese in the summers is just right for now. With two school-aged children it's all I can manage." At one point the Cheesiry's pecorino was available throughout the province. Let's hope this food artisan and shepherdess ages more of her delicious cheeses as her children age.

Winding Road Artisan Cheese | Smoky Lake | 1-855-475-6757
windingroadcheese.com

*Ian Treuer with his award-winning cheese
at City Market Downtown in Edmonton.
Photo by Karen Anderson.*

Growing up in the '70s on processed cheese, Ian Treuer had a cheese epiphany at age 13 when visiting Paris with his Austrian-born father and French-Canadian mother. The cheeses they would order in cafés had come from the farms where they'd been made that morning. Treuer's young palate was forever shaped by the difference in taste.

He came to Edmonton in 1993 for university, but left after a year, found a job he liked in printing, and stayed. "In about 2007 I decided I needed a hobby. It was either cheese or beer making and my passion for cheese won out."

Treuer found a home cheesemakers' community online and started sharing his failures and successes with a blog called *Much to Do about Cheese*. He became a consultant in the cheese industry after emerging as a leader in a Cheesapalooza blogging event. He began working with a company to prove that plant-based cardoon rennet could work in home cheesemaking kits. Cardoon is a thistle from Portugal, where it's been used for this purpose for centuries. "Regular rennet usually comes from the fourth stomach of a baby cow, sheep, or goat. I wanted to work with something more sustainable that didn't rely on the slaughter of animals and cardoon made that possible."

Treuer also began volunteering at a cheesemaking company in Smoky Lake and when the owners wanted to sell in 2015, he and friend Aurelio Fernandes took the leap and bought their facility. Treuer now makes several cheeses from milk supplied by Vital Green Farms (see page 247). "It's pasteurized but not homogenized so we've got that nice creamy layer to work with," he says.

"Gone are days where you can survive on just farmers' market sales, so we got all certifications and proper labelling to be able to sell across Canada." In July 2017, Treuer's RDB washed rind cheese won second place at the American Cheese Society awards. Check out all the cheeses and where to find them on the website.

Debra Poulin | Twisted Fork | 4914 50 Avenue, St. Paul | 780-614-3276
facebook.com/twistedforksp

Debra Poulin. Photo by Karen Anderson.

"I married a community when I married my husband," says Debra Poulin, chef of Twisted Fork. Growing up in Niagara's lush fruit-growing belt, she loved her summer jobs picking produce—especially grapes (she's attained level two with the Wine and Spirit Education Trust). But, after meeting her husband on a business trip, she moved to St. Paul, a town that she feels lives by its motto: "a people kind of place."

Poulin's been cooking professionally for 35 years and has Red and Blue Seals as well as a bachelor of arts in culinary management. She's been a culinary instructor and, at one point, ran an oilfield services camp that fed 1,800 workers daily.

"I opened Twisted Fork in July of 2017 because I want to give back to the community that has given me so much. There are over 200 farmers in this Lakeland region of Alberta. People are looking for local food and I want to provide that and support our farmers."

Over 20 local producers supply feature ingredients for the restaurant including beef and grains from Next Level Organic Farm, vegetables from Farm Chic, Emjay's Prairie Berries, Kyle's Greens, fruits from Flying Rabbit Farms, and cheeses from Old School Cheesery.

Menus change with the seasons and staff are empowered to be part of the creativity. "I want the chance to train other chefs. Flavour comes first always. We can make it pretty after the flavour of the food shines through. We ask customers for suggestions and we hope they'll try new things."

The walls of the 66-seat room are decorated with paintings by her father-in-law, noted Alberta sculptor/painter Herman Poulin—another authentically local touch. The place starts to fill, and two tables over, a woman is eavesdropping on a server describing the many local and house-made components on a charcuterie board. When it comes her turn to order she says, "I'll try what they're having." Poulin's success will come one palate at a time.

Red Cup Distillery | 210-5341 50 Avenue, Vegreville | 780-603-3040
redcupdistillery.ca

Left to right: Jerry Reti, Rob de Groot, and Sam Stewart. Photo by Karen Anderson.

Visiting Red Cup Distillery is a lesson in pop culture and history. The name comes from those red Solo cups that are synonymous with parties. Singer Toby Keith wrote a very "sticky" song about them. That's the pop culture part.

The history comes from owners Rob and Barb de Groot's wish to make something that pays homage to the people that settled Alberta. Moonshine was their liquor and the women made it. "Women weren't recognized as persons until 1929 so they couldn't be arrested. A group of five Alberta women known as the Famous Five got the British North American Act changed," says Rob de Groot. "With no sugar in their budgets they learned to make their liquor in pot stills from sprouted grain and that is what—after much trial and error—we've been able to recreate."

A gleaming copper still sits front and centre. Distillery manager Jerry Reti, a farmer and jack of all trades, had the skill set to braze the massive sheets of copper and weld it into being. "It's the only *legal* made-in-Canada still. It did not come from a catalogue," says de Groot.

"We work with 100-bushel batches. The grains come from George Olynyk's farm 10 miles away. It's cleaned and aged. Sprouting allows the sugars within the wheat to develop. Malting takes place on the concrete floor—like the best distilleries in Scotland. Fermentation is open. Distillation happens twice and the copper allows the taste of the grains to shine through. There's no filtration because we don't need to. The output per bushel of grain is low because we don't use any chemicals like commercial malters do. That's why we end up with pure essence. The time and temperature we distill at are proprietary," says Reti, in a quiet moment when the endearingly frank, honest, passionate, and politically charged high-voltage tower that is Rob de Groot runs out to do an errand.

And then de Groot is back. He pours a tasting round (in shot-size red Solo cups). Drinking is believing. It's easy to see what the excitement is about.

Broken Tine Orchard | Rio Grande | 780-518-9115 | brokentineorchard.ca

Kreg Alde with his haskap berries.
Photo by Karen Anderson.

"There are 20 different haskaps on the market. I've bought about 20,000 plants from the University of Saskatchewan over the last five years. They are Borealis, Indigo Gem, and Aurora varietals and they are doing well here in Peace Country." Haskap is the Japanese name for *Lonicera caerulea*. The oblong berries are also known as blue honeysuckle or honeyberries.

Kreg Alde's family homesteaded this land near Beaverlodge in 1926 and he owns 2,400 acres. His own children are weeding the family vegetable garden as we tour the fields and facilities. Inside the family home, we try haskap muffins, cheesecake, and ice cream. There are smiles all round on this hot day in late July.

Alde has returned to the farm from a career in oil and gas marketing. "My accountant told me that if I wanted to farm, I had to find a way to increase the revenue on the land that I have. I want to go large scale so I've started a haskap growers' co-operative. We're finding a way to get local food to local people."

Networking is like breathing for Alde. "I believe haskaps could be as good for farmers as canola was—only without all the chemicals. Haskaps have natural pesticides in their leaves called iridoids. They have twice the antioxidants of blueberries and none of the diseases that have plagued saskatoon farms."

Dr. Bob Bors, head of the University of Saskatchewan domestic fruit program, went to Japan, where haskaps are big, to study them. Through natural breeding methods he has developed the varietals available here. "He really hit a home run. They add an early fruit to our growing season."

Alde has invested in an on-farm processing facility and can clean 500 pounds per hour. He blast freezes them to minus 23 Celsius for storage. He's partnered with Village and Mackay's Ice Cream and Foothills Creamery for products and Mo-Na Food (see page 79) for distribution. He's also hired one of the best fruit wine makers in the world, Quebec's Dominic Rivard, to make a melomel haskap and honey wine. Expect more blue fruit in your future.

Red Willow Gardens | Beaverlodge | 780-354-8211

Eric and Carmen De Schipper on their organic farmland. Photo by Karen Anderson.

On the banks of the Red Willow River, a few kilometres south of Beaverlodge, lies a farm with cherry-red buildings encircling an asphalt loop of driveway so clean it looks like a fresh chalkboard. There's a cold storage facility, tidy chicken coop, and cheery new farm store where you can buy popcorn and lemonade along with your vegetables.

Eric De Schipper, a tall blond man with a ruler-straight back and measured gait, appears along with a few of the farm's dogs and we're off on an ATV to tour the 45 acres in cultivation. Eric and his wife, Carmen, own a total of 110 acres but the others are left natural with ponds and forest that work together to cool the land and provide water for irrigation. A red fox glances over its shoulder and flicks its showy tail before slipping into the bushes as we round a corner.

We find Carmen in a far field, weeding with the crew of Mexican workers the De Schippers credit as the key to their survival as farmers. Eric moves carefully as he joins Carmen for a photo. He's a cancer survivor and lives in chronic pain related to a series of accidents and eight back fractures since his 15th birthday. A few instructions in Spanish to her staff and Carmen rides back with us to the main yard to pick strawberries fresh from the field.

The De Schippers bought this land in 1984 with Eric's parents and then bought them out so they could retire. Eric has kept a journal every day since he began the farm. He has not sprayed the land with pesticides or fertilizers since 2008. "We use regenerative methods here now. Potatoes get two years back to back and are not replanted in that field for six years. With carrots, we keep four years between planting in the same field. We sow and mow oats to build the soil nutrients in fallow years."

The carrots are their most famous crop. "I'd like people to know that they taste so good because it's a specialty carrot that's been grown in regenerated soil with the pristine air, water, and climate of Peace River Country." A hug goodbye comes with a bag of carrots for the road. You can find the De Schippers' produce here or at the Grande Prairie Farmers' Market.

The Homestead Farm | Goodfare | 780-356-2744 | thehomesteadfarm.ca

Lisa Lundgard. Photo by Donovan Kitt.

"Food is medicine." When a farmer starts quoting Hippocrates, it's time to listen.

Lisa Lundgard and her partner Donovan Kitt own a quarter section of land next door to Donovan's father, Jerry Kitt of First Nature Farms (see page 36). Of the 160 acres, 30 are cleared for pasture where they are raising a few cattle, sheep, and laying chickens. Their log home has a small greenhouse attached to lengthen the growing season here in Peace Country where the seemingly endless days of summer light and warmth vanish harshly with October blizzards.

A large vegetable garden—as lush as Jurassic Park—is visible over tall deer fencing. Two old yellow school buses are parked on the property. One houses freezers for meat storage and the other is converted to an animal transport unit. Inside the cabin, trays of sprouts are parked under the skylight's beams of sunshine and books on farming fill an entire wall in one corner of the kitchen.

Both Lundgard and Kitt were raised on organic farms and both have returned to farming after earning degrees. Kitt still works off farm to pay down the purchase of the land. A quarter section of land here runs anywhere from $200,000 to $500,000. This is Alberta's prime canola-growing territory, and that has doubled and quadrupled land prices over the last decade.

Lundgard and Kitt met at a holistic management course. "Now we're creating a farm from scratch and we're focusing on diversity and anything we think will add value to the farm." Though only a few years on this property, they've attained certified organic status and take every opportunity to explain why they go to that effort and expense to their customers at the Grande Prairie Farmers' Market where they sell eggs, beef, pork, lamb, bison, vegetables, and pea, radish, and sunflower shoots. "I tell people the consumer dollar is mighty. If you seek out local small-scale farms, and put your dollar there, it doesn't take much for us to be able to have a business and survive."

With their peers in the Young Agrarians of the National Farmers' Union, they are making changes so that farms can become viable businesses again. You can find produce from the Homestead Farm at the Grande Prairie Farmers' Market.

Lakeland Wild Rice Ltd. | Athabasca | 780-387-3389
aptolemy17@gmail.com

The Ptolemy family. Photo by Karen Anderson.

Alice and Wayne Ptolemy have been growing wild rice near Athabasca since 1989. At that time, there was an annual Wild Rice Growers convention in Lac La Biche and, along with a neighbour, they went to check it out. Alice describes her husband as "someone who can do or make just about anything he sets his mind to. He even built our airboats."

Wild rice is an aquatic grass native to Canada. The Ptolemys have 1,000 acres planted on four lakes Alice describes as "back in the bush." They lease the land from the Department of Forestry and plant the seed annually. "It can be planted in spring or fall—either way we lose a lot to moose and birds or if there aren't enough rains and the water in the lakes is too low."

Each fall they use a scoop Wayne welded to the front of the boats to plow the wild rice kernels ashore to Alice, their family, and friends who volunteer to hand scoop it into buckets. The rice is then shipped to the Great Northern Wild Rice company in Manitoba to have the kernels rubbed off and then dried and packaged. "It's also grown in Minnesota and California in rice paddies but that's not the real rice like ours."

The Ptolemys are the last wild rice growers in Alberta. Slowly their friends in the business have quit, moved, or died. "My husband was attracted to this idea because of his great passion for the outdoors. We're retired now and though it is incredibly hard work—each bucket we fill is 60 pounds—we both still love working in the great outdoors."

You can order your Alberta-grown wild rice directly from Alice by phone or email for five dollars per pound plus shipping.

First Nature Farms | Goodfare | 780-356-2239 | firstnaturefarms.ab.ca

Jerry Kitt with a young turkey out on the pastures of First Nature Farms. Photo by Karen Anderson.

First Nature Farms is surrounded by land preserved by the Nature Conservancy of Canada and Ducks Unlimited, a few other organic farmers, and Crown land. Driving west past Beaverlodge's roadside giant beaver attraction (south off the main highway), tracks of heavy gravel and towering aspens narrow the sky to a lean strip of blue. On the farm, machinery sits where it's needed and animals raise their heads from the lush green grass along a rut-filled lane leading to a log home. "There isn't another farm west of here until you hit Russia," says owner Jerry Kitt. As that sinks in, he pours a cold draught from a specially designed tap and keg beer fridge in the dining room.

Walking the near pastures with pints of ice-cold draught in hand, we meet the menagerie of animals in Kitt's care including bison, Berkshire and Tamworth hogs, laying and broiler chickens, turkeys, Muscovy ducks, a goat, a few milking cows, cats, fish, a turtle, and Sixty, an intensely smart farm dog who is part border collie, part Great Pyrenees. The cattle are grazing 2,000 acres of leased land to the west.

Using Holistic Management International principles, Kitt has farmed this land since 1980. Born and raised in Edmonton, he left a zoology degree behind to join his cousin and a few friends in buying this property. He's the only one left. His six quarter sections have been certified organic and humane since 1990 with 90 percent untouched. Over 400 WWOOF (World Wide Opportunities on Organic Farms) workers have poured through in the last 20 years.

We learn how each animal helps keep the "farm in harmony with the natural surroundings to sustain and enhance its natural biodiversity." Whole Foods in BC takes lots of Kitt's product and his stall at Old Strathcona Farmers' Market in Edmonton thrives.

Over a meal of wood-fired ranch-raised bison, garden greens and potatoes, and haskap berries from neighbours, he shares stories of a well-lived life. He's proven that a farm can be kind to the ecology and economically viable. Exuberant and involved, he's a reflection of the vibrant life surrounding him.

Hog Wild Specialties | Mayerthorpe | 780-786-4627 | hogwild.ab.ca

Earl Hagman in a field of barley that will become feed for his wild boar. Photo by Karen Anderson.

Since 1992, Earl Hagman and his family have raised wild boar on their 1,800-acre ranch just off the Cowboy Trail south of Mayerthorpe. Almost as though he had a crystal ball, Hagman began to diversify his operations long before BSE, or mad cow disease, hit in 2003. He had already reduced his cattle operation from 300 head to 50 while bringing a dozen sows from Germany and one boar from Russia to begin his enterprise. "Our wild boar saved our farm—it's as simple as that," he says.

"It took about 11 years of investment before we started turning a profit and paying off what we'd borrowed—you know, we're your typical overnight success. Chefs like Glen Manzer, Angelo Contrada, and Sal Howell, owner of the River Café, have been our greatest support from day one."

Having grown up cattle ranching, handling these animals did not intimidate him. "In all this time, I've only been hurt once." Moving the hogs for processing requires strategy, but he's an expert at it now. Demand for his product is such that he is also supporting four other wild boar farms throughout the province by ordering from them with increasing frequency. "There used to be 200 farms raising these animals. Now there are 12."

Hagman puts about 60,000 kilometres on his vehicle each year delivering product and moving the animals from the various farms to abattoirs for slaughter. Hogs destined for barbecue pits are processed at nearby Sangudo Custom Meat Packers (see page 40). A processor near Red Deer makes his bacon, smokies, and jerky. A company in Vancouver makes prosciutto for him.

"Monday is the day all the restaurants place their orders." The phone rings steadily. Chefs across Alberta, BC, and Saskatchewan love to cook with this product.

In another fenced and forested section of the ranch, about 150 hunters each year pay to come on a hunt. Hagman, his son, and a neighbour offer guiding services. Many of their long-standing customers come in the off-season to help with fencing. "It's the biggest job on the ranch and a vital one. I feed and water them well and they like to come and hang out."

Though the hogs have lots of room to root and forage, about 400 bushels of oats, wheat, or barley are set out as feed each week. Hagman leads the way to a nearby barley feed waving its golden fronds in the late afternoon sun. "I just want people to know they can count on us."

Meadow Creek Farms | Waskatenau | 780-650-2047
meadowcreekfarms.ca

Geoff Maki and owner Mandy Melnyk at Meadow Creek Farms. Photo by Karen Anderson.

"My friends in Edmonton used to have chicken parties for me like some people have Tupperware parties for their friends." The first frost has fallen overnight and we're taking a break for coffee on Mandy Melnyk's front deck after picking a few dozen cases of tomatoes. They'll be safe from further threats now. Since 2011, Melnyk has been working hard to make her farm work. "Every day I get up and do my best. That's all I can do.

"If my workers had shown up yesterday these tomatoes wouldn't have been an issue, but it is hard to get help this far north of Edmonton." Melnyk grew up a mile up the road and had moved to Peace Country after her parents sold off their cattle and retired. She was set to marry a conventional farmer there but couldn't do it in the end. "Such different values." She shrugs.

"I decided to market to the North, to Lac La Biche and Fort McMurray. I set up a farmers' market at MacDonald Island Park and drove nine other producers' stuff up there with me. Everything was going great until May 3, 2016. I lost 150 Community Shared Agriculture customers the day the Fort McMurray fire started. They lost everything.

"Community-supported shares are vital but difficult when I am a two-hour drive to Edmonton. I can't get into farmers' markets. They are too political. I used to just drive to St. Paul to a great abattoir but they retired. But, my animals are well cared for and everything is organic here. People think because I'm broke, I'm doing something wrong."

Meanwhile there are pigs to be fed and turkeys to keep warm. Melnyk and the farm's animal manager, Geoff Maki, need to make a run to the Co-op. "Farming isn't rocket science," she says as they leave. "It's harder. Food is power and with every farm we lose, our country is losing its power." Melnyk is an activist who's been a member of the National Farmers Union since she was a teen. Catch her podcast, *What's Food Got to Do with It?*, for more of her farming life lessons.

Nature's Way Farm | Grimshaw | 780-338-2934
facebook.com/Natureswayfarm

Peter and Mary Lundgard at the kitchen table in their home near Grimshaw. Photo by Karen Anderson.

Rolling into the farmyard on a section (640 acres) of land near Grimshaw, we wait for the cloud of dust to settle before entering the ranch house where Mary Lundgard is finishing preparations for lunch. There are places set around an antique oak table. The noon meal is a creamy ground beef and beet green borscht, fresh rye bread, farmstead cottage cheese and bright yellow grass fed butter, still-warm berry compote, and sun-brewed iced tea sweetened with honey. One by one the farm manager Lilli Klamke, WWOOF (World Wide Opportunities on Organic Farms) workers, and ag student interns take a place at the table. The last to appear is their mentor, Peter Lundgard.

Lundgard's grandparents were homesteaders from Norway. He knew at age 17 that he too wanted to farm and when he and Mary hit financial hard times and lost their first farm, instead of giving up and leaving the community, they stayed and searched for sustainable models with ways to secure sources of steady income.

In 1991, they took a Holistic Management International course where they learned values-driven goal setting and planning skills that allowed them to live securely at last. They began managing the farm by putting the ecology of the soil first. Aiming for a specific balance between the calcium, magnesium, and sodium, they farm organically, creating a strong bacterial and fungal microbiome, which enables the soil to release maximal nutrition. The strong, healthy plants naturally repel insects and beat out weeds.

"Creating maximal nutrients in the food we eat creates healthy humans, which makes for the strongest of countries. This is why agriculture is the backbone of any nation," says Peter. Mary expands: "We believe there's a need for a system that focuses on local food and allows for farm-gate sales that are not governed by restrictive health board rules and regulations."

The Lundgards openly share the knowledge needed to run a completely organic operation and have welcomed over 20 agricultural degree students for internships and 40 WWOOFers since 2005. They have cattle, sheep, pigs, dairy cows, chickens, and a farm garden, and along with an alfalfa seed and leafcutter bee operation, everything on the farm is certified organic and humane. Products are for sale by appointment at the farm gate and at Simply for Life in Peace River.

Sangudo Custom Meat Packers | 4930 49 Avenue, Sangudo
780-785-3353 | facebook.com/Sangudo-Custom-Meat-Packers

Jeff Senger. Photo by Kevin Kossowan.

Highway 43 is Alberta's major route to the BC border west of Grande Prairie. A little over an hour along its twin grey ribbons from Edmonton lies the hamlet of Sangudo on the banks of the Pembina River. Like many rural towns, Sangudo is diminishing in population and has lost many of its businesses.

When the owner of the local abattoir, in operation for 50 years, was ready to retire, the town faced another challenge. To lose it would mean loss of jobs and ease of access for the hunters and ranchers who depend on its proximity to process the animals that are their source of food and/or income.

"I bought the business, Sangudo Custom Meat Packers, with a partner in 2010 with some financing help from a community investment co-operative that I helped found a year earlier. We bought it to preserve an important service to the community and to protect this aspect of rural food culture," says Jeff Senger.

Senger was a finance-savvy accountant working in nearby Whitecourt. He craved connection with the land and community for himself and his family so he left the oil patch and with his wife, Heather, and their four daughters moved to a quarter section (160 acres) north of the town. Here they raise hogs, cattle, a Jersey cow, rabbits, laying hens, goats, and horses. With the meat packing plant, Senger wanted to increase the chances that his own children will be able to stay in Sangudo.

Several years on, the business's animal handling system has been completely updated using the humane principles developed by Temple Grandin, the co-operative members are paid handsome dividends, and the business has created six to eight full-time jobs depending on the season. "We kill about 700 beef, 100 hogs, 500 rabbits, and 450 sheep a year. We also typically kill and process a few dozen bison, deer, and elk and 50–100 wild game from hunters." The numbers say it all. This small Alberta abattoir provides food and a trust factor in a day and age where bigger isn't always better.

Serben Farms | Corner of Highway 28 and RR 180, Smoky Lake
780-656-5244 | serbenfarms.com

Jered and Julia Serben with their children Jedd, Jacob, and June. Photo by Hayley Prusko.

If you drive Highway 28 through Smoky Lake you will find a new shop featuring the produce of two of our Alberta food artisans. Jered Serben is a fourth-generation farmer and the third generation to farm a quarter-section piece of his family's original homestead. He and his wife, Julia—whom he describes as a person who can do anything—raise hogs, turkeys, laying and broiling chickens, and lamb on pasture.

"I farmed with my dad but he wanted to specialize in hogs. He needed more land and grew debt along with everything else. I didn't want to farm like that so I split off and started raising animals on pasture. I know good breeding stock, feeding rations, how to raise animals outside with shelter and water, and how to let sows farrow in comfort—not stuck in a farrowing crate. Julia and I base our business on feeding families instead of growing commodities. The commodity game is not farming to me. You are just the bottom piece of a huge company. You take all the risk and they take all the profit."

Julia has a PhD in nutritional sciences but now farms full-time, does meat cutting and grows a one-and-a-half-acre market garden in summer with her ten-year-old and five-year-old. "Jedd and Jacob are seriously into growing things and have gotten us into beekeeping as well."

"When we decided that we needed to add value to our products by doing our own butchering and meat cutting, we built our own shop in a sea container and had a British butcher friend come and teach us. We'd watched some YouTube videos but it was crazy how hard it actually was. Julia's an amazing cook and came up with all our sausage recipes. She makes several different kinds—about 350–400 pounds a week."

Serben Farms has a stall at City Market Downtown in Edmonton from May to Christmas each year. "I love to connect with the people we grow for. I'll always find time for that."

FARMERS' MARKETS

Check the website for current hours prior to your visit.

ATHABASCA FARMERS' MARKET

Athabasca Multiplex (October to May), Riverfront Park (June to September)
Saturdays fall/winter 10:00 A.M.–2:00 P.M., summer 10:00 A.M.–2:00 P.M.
780-675-4398 | facebook.com/Athabasca-Farmers-Market-386200578073207

FORT MCMURRAY URBAN MARKET

9909 Franklin Avenue | Wednesdays 11:00 A.M.–6:00 P.M., June to September
every second week | 780-215-2669 | rmwb.ca/urbanmarket

GRANDE PRAIRIE FARMERS' MARKET

Big Red Barn, 10032 101 Avenue | Saturdays 10:00 A.M.–3:00 P.M., Fridays 4:00
P.M.–8:00 P.M., year-round | 780-814-8224 | gpfarmersmarket.ca

LAC LA BICHE FARMERS' MARKET

Lac La Biche Agricom, Highway 881 | Fridays 3:00 P.M.–5:30 P.M., April to
December | 780-623-8002 | albertafarmersmarket.com/farmers-market/lac-la-biche

PEACE RIVER FARMERS' MARKET

Senior's Centre, 10301 101 Street | Saturdays 10:00 A.M.–2:00 P.M., February to
December | 780-274-0536 | peaceriverfarmersmarket.com

SMOKY LAKE FARMERS' MARKET

Smoky Lake Ag Complex, 4612 54 Avenue | Saturdays 10:00 A.M.–noon, April to
December | 780-656-2463 | www.smokylake.ca/Farmers-Market

ST. PAUL FARMERS' MARKET

St. Paul Centennial Senior's Centre, 5114 49 Street | Fridays 10:00 A.M.–2:00 P.M.,
February to December | 780-614-7700 | facebook.com/St-Paul-Farmers-Market

WATERING HOLES

Check the website for current hours prior to your visit.

BENCH CREEK BREWING

53527 Range Road 181A, Edson | 780-517-7008 | benchcreekbrewing.com
⇒ Tours: Saturdays by appointment.
Favourite beer here: White Raven—it's elegant.

BROKEN TINE ORCHARD (SEE PAGE 32)

Rio Grande | 780-518-9115 | brokentineorchard.ca
⇒ Tours: Check their Facebook page for their annual U-pick days.
Favourite wine here: Award-winning haskap Melomel wine.

COLD LAKE BREWING AND DISTILLING

7-5109 51 Avenue, Cold Lake | 780-201-1611 | coldlakebrewingdistilling.com/distillery
⇒ Tours: Available on request with notice.
Favourite beer here: Cold Lake Lager. Their Honey Shine will send you over the moon.

DOG ISLAND BREWING

250 Caribou Trail, Slave Lake | 415-255-0212 | dogislandbrewing.com
⇒ Tours: By appointment.
Favourite beer here: Try the 1965 Old Town Porter to warm you up.

THE GRAIN BIN

104-8504 112 Street, Grande Prairie | 780-380-6532 | grainbinbeer.com
⇒ Tours: By appointment.
Favourite beer here: Willie the Wit, 2017 Canadian International Beer Award winner.
No taproom, but growler fills are available at this triple-gold Canadian
International Beer Awards winner.

LAKELAND BREWING COMPANY

4227 50 Avenue, St. Paul | 780-614-9466 | lakelandbrewing.wixsite.com/beer
⇒ Tours: By appointment.
Favourite beer here: Gypsy Grapefruit Radler. It's very refreshing.

RED CUP DISTILLERY (SEE PAGE 31)

Vegreville | 780-603-3040 | facebook.com/RedCupDistillery2015
⇒ Tours: By appointment.
Favourite spirit here: Alberta Moonshine made from sprouted wheat.

SHADY LANE ESTATE WINERY

58029 Range Road 44, Barrhead County | 780-282-0128 | shadylaneestate.com
⇒ Tours: By appointment.
Favourite wine here: Junibeeren—it's also a refreshing way to enjoy one of Alberta's signature foods, saskatoon berries.

WOOD BUFFALO BREWING COMPANY

9914 Morrison Street, Fort McMurray | 587-276-0022 | woodbuffalobrewingco.ca
⇒ Tours: By appointment.
Favourite beer here: Lift Kit Lager.
One of the largest brew pubs in Canada and Alberta's first craft distiller.

Facing page: photo courtesy of Edmonton Tourism

EDMONTON

E dmonton, Alberta's capital city, is our province's City of Festivals. It was originally a fur trading post for the Hudson's Bay; settlers began homesteading in the fertile river valley of the North Saskatchewan River, which now divides the city north and south, in the late 1800s.

While the city was incorporated in 1904, its downtown city farmers' market was founded in and has been in continuous operation since 1903. To this day, it is a place for city dwellers to connect with the people that grow their food. Many of the producers in this book have kiosks there or at Old Strathcona Farmers' Market and at both locations they enjoy loyal relationships with their patrons. The 124 Grand Market, and St. Albert Farmers' Markets are some of the other popular links to fresh, local produce.

The Strathcona neighbourhood on the south side of the river was a separate town until 1910. It was the terminus for the Grand Trunk Railway from Calgary. Today, it is known for theatre, arts and music venues, hip bars and eateries, and of course its Saturday market.

The University of Alberta, also on the south side, has a quarter-section farm on campus that has spawned both community gardens and urban chicken-keeping movements in the city. Northlands Agricultural Society, back on the north side, has a one-acre urban farm called Lactuca (see page 78). Families like the Kuhlmanns have been market gardeners within the city limits for generations. Riverbend Gardens' (see page 81) Janelle Herbert was raised on her family's farm along the river and is a vital vegetable producer for the city and its restaurants.

Diverse cultures have settled here. Downtown Edmonton has a small Chinatown. East of the city, Ukrainian Village pays homage to this cultural group and the important food heritage it has contributed. Italians and Europeans have been stocking up on their favourite items at the Spinelli family's Italian Centre Shop on 95 Street since 1959.

West of downtown, 124 Street is becoming a destination for food lovers thanks to world-class Duchess Bake Shop (see page 59), nearby

Previous spread and facing page: photo courtesy of Edmonton Tourism

hyperlocal Rge Rd (see page 69), and fun bars like North 53. Distilleries and breweries are popping up all over.

Jasper Avenue in the downtown core was once deserted due to the popularity of the world's largest shopping mall, West Edmonton Mall. But it is quickly being revitalized by chef-driven restaurants like Daniel Costa's Uccellino, Bar Bricco and Corso 32; owner Patrick Saurette's legendary hospitality at the Marc; and daring leader chef Larry Stewart at Hardware Grill (see page 67).

Elk Island National Park, home to herds of purebred plains bison, elk, and moose, is a mere 30 minutes from the heart of the city and a great place to take in a picnic or one of chef Brad Smoliak's (see page 68) long-table dinners held throughout the summer.

Edmontonians love to be outdoors and they love the festivals the city is known for. Taste of Edmonton draws people to Winston Churchill Square in front of city hall. What the Truck festival celebrates the city's vibrant food truck culture. Folk Fest, Fringe Festival, and Ice on Whyte all illustrate how closely linked food and culture are. This section of the book celebrates a slice of Edmonton's lively food culture.

Travel Tip

➤ Food lovers can cut to the chase and book a food tour upon arrival in Edmonton. You'll meet locals, taste a variety of curated foods and beverages, and learn about the history and culture as you stroll a neighbourhood together. Check edmontonfoodtours.com for dates and times.

Facing page: photo courtesy of Edmonton Tourism

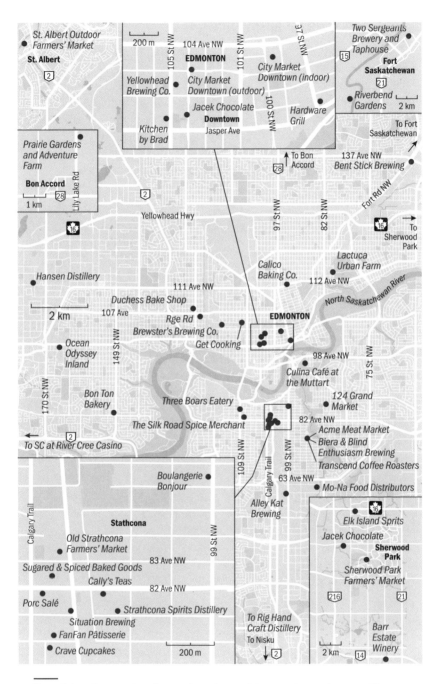

St. Albert Outdoor Farmers' Market
St. Albert

200 m
105 St NW
104 Ave NW
101 St NW
EDMONTON

Yellowhead Brewing Co.
City Market Downtown (outdoor)
97 St NW
City Market Downtown (indoor)

Jacek Chocolate
Downtown
Jasper Ave
100 St NW
Hardware Grill

Kitchen by Brad

Two Sergeants Brewery and Taphouse
15
Fort Saskatchewan
21

Riverbend Gardens
2 km

To Fort Saskatchewan

Prairie Gardens and Adventure Farm
Bon Accord
28
1 km
Lily Lake Rd
2

To Bon Accord
28
137 Ave NW
Bent Stick Brewing

Yellowhead Hwy
97 St NW
82 St NW
Fort Rd NW

16
16
To Sherwood Park

Hansen Distillery
111 Ave NW
Duchess Bake Shop
2 km
107 Ave
Rge Rd
Brewster's Brewing Co.
149 St NW
Get Cooking
EDMONTON

Calico Baking Co.
Lactuca Urban Farm
112 Ave NW
North Saskatchewan River

Ocean Odyssey Inland
170 St NW
Bon Ton Bakery
Three Boars Eatery
The Silk Road Spice Merchant

98 Ave NW
75 St NW
Culina Café at the Muttart

124 Grand Market
82 Ave NW
Acme Meat Market
Biera & Blind Enthusiasm Brewing
Transcend Coffee Roasters

To SC at River Cree Casino
2
109 St NW
Calgary Trail
99 St NW
63 Ave NW
Mo-Na Food Distributors

Boulangerie Bonjour

Alley Kat Brewing

16
Elk Island Sprits
Jacek Chocolate
Sherwood Park
Sherwood Park Farmers' Market

Calgary Trail
Stathcona
Old Strathcona Farmers' Market
99 St NW
83 Ave NW
Sugared & Spiced Baked Goods
Cally's Teas
82 Ave NW
Porc Salé
Strathcona Spirits Distillery
Situation Brewing
FanFan Pâtisserie
Crave Cupcakes
200 m

To Rig Hand Craft Distillery
To Nisku
2
216
21
Barr Estate Winery
2 km
14

Note: Only artisans and producers who welcome visitors on site are shown on this map.

FOOD ARTISANS OF EDMONTON

Fruits of Sherbrooke | 780-244-0129 | fruitsofsherbrooke.ca

Left to right: Christina Piecha, Al Cosh, and Carol Cooper in Carol's rhubarb patch. Photo by Karen Anderson.

Fruits of Sherbrooke founders Christine Piecha, Al Cosh, and Carol Cooper are unintentional food artisans. The three met at their neighbourhood gardening club. One day when they were walking the back lanes of their community, Sherbrooke, and saw fruit rotting on the ground and headed to the landfill, Christina challenged her friends: "There are hungry people in this city; why aren't we doing something about it with all this fruit?" That was in 2010.

"We started with neighbours and our gardening club and asked if we could harvest their excess," says Christina. The trio went on to mastermind a network of volunteers devoted to harvesting the bountiful fruits that grow in Edmonton, St. Albert and Sherwood Park. Rhubarb, raspberries, saskatoon berries, apples, and pears are given to charities, not-for-profits, community kitchens, school programs, and individuals in need. Remaining amounts are used to teach preserving classes. "Carol's an amazing cook. Her grandmother cooked for the king of Denmark. She makes all the jams, jellies, sauces, and condiments which we sell to support the costs involved in our not-for-profit society," says Al (check website for retailers and markets).

In 2015 alone, they rescued over 15,000 kilograms of fruit. "We're starting to focus on people of low incomes and new immigrants to Canada—people who will really benefit from learning preserving skills and receiving the fruit," says Carol. In the two years since they started making dried apples and applesauce snack tubes for inner-city schoolchildren at risk they've fed 27,000 children.

Carol and Al are retired but work more than full-time at these volunteer jobs. "Our drive comes from Christina's immense respect for nature," says Carol over homemade iced tea and fresh baked goodies in her cozy kitchen. There's a batch of something she's recipe testing bubbling away on the stove. "Christina inspires us to keep on making a difference." Al agrees. Instead of taking any credit, they deflect it to the non-retired one who has quietly slipped out to go to her paying job. Aware of the fragile nature of life, they now put equal efforts into ensuring their work is sustained. That makes them eternal fruit stars in our books.

Bon Ton Bakery | 8720 149 Street | 780-489-7717 | bonton.ca

Hilton Dinner (left) and Gerry Semler in the shop at Bon Ton Bakery. Photo by Karen Anderson.

A petite, elderly woman with fresh lipstick, elegantly coiffed hair, and a spotless black wool coat slowly makes her way to the cashier's counter, a pleasant smile on her face. "Do you know who that is?" asks Hilton Dinner, co-owner of Bon Ton Bakery with his wife Michelle and manager Gerry Semler. Dinner excuses himself to pay respects to the woman in question. She is the original owner, Mrs. Judy Edelmann, who along with her husband, Eugene, started this bakery in 1956.

The Edelmanns ran the bakery until the Dinners took over in 1998. The older couple trusted that Dinner would carry on their commitment to quality. "When I asked Eugene Edelmann about measurements for his recipes he told me that when it comes to bread you had to feel it. Our bakers still tell me they do what they do—by feeling it."

In the back of the house, there are stations for bread, patisserie, and *viennoiserie*, and staff from 11 countries in a "ballet without music," says Dinner. Past shelves piled high with huge bags of flour, he pulls out a three-level supply cart loaded with five-gallon pails. "There's one for every sourdough we make. You feed your children, we feed our sourdoughs every day." And for their rye bread, they've done that every day since 1956.

Bon Ton uses flour from Alberta, with some from Saskatchewan and heritage grains grown by John Schneider of Gold Forest Grains (see page 83). Dinner was delighted to buy hundreds of pounds of raspberries from Shady Lane Orchards in Strathcona County throughout the summer. The bakery serves as a Community Supported Agriculture pickup location for Riverbend Gardens (see page 81). It seems they are as artful at shaping community as they are at shaping loaves of bread.

Back in the bakery shop, Semler is standing with a shopping bag of bread and goodies. There's a loaf of heritage grains, potato bread, and that original rye. "You need to taste the quality yourself and know there's no compromise." Add generosity to the list of things that make Bon Ton such a success.

Boulangerie Bonjour | 8608 99 Street NW | 780-433-5924
yvanchartrand.com

Yvan Chartrand with his Osttiroler stone mill.
Photo by Karen Anderson.

"We do our own milling to get the exact flour we want," explains Boulangerie Bonjour owner Yvan Chartrand. He bought Bonjour in Edmonton's Mill Creek area in 2009 after spending 17 years owning and running two bakeries on Hokkaido in Japan, where his wife Ritsuko is from.

"Commercial flour mills remove the wheat germ. The germ is full of healthy fats but can go rancid if it sits too long so that's why they take it—and all its fibre—out. Sometimes they bleach it too. Commercial flour has very little vitamins or minerals." Chartrand is explaining the bakery's operations as we tour the back end on a quiet Monday morning. "We only use organic because we don't want to use anything that was sprayed with glyphosates (Roundup) and milling the whole wheat allows us to retain its nutrients. My son Kenny, who is also a baker, got us into doing our own milling. Now we mill six to seven tonnes each year."

The *levain* (sourdough) at Bonjour is over 20 years old. Breads take three days to make. Chartrand calls it "slow dough." White flour comes from Anita's Organic Mill in BC and he uses Mark Gibeau's Marquis wheat from Heritage Harvest in Strathmore (see page 273) for wheat loaves.

Back to visit on a Saturday morning, the lineup is almost out the door. "Small is good," says Chartrand. "The first thing everyone should see when they enter is a smile. My wife Ritsuko is on a first-name basis with 70 percent of our customers."

The Chartrands originally met in Edmonton and his mother's family are from Peace Country. "We were happy to come back here. There's a surprising number of people in the francophone community too." He's tending the ample French cheese counter as loaves of their big round "Miche" are sliced to the size that suits each customer's needs.

Leaving without some would be unthinkable after hearing all that went into its crafting. You can also enjoy Chartrand's breads at restaurants like Uccellino, Bar Bricco, Corso 32, Woodwork, and Cavern.

Calico Baking Company | 11068 95 Street | 587-520-0028
calicobaking.com

Zinovia Hardy (left) and Laurel Ferster.
Photo courtesy of the subjects.

Sometimes people doubt the power of a local food economy but Calico Baking Company is a good example of cause and effect in a local supply chain. You buy from them. They buy flour from Sunny Boy Foods in Camrose. Sunny Boy buys strictly from small organic grain farmers in the Camrose area. The grain growers buy their seeds and supplies locally, and on it goes.

Sunny Boy is an interesting choice for a flour source. That Alberta company has been making its hardy Prairie hot cereal mix since 1926 using wheat, rye, barley, and flax from nearby fields. Ferster and Hardy needed a local and organic source for their flour, and in Sunny Boy they found both.

"Currently we are waiting on this year's wheat harvest to come in so that we can pick up our next order," says Ferster. That's fresh flour. Both Ferster and Hardy have family farming roots that go back over 100 years. Flour is not the only local ingredient they use.

"Our baking uses real ingredients—grains from the field, milk and butter from the cows, eggs from the chickens—and so we try to source these things from Alberta producers as much as we can." Strathcona Stoneground Organics, K and K meats, and Foothills Creamery butter are other sources.

The pair have amassed a wealth of skills and knowledge related to artisan baking over the course of their careers but lacked a venue and opportunity to put them to use. "We also couldn't find the kind of breads and baking we wanted in the local marketplace so our decision to start our own business developed organically from there." Their croissants, breads, cookies, and hand pies disappear quickly at their year-round Old Strathcona Farmers' Market stall.

"We would love for Calico to be afforded some of the same reverence given to craft beer brewers and we'd love our bread to be served at all the best restaurants. In the meantime, we've only just started to scratch the surface of the wealth of baking traditions we'd like to explore."

Cally's Teas | 10151 82 Avenue | 780-757-8944 | callysteas.com

Cally Slater Dowson. Photo by Karen Anderson.

Cally Slater Dowson knows tea. Her parents immigrated to Quebec from England and sharing a cup of tea was central to their family's communications—good, bad, happy, or sad. Slater Dowson started selling her handcrafted tea blends out of a stall at the Old Strathcona Farmers' Market in 2003, graduated to a shop on 99 Street, and then moved to her current location on Whyte Avenue in 2012.

Cally's sells over 250 teas and tisanes (herbal infusions) from around the world. "And, from Flatbush, Alberta's Chickadee Farms we source spearmint, peppermint, and wild mint as well as calendula (marigolds), lemon balm, horsetail, Labrador tea from the Arctic, and Alberta chamomile. I'm quite partial to the Alberta chamomile—it smells like a meadow." The owners of Chickadee are wild crafters. "That means they harvest and use wild plants in ways that protect the plants and the environment. Our Mill Creek Sunshine Blend uses a lot of herbs from that farm."

British tea time would not be complete without specialties like cucumber sandwiches, shortbreads, scones, and clotted cream. Those items and light supper comfort foods like "dippy eggs" with toast soldiers, beans on toast, Welsh rarebit, and beef and porter pie are all made in-house. "We use organic eggs from Sunworks Farms (see page 134) in our baking and instead of importing Devonshire cream we use Vital Green Farms (see page 247) heavy cream as our clotted cream."

Cally's Teas keeps a bit of English (and Irish) culture alive for Edmonton with regular tea parties and themed Harry Potter, Mad Hatter, and Jane Austen events. They also celebrated Canada's 150th birthday with Nanaimo bars, butter tarts, flapper pie, and even poutine. A future visit might provide a chance for you to choose the truly Canadian Labrador tea over the Lapsang souchong. Slater Dowson has worked to give us these choices.

Duchess Bake Shop | 10718 124 Street | 780-488-4999
duchessbakeshop.com

Giselle Courteau. Photo courtesy of the subject.

Duchess Bake Shop hasn't yet celebrated a decade in Edmonton but it is hard to imagine the city without it. Fine French patisserie meets Prairie kitchen home-cooked goods, and even on the coldest winter mornings there's a lineup at the door at opening. "We have 550 spots in our Duchess Atelier cooking school classes for a three-month period and they sell out in less than a minute. According to our calculations we have about 3,000 people vying for those spots. I think there is a real lack of people to teach baking to home cooks and we are definitely filling a void," says owner/baker Giselle Courteau.

Courteau and her then husband Garner Beggs were living in Japan deciding their "what next" after teaching ESL when the idea for a café and bakery inspired them to go the distance and start their business in 2007. After much research and testing they opened their doors in October of 2009 to instant success. They credit experienced baker and business partner Jacob Pelletier, who is Courteau's husband now, for helping them get to the point of thriving, not just surviving. The business has grown from 1,500 to 4,500 square feet and now employs 65 staff.

"We use 125 kilograms of butter a day which we import from New Zealand and Ireland for the 84 percent milk fat content. That works out to 22 tons of butter a year. We will only use organic flour and are loyal to Anita's Organic Mill from BC because they are consistently able to supply the vast quantities we need. All of our eggs come from Four Whistle Farm (see page 85), we use fresh local saskatoon berries in season and rhubarb and strawberries from Sparrow's Nest Organics (see page 82)."

Courteau's proudest achievement for Duchess Bake Shop is that their eponymous cookbook won a gold medal at Taste Canada's culinary writing awards. "We self-published, so it really meant a lot to us. I am working on another cookbook now specifically for home cooks. That's what I love the most—baking, testing recipes, and teaching others." Baking is, after all, meant to be shared.

FanFan Pâtisserie | 10330 80 Avenue | 587-524-9899
fanfanpatisserie.com

Franck Bouilhol with one of his mille-feuilles.
Photo by Karen Anderson.

Lyon has been called the gastronomic capital of the world. Now, a little bit of Lyon has come to Edmonton. Franck Bouilhol, owner of FanFan Pâtisserie, is a pastry chef graduate from the Alain Ducasse Formation et Conseil—Ducasse Institute Nationale Supérieure de la Pâtisserie in Yssingeaux, near Lyon.

Bouilhol was born near Lyon, and his stepfather was a baker. "I stopped at the same bakery every day of my school life for *pain au chocolat*. Even at 15 years old, when my friends were all into cigarettes, this is what I spent my money on. When I think back to how good that pastry was, every single day, I realize how good that baker was. It's hard to achieve that kind of consistency."

Bouilhol admits to being a perfectionist. "I love the technical aspect of pastry and the more I do something, the more I want to improve. My wife calls it a sickness." His wife is a neonatologist, specializing in the care of premature infants and their families. "If I have a bad day baking, I just have to talk to my wife to put everything in perspective."

After Bouilhol arrived in Edmonton in 2014, Culina's Brad and Cindy Lazarenko (see page 66) were the first customers for his wholesale business. By 2017 he was able to move to a new space with an 80:20 split of small kitchen to tiny retail outlet, and he is very happy to have a storefront.

The display cabinets are jewel boxes of *viennoiseries* (the croissant, *pain au chocolat*, and brioche family), *pâtisseries* (the cake family), macarons, and containers of gelato and sorbet. Bouilhol imports Irish butter and French Valrhona chocolate but uses Alberta ingredients otherwise. "We are happy to have a loyal clientele already. Our staff know everyone by name. We know people are coming for coffee, pastry and an experience."

Seeing customers leave with their pastry picks carefully tucked into boxes so elegant they could double as evening bags and hearing Bouilhol's warm "*à bientôt*," it seems like the creation of that experience factor is a *fait accompli*.

Sugared & Spiced Baked Goods | Rear-10334 82 Avenue | 780-244-2253
sugaredandspiced.ca

Jeff and Amy Nachtigall. Photo by Karen Anderson.

For Amy and Jeff Nachtigall's Sugared & Spiced bakery in Old Strathcona, community is where their story starts and ends.

Amy was asked by a friend if she'd sell her baking at the Highlands Farmers' Market in their close-knit inner-city neighbourhood. That was 2012 and after selling out her home-baked cookies weekly, and enjoying the process more than she ever imagined, she enrolled in the Northern Alberta Institute of Technology's Baking Certificate program the following year.

Custom orders—prepared in a shared rental kitchen—began rolling in. Using the Alberta Treasury Branch BoostR crowdfunding platform and the support of the community contained in their email list, the Nachtigalls raised a record $57,000 in funding toward opening their own bakery.

"Finding our location in Old Strathcona was gold for us. This is the kind of neighbourhood we seek out when we travel. We are close to the farmers' market and all the festivals here," says Jeff.

A variety of cookies, macarons, meringues, and cakes made with all of the above on top—epic cakes—burst with colour against the sleek black and white of the bakery nestled into the alley behind Whyte Avenue. All the baking is done with real flour, eggs, butter, and milk—and no mixes ever. "Right now, we use eggs from Four Whistle Farms (see page 85) and ham from Irvings Farm Fresh (see page 128), but I see us sourcing local a lot more now that we have the shop," says Amy when asked about Alberta ingredients.

The future looks bright for this pair. Originally from Winnipeg, they love Edmonton's long summer nights and exploring the trail systems in the river valley and beyond. It must be how they can eat Amy's peanut butter chocolate chip bacon cookies and stay looking so fit and happy. "I love creating and using my hands every day," she says. "I used to paint and draw; now this has become my art form. We love being part of our community's celebrations and their joy."

Transcend Coffee Roasters | 9570 76 Avenue NW | 780-430-9198
8708 109 Street | 780-756-8882 | transcendcoffee.ca

Poul Mark at the Ritchie Market Transcend Coffee Roastery. Photo by Karen Anderson.

"Ninety-five percent of coffee beans are purchased at below the cost of production. It means it is an industry that relies on exploitation to survive. I got into it to be part of the solution, and not contribute to the status quo."

Poul Mark has a law degree from the University of Alberta specializing in Aboriginal rights. He loved his clients but not the practice. When he got into the coffee business he wanted to be able to trace the coffee his company sold from seed to cup. This is where he discovered that the industry "was built on the backs of the world's most impoverished people." His deeply ingrained sense of social justice was awakened and he decided to build a different kind of coffee company.

"I spent three years travelling as a coffee judge so that I could meet the best growers in small coffee-growing countries. We pay them an amount that allows them sustainability for themselves and their workers. The quality of bean we get in return is phenomenal."

Transcend is making a small but important difference. "To put it in perspective, we roast 150,000 pounds of coffee in a year. Tim Hortons goes through 300,000 pounds a day. But, our wholesale business keeps growing and we're up every year. People can help by asking coffee shops if they know how much their producers get paid and whether they can trace from cup to bean."

Mark has opened five cafés and closed three. "I'm not really a business guy. Things will improve for us now that I hired an operations manager." He laughs. "We love our Garneau and Ritchie locations. Ritchie Market is a chance for us to bring the manufacturing of goods back into the public domain. With our Probat roaster here, people can see the coffee being made. For me, this has always been about being embedded in our community."

Fuge Fine Meat | fuge.ca

Steven Furgiuele. Photo by Curtis Comeau.

"Fur-jew-elly." That's how you pronounce the last name of this talented *salumiere*—sausage and salami maker. Steven Furgiuele grew up in Sault Ste. Marie, Ontario, making sausages with his Italian immigrant father and French-Canadian mother.

While other kids were out playing Furgiuele and his siblings had to help can tomatoes and make sausages. With a prodigal palate, he admits that he always secretly liked helping. "When we got to eat what we had made, the rewards tasted so sweet to me.

"My skills were graduated. Each year my father gave me more to do. There were never any recipes. We drank a bit of wine, chopped and ground while my father put in a few handfuls of spices. We are incredibly close and now after my professional training, I understand the science behind all we did and can share that with him."

After a career in music, Furgiuele remembered his love of food and cooking and attended culinary school in North Bay. "They let me teach what I knew to the other students and they featured my cured meats and charcuterie on our graduation buffet."

After stints in Waterton and a hotel in Edmonton, Furgiuele went to work at Culina Mill Creek and went from lunch chef to general manager and head chef in the four years before it closed. "I learned to love our local suppliers working with owner/chef Brad Lazarenko (see page 66)—he's been my greatest mentor."

Closing that chapter allowed him to open a new one and now that he has secured his own facility with a drying chamber he designed, he's able to make and offer a broad array of cured meats, charcuterie, sausages, and salami including the Kielbasa Lazarenko as a nod to his former employer and his Ukrainian heritage. Furgiuele wholesales to many restaurants and markets (check website for retailers) and makes all the sausages for Otto Food and Drink, a place devoted to local beers and meats. Customers that want to meet him in person will find him at farmers' markets listed on his website. "The markets have turned Edmonton into a small-town community for me. I love meeting my customers—especially the kids—and I'm really thrilled with how much sausage people in Edmonton can eat."

Porc Salé | 10351 82 Avenue | 780-717-7111 | porcsale.com

Mark Kalynchuk at the Almanac bistro, where he is the executive chef. Photo by Karen Anderson.

It's a quiet Sunday morning. The sunlight streams into the Almanac bistro, through the fresh green leaves of spring on tree-lined Whyte Avenue. Though he worked into the wee hours the night before, executive chef Mark Kalynchuk offers a coffee and excitedly leads the way down a back set of creaky stairs to the basement. It feels a bit like one of Harry Potter's secret passageways.

We arrive in a small butchery and meat processing facility that he has built himself. There are knives and saws and a meat cutter on one wall, a huge walk-in cooler for aging his cured creations, and a refrigerated showcase for the customers to view the meats he's cut or cured or the sausages he's stuffed. A few shelves behind us hold locally made jams, jellies, and mustards. "I'm looking for more local to sell here." He knows a lot about local.

This Northern Alberta Institute of Technology culinary apprentice grad grew up eating great kielbasa and sausages from his Ukrainian culture and family home east of Edmonton. "I was frustrated at culinary school because they were teaching ice sculpture instead of things chefs need like how to clean a hood fan or fix plumbing. Getting out and having a chance to work as the sous chef for chef Andrew Cowan was fun because he was so passionate. He knows a lot about charcuterie and started me off with the easy stuff, like making fresh sausages. From there, I've read every book I could get my hands on."

Particular about ingredients, Kalynchuk sources his animals from farmers he trusts for quality like bison from Jerry Kitt of First Nature Farms (see page 36) and pork from Irvings Farm Fresh (see page 128) and Bear and the Flower Farm in Irricana. "Because I use so much less salt than commercial brands, you can really taste the flavour of the meat."

Look for charcuterie, made from whole muscles, to salamis, terrines, and pâtés, and dry-aged steaks. Leave with a ham, bacon, or back bacon hand sliced to the thickness you like. "Prosciutto is coming!" Food artisans need time to work their magic.

Christine Sandford | Biera in Blind Enthusiasm Brewery
9570 76 Avenue NW | 587-525-8589 | blindenthusiasm.ca

Christine Sandford at Biera.
Photo by Karen Anderson.

Christine Sandford grew up in Edmonton. "I thought I wanted to be an interior designer but I got an Easy-Bake oven when I was little. Instead of making the cakes, I tried to recreate my mom's fanciest meals in it."

On a post-high school trip to Europe, her favourite thing was exploring the markets. "There were so many things I'd never seen. I came home and went to the Northern Alberta Institute of Technology culinary program.

"Working at Culina Mill Creek shaped me. Brad Lazarenko (see page 66), the chef/owner, was far ahead of his time. From technique to use of local, I learned that these are the investments that pay off. Customers would say, 'How'd you make this taste so good?' and we'd get to explain that it was the taste of good quality food in season."

In 2014, Sandford went back to Europe for a few years. She worked in Belgium at La Buvette and then at Michelin-starred In de Wulf where they had their own farmer. Another stint in Gent's De Superette brought her skills in baking and charcoal grilling. Returning to Edmonton she worked as a meat cutter at Acme Meat Market (see page 84) for two years before being recruited by the owner of Blind Enthusiasm brewery to be the executive chef of its restaurant, Biera. Before opening in July of 2017 she did *stages* with the world's most famous butcher, Dario Cecchini, in Chianti, and at Relae in Copenhagen.

"We don't make pub food. It's food to complement great beer. We get all our meats from Acme. I took the staff on a farm tour with Galimax Trading (see page 250). I wanted them to see the work the Mans family does to grow organically. We get herbs from Prairie Gardens (see page 80) and support August Organics (see page 77), Sundog Organics, Mo-Na Food Distributors (see page 79), and Effing Seafoods.

"Nothing makes me happier than when somebody says, 'That was delicious'—or when I get the chance to educate people about food."

Brad and Cindy Lazarenko | Culina Restaurants and Catering
Culina Café at the Muttart | 9626 96A Street NW | 780-466-1181
culinafamily.com

Siblings Brad and Cindy Lazarenko at Victoria Park Golf Course in Edmonton's lush river valley. Photo by Karen Anderson.

The food sensibilities of this savvy pair of siblings were developed as teens with jobs as servers and dishwashers. Both left the industry for the lure of more regular nine-to-five office jobs but soon returned, craving the excitement they got from the restaurant lifestyle.

While bartending, Brad volunteered in the kitchen at then newly opened Normand's Bistro. He wanted to learn technique from a classically trained chef. "Nobody in Edmonton at that time even knew what a bistro was."

Chef Peter Johner took him under his wing at Boccalino and later at Packrat Louie where Brad worked as host, server, and bartender in the front and as a cook in the back end. Watching Edmonton's food scene evolve, with places like Jack's Grill serving fresh mesclun greens, Boccalino having an in-house microbrewery (years before it was trendy), Bruno's Italian having a stone oven for pizzas, and Savoy bringing small plates and martinis to Edmonton, inspired Brad to go out on his own in 2004.

He started sourcing local ingredients when the term didn't exist. "I just wanted to support other small businesses. They were owners like me who came to dine in my restaurant. It just made sense to build our community." Fuge Fine Meat (see page 63), Boulangerie Bonjour (see page 56), Pinocchio Ice Cream, and Cally's Teas (see page 58) are businesses his purchasing power supports, rather than reinventing their skill sets in his own restaurants.

Cindy started as a host at Hardware Grill (see page 67) and as a server at Il Portico before partnering and then buying her own restaurant, which became Culina Highlands in 2007. Her food is Ukrainian modern and she earned a spot among *enRoute*'s top 10 restaurants in Canada. She worked with Brad as head of catering and manager of Culina Muttart. With a love of design and marketing, she also owns a company called OnOurTable with her husband Geoff Lilge, an award-winning local designer.

The Lazarenkos have both proven themselves, are comfortable with their skills and whatever project they are working on, and serve the food they love to eat. It's a reflection of them—completely genuine.

Larry Stewart | Hardware Grill | 9698 Jasper Avenue | 780-423-0969
hardwaregrill.com

Chef Larry Stewart. Photo by Christophe Benard Photography.

Larry Stewart is a self-taught master of cooking who grew up on a farm in Ontario and started his career as a dishwasher at the age of 16. "That's where I got the bug." He had a brief stint in university to study business before starting up with Canadian Pacific (CP) hotels in Winnipeg. In their grand style of hotel, he learned everything from butchery to baking, and after transferring to Calgary's CP hotel at the airport he even ran their airline food program for a time.

In the '80s he became the opening chef at an immensely popular restaurant called 4th Street Rose. The owners were Californian and the menu items like the Burger Queen and Caesar salads served in large glass jars became instant classics.

He joined the Earls restaurant chain in '84 and when he moved to Edmonton to open a restaurant there, he stayed. After a decade, tired of the corporate chef life and longing to cook again, he opened Hardware Grill. His wife had found the location a block from the convention centre, surrounded by hotels, and they dove in.

"I like to be on the leading edge." There was no downtown dining scene in 1996 but with so much travel to California, he wanted a place that would celebrate all things local, from the construction company to artists and tables by a local welder. He scoured for suppliers and cooked seasonal cuisine. When others were flying in strawberries in Edmonton's long cold winters, he was serving rhubarb compote. Everything was artisanal-style and made in-house.

"I wanted to go back to providing a kitchen that cultivated a culture to develop great chefs." And that he did. So many of Alberta's great chefs have come out of Hardware Grill, including Cam Dobranski, Andrew Fung, Cory Walsh, Evan Robertson, Sean O'Connor, Jordan Wiggins of Alta and Alder Room, and Peter Keith of Secret Meats.

Now that so many restaurants understand that ingredients taste better when sourced locally, Stewart finds the suppliers are stretched thin. He hopes for more and loves to support Wild Game's Warren Smith for bison and Alberta lamb.

He's had a long and distinguished career, but you'll still find him on the line each night because he still finds it exciting. "I love the lifestyle, it's still fun for me and when almost every night someone sends a message back to the kitchen that they just had the best meal of their life, that's what keeps me going."

Kitchen by Brad | 101-10130 105 Street | 780-757-7704
kitchenbybrad.ca

Kitchen by Brad's Brad Smoliak in his dream teaching kitchen. Photo by Karen Anderson.

Born in Edmonton and often unwell as a child, Brad Smoliak credits TV shows like *The Galloping Gourmet* and Julia Child's *The French Chef* for creating his longing to cook. "They had so much passion and were really fun." He also had two Ukrainian *bubbas* (grandmas) nearby. Both were great cooks and his bubba in Vegreville, where the family went for Sunday dinner each week, always took the time to explain where each part of the meal had come from. Smoliak's palate understood at an early age the difference local makes to the taste of food.

Out of high school he apprenticed under chef Larry Stewart (see page 67) and the two co-founded and owned Hardware Grill in 1996. Prior to opening he spent time at the Culinary Institute of America to learn sausage making and charcuterie.

A love of product development was born out of the skills he acquired and in 2012 he opened Kitchen by Brad to consult and offer his expertise in commercial food development. He offers a cooking school component—a place for people to gather and enjoy cooking as a skill that will nourish them through life.

In 2014, one of his cooking class guests who worked with Parks Canada suggested a collaboration with nearby Elk Island National Park and an annual long-table dinner series was born. "It's good for the park because it gives people a reason to go out there." He sees that food can be a driver for tourism and that Alberta has a bounty of excellence to offer the world.

Favourite local food producers include Irvings Farm Fresh (see page 128) pork products, Winding Road Artisan Cheese (see page 29) from Smoky Valley for his perogy stuffing, and Fairwinds Farm (see page 244) goat cheeses for salads. He trolls the weekly City Market Downtown on 104 Street for vegetables from vendors like Sundog Organics, Coleman's, and Steve and Dan's BC fruits. He uses Highwood Crossing (see page 274) canola out of High River, Graham's honey and Kobe classic Wagyu beef from Camrose or Acme Meat Market (see page 84) for other special cuts. Having more local to choose from is the biggest and best change he's seen in Alberta's food scene and he intends to keep working with tourism to bring more people here to enjoy it.

Blair Lebsack | Rge Rd | 10643 123 Street NW | 780-447-4577 | rgerd.ca

Chef Blair Lebsack. Photo by Kevin Kossowan.

"I grew up on a farm in Joffre with milk cows, chickens, pigs, and a huge garden. We grew and cooked all our own food. I didn't know how good our food was until I moved out." Blair Lebsack, the award-winning chef of Rge Rd restaurant, got into cooking after too many bad pizzas with his college roommates.

"People told me if I was going to get into cooking, I should go straight to hotels because back then they still made 95 percent of their own products. My first five years were about learning technique in Canmore, Banff, and Calgary. When I came back to Edmonton I was at the Union Bank for five years and ended up at the Northern Alberta Institute of Technology culinary program." People thought Lebsack wouldn't leave such a cushy position, but he was determined to have his own place.

"In 2011, I started hosting on-farm dinners with Nature's Green Acres (see page 129). We'd set the dates, harvest the gardens, kill a pig or chickens, and that's when I knew what kind of restaurant I wanted to be. Rge Rd opened in July of 2017 with our own butcher shop for the whole beef, pigs, ducks, rabbits, lamb, and goats on the menu."

Once monthly, Lebsack retails mortadella, smoked hunter sausages, fresh sausages, pâtés, rillettes, bresaola, capicolla, prepared hamburgers, and pork pies. "We have to use a whole animal before we cut into the next one.

"I do it because I love cooking for people. My wife, Caitlin Fulton, who is also my business partner in charge of the front of the house—we love the hospitality. It's like a party every night."

Lebsack doesn't forget about vegetables. He enlists Tam Andersen of Prairie Gardens (see page 80) to grow specific vegetables as well as August Organics (see page 77) and Riverbend Gardens (see page 81).

"Alberta is bigger than France from a land perspective—why should we try to lump ourselves into a few foods? We have boreal forest and the north and south are different. It's time to explore that."

Shane Chartrand | SC at River Cree Resort and Casino | 300 East Lapotac Boulevard, Enoch | 780-930-2636 | rivercreeresort.com/dining

Chef Shane Chartrand. Photo courtesy of the subject.

Shane Chartrand was born Enoch Cree but was adopted into a Métis family near Penhold as a young boy. His adopted father wanted him to know as much of his Cree culture as possible so he taught Chartrand to fish, hunt, and butcher game. "We didn't have a lot of money but I got to grow up close to the land."

Chartrand dreamed of studying the visual arts. "Even though I didn't really even know what that meant. I just wanted to focus on the arts." To earn money, he started cooking in truck stops near his home. "I really liked it so I went to NAIT (Northern Alberta Institute of Technology) for culinary school and after that I worked in every kind of restaurant imaginable in Calgary, Edmonton, and Toronto."

Chartrand is currently the chef de cuisine of SC restaurant at the River Cree Resort and Casino. He uses his time off to learn as much as possible about indigenous food and cultures. "I travel from nation to nation to study their sovereignty. The more nations I meet, the more I learn."

With his friend, country music star Paul Brandt, he's spent time with the Siksika. Also in Alberta, he's befriended the people of the Beaver, Lac La Biche, Blackfoot, and Kainai nations. In BC, he spends time with the Haida, the Salish, and the Penticton band, and in Washington, the Lummi. "Each nation has protocol and etiquette to be respected and learned from. I want to share each nation's stories because they are inspirational and unforgettable."

Chartrand will share these stories and the food of our Aboriginal people in a book he is writing with Jennifer Cockrall-King. "I had to write it with someone I could trust—a close friend. We will tell stories that people will want to read five times."

And the food? "There will be recipes for home-cooks—my mom and dad's recipes—but there'll also be recipes for chefs." Examples? "Bannock of course, but tweaked, preserves, prairie chowders, and lots of bison, I always have a freezer full of bison. For chefs—how to cook bear liver.

"The crux of information our indigenous culture holds is too valuable to be lost. The book will be called *Marrow: Progressive Indigenous Cuisine*." Watch for it.

Brayden Kozak | Three Boars Eatery | 8424 109 Street NW
780-757-2600 | threeboars.ca

Brayden Kozak at Farrow Sandwiches in Ritchie, Edmonton. Photo by Karen Anderson.

"Growing up in Wainwright, the entire town was my playground." Brayden Kozak got a job pumping gas across the street from a roadside diner during high school. "I liked the atmosphere at that diner and saw how food, even a well-made club sandwich, could shape somebody's day. They gave me a job as a dishwasher and when one of the servers left, I asked if I could give that a try." He laughs. "I was pretty awkward socially so I wasn't very good. But they didn't give up on me. Eventually they put me on the line. To this day, I still love making something over and over, trying to make it better each time. When you're really busy, that's a rush."

After a gap year Kozak attended the Northern Alberta Institute of Technology culinary program. "I could cook but I really upped my knife skills there. Working at a place called Savoy with Brad Lazarenko (see page 66) set the bar for me as a chef. I got interested in running small kitchens working in Vancouver and Victoria but came back to Edmonton to help raise my daughter Davey here." He worked as the head chef at his friend Abel Shiferaw's Sugar Bowl Café in Garneau for three years.

"One day I was walking by a little place near there and saw a sign, 'Pints and Plates—Opening Soon.' I sent in my resumé. Nobody else wanted to run it. It was so tiny. It became Three Boars and I started going to the farmers' market weekly and contacted all the local producers I could find. Jeff Senger of Sangudo Meats (see page 40) and Kevin Kossowan (see page 75) had made films featuring farms and I just followed their path."

Kozak contributed to Alberta's food story as a chef in 2015's Cook It Raw Alberta produced by Alberta Culinary Tourism Alliance. "It made me proud to be from Alberta. I was up to my neck in local anyway. I can't imagine owning a restaurant and not using local ingredients."

You can also find Kozak at both locations of Farrow Sandwiches (8422 109 Street NW | 780-757-4160 / 9855 76 Avenue NW | 780-757-0132 | farrowsandwiches.ca) **and at Wishbone** (Upper Level, 10542 Jasper Avenue | 780-757-6758 | eatwishbone.ca).

Jacek Chocolate | jacekchocolate.com

Jacqueline Jacek. Photo courtesy of Jacek Chocolate.

Jacqueline Jacek has been creating chocolate confections in Alberta since 2009, releasing a new line of chocolate fashions every season and calling herself a "cocoanista" chocolate designer. This marketing pro, with a love of fashion and chocolate, designed a business that brings together all her passions and now she's on a mission to spread joy (her personal raison d'être) with haute couture chocolate style.

One of Jacek's staff, chef Curtis Jones, had experience as a bean-to-bar chocolate maker so in 2015 the company began sourcing beans to create their own "fabric" for use in their design process. "For our chocolate to be joyful it has to be ethical. It was important for us to go to the source and see if they were truly joyful beans."

In the summer of 2017, Jacek went to Costa Rica to see for herself the conditions of the chocolate producers there. "I knew they worked really hard, but I didn't know how much pride they take in producing high-quality chocolate for us. That was joyful to see. The children on the farms, which are only one to two hectares, are now looking at cacao as a business they'd like to get into. That comes from chocolate makers like us paying more for their 'A' grade beans. They are motivated."

All this talk about joy might seem a bit esoteric but Jacek has set a "BHAG" for herself. "My Big Hairy Audacious Goal is to bring joy to 1 million people by July 31, 2024. We are keeping track by counting the number of six-piece (or larger) boxes that we sell."

Jacek is stepping up her progress on the runway to her dream. She plans to triple the size of her Sherwood Park workshop so that guests can come and tour and engage in chocolate experiences. "They'll be able to watch us sort and roast the beans and, of course, there will be tastings." Now there's a surefire way to spread joy. Check the website for Jacek's boutique and retailer locations and online shop.

The Ruby Apron | 780-906-0509 | therubyapron.ca

Kaelin Whittaker with a loaf of her Real Bread sourdough. Photo by Karen Anderson.

Ballymaloe is a 100-acre farm and cookery school in County Cork, Ireland. The only cooking school in the world to be so endowed, it is on the leading edge of sustainability, closing the gap between farming and what we cook. Kaelin Whittaker, founder of the Ruby Apron, attended Ballymaloe's 12-week intensive immersion cook's certification program for a true farm-to-fork education.

"I had finished an arts degree and always loved to cook. I admired the connectivity Ballymaloe has created within their community and the incredible food culture of Ireland. I thought, that's what I'd like to bring back to Alberta, that's the kind of teacher I'd like to be. I decided it was now or never and took the plunge."

Whittaker fell in love with sourdough bread making during her time in Ireland in 2015. She struggled initially when she returned to Edmonton to get a loaf to rise but when she found Highwood Crossing (see page 274) organic flours, "it was magic." She blends Highwood's flours with Red Fife, Park, and einkorn wheat flours from Gold Forest Grains (see page 83) for the breads and pastas that she creates with her students. She now has five different sourdough starters "mothering along."

"The biggest thrill for me is when my students send me photos of their successes—then I know I've truly made a difference in someone's life and the transfer of skills and knowledge has taken root." To foster our Alberta food culture, Whittaker is the driving force behind Real Bread Edmonton, a forum to connect bakers of all levels, grain farmers, and anyone who wants to learn more about making bread by hand with or without the help of commercial yeasts. She organizes bulk flour purchasing, mentors and fields questions, and is hopeful that interest will rise with each successful loaf of bread group members produce.

Get Cooking | 11050 104 Avenue NW | 780-566-2106
getcookingedmonton.com

Doreen Prei (left) and Kathryn Joel.
Photo by Karen Anderson.

Like mother, like daughter. Kathryn Joel's mother had never cooked a meal when she arrived on a plane from England to be married in Canada. Once she started she loved it so much that she attended George Brown Culinary Institute and started her own catering company. Joel grew up cooking at her mom's side but left Canada for a career in banking back in her mother's homeland. "I was in banking but taking days off to attend specialty cooking classes at Notting Hill's famous Books for Cooks culinary studio."

She decided to follow her joy and, at age 28, she signed up for Le Cordon Bleu in London. A decade later, after extensive travel and two children, she attended Leiths School of Food and Wine, where she fell in love with teaching cooking. Her love of local, fresh, approachable food was solidified with three months at Ireland's Ballymaloe Cookery School.

Moving to Edmonton and starting Get Cooking in her own home kitchen was her way to support the local food supply chain, realize a dream of teaching people to cook, and stay close to her children until they launched. Through patronage at Edmonton's farmers' markets she sourced a truly local supply chain including farms like Tangle Ridge Ranch, Riverbend Gardens (see page 81), Reclaim Urban Farm, Vesta Gardens, Moose Wood Acres, and Gold Forest Grains (see page 83). "I love when our students taste the difference in flavour that local fresh food produces. Then we don't have to convince them why spending a few dollars more matters."

In 2014, Joel moved Get Cooking to a commercial space at Grant MacEwan University and in 2016 she partnered with chef Doreen Prei to continue teaching, but elevated the offerings based on Prei's extensive Michelin-star restaurant experience. The two hope to eventually write their own cookbooks and perhaps open a restaurant and food store to complement their cookery school.

Kevin Kossowan | kevinkossowan.com

Kevin Kossowan. Photo by Jeff Senger.

While discussing his career as a food-centric filmmaker, Kevin Kossowan reveals the driving force behind his work: "I'd like people to be at ease in nature." His passion for inspiring people to reconnect with Alberta's bounty stems from his own personal journey of rediscovering our wild places and all they have to offer. While the one-time financial planner grew up hunting and gardening with his family, he drifted away from the land in his 20s. While visiting relatives in Europe, he was asked what a typical Albertan meal would be and realized that beyond the beef and pork he'd grown up with, he didn't have a clue. He couldn't even name an Alberta farmer.

In 2005, inspired by Minnesota chef/ filmmaker Daniel Klein at theperennialplate.com, he began documenting what socially responsible adventurous eating looks like in Alberta. Since 2007, he's been sharing his journey with critically acclaimed internet videos that he says are "more learn along with than how to." They cover backyard farming, growing and gleaning fruit, cooking with fire, sourdough bread, preserving and cellaring food, butchering your own meat, making charcuterie, and fermenting cider.

Kossowan veered onto a wilder path when he realized he could fill a knowledge void for the skills required to hunt, fish, and forage wild game and plants. He now spends 40–50 days a year in the field documenting those skills. Going forward, he plans to strike a balance with a new series of affordable online video workshops on food skills.

Kossowan has crunched the numbers right along with his homegrown carrots. Turns out, 20 cents' worth of seeds will grow you more carrots than you can consume. His legacy will be showing people that acquiring skills is the key to food abundance and economy—not more big-box stores. He'd also like to deepen our understanding of the Aboriginal people's culinary knowledge of food and to celebrate their ancient ways, fusing them with modern skills.

Hens and rabbits peck and nibble in his backyard. Raised garden beds and a food forest featuring 10 different fruit species grace his front yard. With his knowledge of how to live off the land, Kevin Kossowan is one Albertan we'd like to be stranded in the wild with.

Strathcona Spirits Distillery | 10122 81 Avenue NW | strathconaspirits.ca

Adam Smith. Photo by Karen Anderson.

"Let the confusion, music, and distilling begin!" This is the introduction to an invitation to a Tex-Mex polka cocktail hour event that Adam Smith, the owner of Strathcona Spirits, is participating in shortly after our visit. Its freewheeling style suits him to a T.

"Distillation is a concentration of everything that's interesting to me—politics, history, science, and nature." Music is also connected as Smith formerly ran a music venue called Baby Seal Club in the space that's now his distillery.

Smith formerly worked in the craft brewery industry on Vancouver Island and at Rig Hand Craft Distillery. He was the first to register a distillery in Edmonton. It was a long road to getting up and running. "There was about two years of paperwork and then the challenge of finding a still. They are very much in demand. Ours came from the Ozarks. It weighs 6,500 pounds. I drove down there to get it with a buddy and ended up staying for a few weeks while we toured the music scene." Again with the music connection.

"I got a lot of help from the other distilleries in the province. Most spirits sold here come from big multinational corporations. It'd be great to have a sliver of that pie for Alberta businesses and to be part of the local movement where people can enjoy spirits made from local ingredients."

Strathcona Spirits uses hard spring wheat from 20 minutes away in Leduc County for their vodka. They distill it 20 times before filtering to get it to the state of smoothness they desire. Their Badland Seaberry Gin has juniper foraged in the Badlands along the Red Deer River as well as sea buckthorn, which flourishes around Edmonton. Both taste like great poetry.

Smith got his licence in 2014, the first bottles hit the shelves of liquor stores in December of 2016, and sales have spread across the province and to Saskatchewan as well. Visit his tasting room and tours—maybe they'll be set to Tex-Mex polka music.

August Organics | Leduc County | 780-987-4338 | augustorganics.com

Dan and Kristine Vriend at the Old Strathcona Farmers' Market in Edmonton. Photo by Karen Anderson.

Dan Vriend's father was one of the founders of Old Strathcona Farmers' Market and was also the first certified organic family farmer in Canada. Vriend remembers his early teen years getting up at four o'clock in the morning on Saturdays to load and drive to the market. He worked the stall until late morning and was then allowed to go to the 50-cent matinee at the Princess Theatre on Whyte Avenue. "We just had to be back by three o'clock to pack up and go home."

After high school, he attended Olds College and then, itching to get back on the land, he worked on other people's farms. When he and Kristine married in 1993, it was time to go back home and help his father. They bought the property they currently own in Leduc County in 2002. It took three years but they were certified organic by Pro-Cert in 2005.

"When my father retired, I was able to buy his machinery and take over his stall at the market. He taught me that organics is doing your best to take care of creation while letting nature work on its own without interfering. Honesty and integrity are vital to everything we do. We don't bend rules or fake certificates. Anyone can call Pro-Cert any time to check our records."

August Organics grows over 25 types of vegetables with more than 150 different varieties on 20 of their 100 acres of land. Sixty of the acres are certified organic to allow for rest and rotation; the rest are leased out.

"I always say that we don't sell vegetables, we make friends. Our customers are our friends and with being our friend you get the opportunity to buy vegetables. Kristine and I do this for the lifestyle. We get to meet people, eat and live well, and be outside every day. We are connected to the big picture of what the food cycle is. It's a higher purpose. We do it for our community." The Vriends make their living from one farm and one market.

Lactuca Urban Farm | 11306 79 Street | 780-218-7270 | lactuca.ca

Travis Kennedy and Vicky Berg at Lactuca Urban Farm. Photo by Karen Anderson.

Travis Kennedy grew up on Salt Spring Island and worked at market gardens as a teen. He attended Olds College for a greenhouse production and nursery management degree and then returned to the island to work with Michael Ableman, learning about mixed cropping from the renowned writer and food activist. In 2005, Kennedy came to the University of Alberta to do a B.Sc. in sustainability. He founded the Edmonton Organic Growers Guild to help others learn organic gardening skills and to grow food for those in need.

After the birth of his daughter in 2012, he still wanted to grow but only had a 30-by-30-foot plot. He knew there was a niche market for lettuce (lactuca) greens and began growing them in rotation for sales at farmers' markets and to food trucks and restaurants. "Duchess Bake Shop (see page 59) bought 40 pounds a week."

In 2014, Lactuca moved to property owned by Northlands, one of Canada's oldest agricultural societies, and became Canada's first urban farm. A little over an acre of lush soil and vegetation now sits where a concrete slab of parking lot previously existed. "The ultimate vision is to create an economic model that can be duplicated."

Kennedy now holds the full-time position of horticultural manager for the City of Edmonton so he has hired Vicky Berg as the farm manager and a few other workers for weeding, watering, and working the 124 Grand Market, and Southwest Edmonton Farmers' Market where they sell their produce.

"We also have a mandate to provide education and for the locals and tourists alike to experience what it means to farm." As if on cue, two women stroll down the lane toward us on a calm and sunny summer morning and Berg goes to greet them. There are beehives, a chicken coop, and rainbows of lettuce and herbs. The garlic, heirloom tomatoes, carrots, peas, beets, and corn are making good progress in a year when spring came late. "Every customer we've ever gained at a market comes back. They love to give 'taste-imony' about the quality. We spoil them for life and they can never go back to produce from a clamshell." Change happens one customer at a time.

Mo-Na Food Distributors | 9320 60 Avenue | 780-435-4370 | monafood.ca

Michael Aventi with some of the fresh mushrooms Mo-Na is famous for. Photo by Karen Anderson.

Sitting down with Michael Aventi is an unexpected lesson in history and ecology. Turns out the University of Alberta has a quarter-section (640-acre) farm in the middle of its campus and Aventi's grandfather was its farmer. His mother's family farmed near Lac La Biche.

"I am Italian so I grew up loving mushrooms and foraging for them with my family. I had dabbled in small business but when I found Mo-Na Food for sale—it's been around since the 1980s—I jumped at the chance to buy it. Mushrooms are a big part of what we sell."

Aventi was also a member of the Alberta Mycological Society (wildmushrooms.ws) and loved their annual outings to the boreal forests around Lac La Biche. "We've got six to eight foragers we work with now. They've got to have the capability to clean, refrigerate, package, and ship their products to us at market grade plus carry invoices."

He reflects on changes in the industry. "I'm concerned about our wild spaces as more roads are built and access goes up. The weather patterns are also more unpredictable for the foragers now. They have such a limited time to harvest and ship when the mushrooms appear—it's much more boom or bust."

We go into the walk-in fridge to drool over the collection of fungi. Giant lobster, chaga, reishi, chanterelle, and lacy-looking cauliflower mushrooms catch our fancy. Freezers contain frozen haskaps and saskatoon berries from Alberta farms and cranberries, blackberries, huckleberries, and currants. Shelves hold dried truffle products, oils, exotic salts and spices, and jars of Brassica mustard (see page 150) from Calgary.

While 90 percent of Aventi's business is to restaurants, he does maintain stalls at Old Strathcona Farmers' Market and City Market Downtown, and consumers can place orders by phone for delivery in Alberta. "Stocking things from around the world allows us the luxury of also carrying small Alberta food artisans."

Note: One of Canada's most famous foragers, Eric Whitehead, has recently set up the headquarters of his Untamed Feast brand in St. Albert. Find their booth at the St. Albert Farmers' Market every Saturday or order directly at untamedfeast.com.

Prairie Gardens and Adventure Farm | 56311 Lily Lake Road, Bon Accord
780-921-2272 | prairiegardens.org

Tam Andersen. Photo by Karen Anderson.

Prairie Gardens sits on about two feet of rich black loam topsoil. For owner Tam Andersen, who was raised on a farm in Rolling Hills near Medicine Hat, this is dream-come-true soil where she can grow just about anything she plants and wow, does she plant.

Since 1956 the farm had always been a tree nursery with greenhouses and vegetable gardens. Andersen bought it in 1981 and in 1986 she planted a two-acre strawberry U-pick. Strawberries yield about 20,000 pounds per acre so when they started coming on she thought they'd never be able to pick them all. She quickly created her first festival to try to attract interest and was thrilled when over 1,000 people turned up and picked the place clean in just four hours. Because only the tiniest berries were left on each plant, and those are called the fairy berries, the annual Fairy Berry Festival was born. It and four other festivals are held at the farm each year.

To increase the sustainability of the farm Andersen now grows 150 different vegetables each year—including 50 kinds of pumpkins—spread over six large gardens on 25 acres. Prairie Gardens is the northernmost pumpkin farm in Canada.

The pumpkin, especially Andersen's favourite blue pumpkin, has become the inspiration for her unique culinary offering called "Fire Roasters Long Table Stories and Field to Fork Dinners." Guests are welcomed to the farm for storytelling around a fire and, much to their delight and surprise, charred pumpkins are lifted from the embers. They split with ease and the sweet juicy flesh is scooped out for all to enjoy. Dinner is then served at long tables fresh from the farm's fields, bolstered by the products of collaborators in the community. Chefs clamour to cook with the in-house culinary team.

Andersen says that Prairie Gardens is a place for people to "take a step back in time and imagine they are spending a day at their grandparents' farm." She loves the joy she sees on children's faces when they dig their first hill of potatoes. She loves the look on chef's faces when they see the abundance and variety her farm produces. Her products are available at the farm-gate store, through the farm's Community Supported Agriculture program, and at fine restaurants in Edmonton.

Riverbend Gardens | 3830 195 Avenue NE | riverbendgardens.ca

Aaron and Janelle Herbert with Evie, Layne, and Carly. Photo courtesy of Riverbend Gardens.

Riverbend Gardens' location provides a lot of positive conditions for a food business. Being situated on the banks of the North Saskatchewan River means sandy soils that are great for root crops. There's also water from the river for irrigation and a longer frost-free growing period due to the low-lying location in the valley. Business-wise, it's good to have Edmonton's million-plus hungry inhabitants to market to. On the flip side, that same population also has the potential to eat up your land instead of your food.

"Because of the threat of development, our wonderful location between Edmonton and Fort Saskatchewan might someday work against us." Janelle Herbert grew up at Riverbend. Her parents originally leased two acres from the city. Janelle, her husband, Aaron, and their team now have 40 45 acres in production and grow food for 550 families in their Community Supported Agriculture (CSA) program. They also grow for a few loyal restaurant chef patrons like Blair Lebsack (see page 69).

"The season begins with asparagus in May and we can have potatoes and peas as early as June because of this special space." While not certified organic, all weeding is done by hand and the crew only sprays occasionally for cabbage moth. There are greenhouses and five hoop houses that extend the season. Each summer, visitors can pick from a two-acre saskatoon orchard on the honour system.

"I came back here in 2006. It was a lifestyle choice for me made possible by my parents' dedication. I watched them struggle and I admire anyone who starts from scratch. I'm able to be here now because they created a financially viable business."

With the City of Edmonton looking for a place to build another bridge over the North Saskatchewan River, will Riverbend be expropriated? "There needs to be policies to protect agricultural lands. Right now, agricultural zones are not defined so all land is just seen as spots for future development. We need to start looking at farms as part of future developments. Farms offer more than just green spaces. They address the need for sustainable food production." Let's hope Janelle's ideas grow as well as her crops. Check Riverbend Gardens' website for farmers' market locations and CSA information.

Sparrow's Nest Organics | Opal | 780-942-2259 | sparroworganics.com

Graham Sparrow at Old Strathcona Farmers' Market. Photo by Karen Anderson.

"People always say, 'Wow, your stuff lasts so long and it's so full of flavour,' and that makes me happy. It's a great place to start a conversation about the nutrients in food raised with organic growing."

Graham Sparrow grows on 20 of the 70 acres of his certified organic farm in the hamlet of Opal in Thorhild County, just a half hour north of Edmonton. "It costs me about $600 per year to certify but business-wise it just makes sense. Especially since the federal government has set standards about what organic actually means and Pro-Cert is there to assure those standards are met. Organic certification means more in Canada than it does in the US."

Sparrow became interested in sustainability and organic food production during a year that he spent travelling and working his way around the UK. In Ireland, especially, he fell in love with the small rural properties and the people's self-reliance.

In 2000, he bought his land and worked toward the certification, which came in 2003. Spud.ca and Earth's General Store have been long-time supporters. "High-end restaurants come around when the economy is good but they've fizzled out lately. Thankfully I have a faithful list of CSA (Community Supported Agriculture) subscribers that keep me going.

"On a typical week in our CSA box, there might be carrots, beets, potatoes, broccoli or cauliflower, kale, leeks, lettuces, herbs, peas, radish, summer squash, tomatoes, and peppers." At Sparrow's stall at Old Strathcona Farmers' Market, customers are mingling with Sparrow and looking at the celery. It's bright green in colour, compact in form, and noticeably different from what's found in a supermarket. A buttercup squash's heft adds up to an impressive $10 sale by its weight. Small cantaloupes are sniffed and their lush fragrance signals their ripeness. From the work of planting, weeding, and watering to harvesting and now selling, Graham Sparrow has brought this food from the field to someone's fork and he loves it.

Gold Forest Grains | Morinville | 780-271-3276
goldforestfarms.blogspot.ca

*John and Cindy Schneider at harvest time.
Photo by Karen Anderson.*

Red Fife, Park, spelt, and einkorn—
Gold Forest Grains owners John and
Cindy Schneider grow "antique" grains.
"Heritage breeds are so important
because they maintain biodiversity in
nature," says John.

John is the sixth generation of his
family to farm in Alberta. The town of
Gibbons is named after his great-great-
grandfather. All that history gives him
the confidence to do things differently.
John and Cindy's fathers both died of
cancer very young—at 23 and 33 years
old respectively.

"We bought this land in 2010 and knew
we had to grow organically. We want to
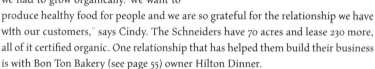
produce healthy food for people and we are so grateful for the relationship we have
with our customers," says Cindy. The Schneiders have 70 acres and lease 230 more,
all of it certified organic. One relationship that has helped them build their business
is with Bon Ton Bakery (see page 55) owner Hilton Dinner.

"Hilton saw us struggle with our flour mill. He financed a larger one and let us pay
him back with each shipment of flour. He just sent us a note that says we own it now.
That was an incredible thing to do," says John. "We are very conscious of the math.
The business can sustain us. I do all the farming and Cindy does the deliveries. We've
got a few people to help with milling and packaging."

With conventional grains becoming Roundup (glyphosate) resistant, new sprays
such as dicamba are being used. According to the *Modern Farmer* website, "One
of the major disadvantages of dicamba compared to glyphosate is that it is much
more 'volatile,' meaning it easily becomes airborne and drifts away from where it is
applied." The Schneiders share reports of dicamba drifts killing Alberta's treasured
shelterbelt trees.

"I want my legacy to be that my great-grandchildren are proud of how I cared for
the earth and how I left it for them," says John. To find Gold Forest Grains' products,
check the website for retail locations.

Acme Meat Market | 9570 76 Avenue | 780-433-1812
acmemeatmarket.ca

Corey Meyer. Photo by Karen Anderson.

Standing in line at Acme Meat Market there's a good vibe. The staff are bustling to fill customer orders for weeknight grilling or Sunday roasting. Owner Corey Meyer is at the back table cutting meat. He looks up frequently and there's always a smile on his face. "When I first started at Acme, I was shy and just kept my head down and worked. One day, I realized that if I smiled I'd put a smile on others' faces."

Meyer is the first owner, since Acme opened in 1921, not from the Pheasy/Eldridge clan. Meyer and his wife, Amanda, bought it in 2009 after he'd put in 21 years with that family. Meyer is a graduate of Northern Alberta Institute of Technology's retail meat-cutting program, but the trade was already in his blood. "My grandfather in Germany was a butcher who travelled between farms to kill, hang, and break down the animals for farmers. My father followed him in that path and I knew from a young age that I wanted to do the same. I like the physicality of it. I always say my wife is the brains and I'm the brawn of the operation."

The Meyers source their chicken, turkeys, pork, lamb, and beef from a handful of Alberta farms in Tofield, Viking, and Wetaskiwin including the Pine Haven Hutterite colony. "They care about their animals and don't use antibiotics or hormones. The animals never leave the farm until they go to slaughter. At least 75 percent of the beef we sell is grass fed and finished. Cows weren't meant to eat grain and grass is better for them and for the humans that eat their meat."

Hams and garlic sausage come from K and K deli on nearby Whyte Avenue, where Acme was originally located. "When we took over and started buying directly from farms, it was good timing as our customers were thinking the same way. Nine out of ten return after their first visit. We don't hide the quality of our meat with marinades. We let the taste of the meat speak for itself."

Acme Meat Market supplies all the meat on the menu at Blind Enthusiasm brewery's Biera restaurant, also located in Ritchie Market in South Edmonton. Chef Christine Sandford (see page 65) is a former Acme Meat Market employee. Meyer says, "She worked with us for two years and is like family. She has her pick of our showcase."

Four Whistle Farm | Millet | 780-499-2726 | fourwhistlefarm.ca

Marius De Boer with a really big duck egg.
Photo by Karen Anderson.

Marius De Boer immigrated to Canada in 1991. He had done two practicums in the Edmonton area while going to agricultural school at Wageningen University in the Netherlands. His thesis work was in animal nutrition and Alberta proved a great place to do research on grains. He also had family here.

An uncle had come to Canada after World War Two and had a farm in nearby Millet. De Boer bought that quarter-section farm in 1997. "When I took over the farm, I applied for a stall at the St. Albert Farmers' Market. They had a few spots open late in the year and when the registrar asked me the name of the farm, I hesitated. All the geographical names were taken by established farms. In that moment, I could hear a train in the near distance. It blew its whistle four times and that's how we got our name."

Four Whistle Farm now produces free-range beef, lamb, pork, chickens, turkeys, and ducks on pasture and free-choice barley (for the cattle). De Boer leases some additional land for grazing and he and his neighbours grow all the feeds so there are no animal by-products, hormones, antibiotics, or soy.

In an innovative partnership with Alley Kat Brewing, De Boer also feeds his cattle the spent grain from their mash tun. "They are happy to give it to us because they would otherwise have to dispose of it. We just have to pick it up. It's about 12,000 pounds a week and the cattle come running when we set it out. They love it. It's good protein for them.

"I love the farming and the selling equally. The whole local thing is dear to my heart." Find De Boer's products at Edmonton's City Market Downtown in the summers and at Old Strathcona Farmers' Market year-round.

Thundering Ground Bison Ranch | 780-719-7774
thunderinggroundbisonranch.com

Larissa Helbig with a few of her yearling bison herd. Photo by Karen Anderson.

Larissa Helbig did a master's degree thesis focused on the reproductive health of bull bison. She grew up on a market garden farm near Devon, and had no experience with animal husbandry until her first university summer job at a bison and elk ranch. She fell in love with the bison and has now spent over 20 years of her life devoted to their conservation and care.

"I had an epiphany at a Slow Food meeting where they said if you want to preserve a species, you have to find a market for it. Essentially, that means we have to eat it to keep it. That hit home for me. If we don't have a use for species, we won't keep them." Helbig and her father initially bought six and now maintain 50 breeding cows and two bulls for a total herd of about 120 bison on a total of 420 acres of land.

Helbig's herd is registered as part of the Treaty Four conservation plan for purebred Great Plains bison. They are raised naturally and she sees their effect on the ecology of the land they graze. As a keystone conservation species, bison increase the nutrient content of soils, help with plant diversity, disperse seeds, and improve nesting for many bird species. The wallows they create retain water after rains, and that creates important habitat for toads and wetland species.

"When I go out to my Wildwood acreage, I just like to sit there and be with them. Watching a dream you've worked hard to bring to life is magic. The meat is a by-product of the bigger goal of their conservation but at the same time, when I see that steak on the plate, if I'm not proud of how it was done then I don't want to do it."

A full 90 percent of Alberta-raised bison are now heading to the US and European markets. "As a producer, I am faced with the question, do I keep supplying my customers and going through the work of taking animals to the abattoir and keeping a stall at the farmers' market or for the same money do I just sell abroad and save myself all the work?"

As more and more bison ranchers slip away from direct retail to Albertans, we hope to see Helbig's stall at Old Strathcona Farmers' Market thriving with customers that understand that access to this species is a privilege that needs to be valued.

Ocean Odyssey Inland | 10019 167 Street NW | 780-930-1901
oceanodysseyinland.ca

Pat Batten. Photo by Karen Anderson.

Darrell and Pat Batten opened for business in 2001 after a fishing trip to British Columbia. They brought sustainable fish to Edmonton from a BC fisherman they'd befriended who had demonstrated his sustainable six-line trolling to them when they were on their holiday.

They began selling at City Market Downtown and then opened their first store in 2005. In 2014, they expanded to a larger space in the West End mostly due to access to fresh fish via Icelandair's regularly scheduled flights to Edmonton. "They called us to see if we'd like to bring their fish here."

The new store also offers Meat Street meat pies, charcuterie and sausages from Fuge Fine Meat (see page 63), and freshly prepared bites of food to take home prepared by their in-house chef including crab cakes, salmon burgers, chowders, and fish stocks.

"My joy is when people say they've found what they were looking for," says Pat. "The quality is here so we get customers who are former coastal people from Iceland, England, and Europe." They are as delighted to find her shop as she is to meet them and she has a long list of regular customers.

"Iceland is a great fishery to do business with. They watch their fish carefully. We get our farmed salmon from there because they are the best in the industry for clean, sustainable practices and healthy fish." Arctic char is the number one seller but she also gets Icelandic cod, haddock, and redfish.

Standing and talking to Pat, it doesn't take long to realize she's an educator and a person who is deeply concerned about fish and the future of our oceans. She talks of big-box chains that pump fish full of water to make more money when they sell it by the pound and of a new virus that's been found in Atlantic salmon (everywhere but Iceland). She's well-informed, transparent, and motivated by sustainability. After the health of our oceans, her customers come first.

FARMERS' MARKETS
Check the website for current hours prior to your visit.

124 GRAND MARKET
102 Avenue at 122 Street | Sundays 11:00 A.M.–3 P.M., May to December
780-463-1144 | 124grandmarket.com

CITY MARKET DOWNTOWN
Saturdays 9:00 A.M.–3:00 P.M. | Outdoor: 104 Avenue from Jasper Avenue to
103 Avenue, May to October | Indoor: City Hall, 1 Sir Winston Churchill Square,
October to May | 780-429-5713 | city-market.ca

OLD STRATHCONA FARMERS' MARKET
Old Bus Barn, 10310 83 Avenue NW | Saturdays 8:00 A.M.–3:00 P.M., year-round
780-439-1844 | osfm.ca

SHERWOOD PARK FARMERS' MARKET
Community Centre, 401 Festival Lane | Wednesdays 4:00 P.M.–8:00 P.M.,
mid-January to December | 780-464-3354 | sherwoodparkfarmersmarket.ca

ST. ALBERT OUTDOOR FARMERS' MARKET
St. Anne Street | Saturdays 10:00 A.M.–3:00 P.M., June to October | 780-458-3660
stalbertfarmersmarket.com

WATERING HOLES
Check the website for current hours prior to your visit.

ALLEY KAT BREWING
9929 60 Avenue NW | 780-436-8922 | alleykatbeer.com
⇒ Tours: Thursday and Friday afternoons.
Favourite beer here: Scona Gold.

BARR ESTATE WINERY
51526 Range Road 231, Sherwood Park | 780-819-9463 | barr.ca
⇒ Tours: By appointment.
Favourite wine here: Try "The Barb" rhubarb wine with some Thai noodles.

BENT STICK BREWING
4-5416 136 Avenue NW | 780-781-3940 | bentstickbrewing.com
⇒ Tours: By appointment.
Favourite beer here: Swap the Hops—because we love hops.
On Fridays and Saturdays you can stop by to enjoy these nano-brews at
the brewery.

BLIND ENTHUSIASM BREWING
9570 76 Avenue NW | 587-525-8589 | blindenthusiasm.ca
⇒ Tours: Growler fills only.
Favourite beer here: ESM 1.4.
The restaurant, Biera, features the food of chef Christine Sandford (see page 65).

BREWSTER'S BREWING COMPANY AND RESTAURANTS
11620 104 Avenue | 780-482-4677 | brewsters.ca
⇒ Tours: By appointment.
Favourite beer here: Rig Pig Pale Ale.
Check their website for their five Edmonton locations.

ELK ISLAND SPIRITS
120 Pembina Road, Sherwood Park | 780-913-1215 | elkislandspirits.com
⇒ Tours: By appointment.
Favourite beer here: A 16 percent creamed whisky called Moose Milk? Yes, please.

HANSEN DISTILLERY

17412 111 Avenue NW | 780-341-0682 | hansendistillery.com
⇒ Tours: Tuesdays through Saturdays.
Favourite drink here: Barn Owl Gold Vodka.
The tours are a good deal at $7 per person with a flight of tastings included.
Designate your driver.

RIG HAND CRAFT DISTILLERY

2104 8 Street, Bay B, Nisku | 780-955-2414 | righanddistillery.com
⇒ Tours: By appointment.
Favourite drink here: The Wildrose Gin. It's made with local juniper, wild rose hips, crabapples, saskatoons, and Alberta chamomile.

SITUATION BREWING

10308 81 Avenue NW | 780-705-1377 | situationbeer.com
⇒ Tours: By appointment.
Favourite beer here: Too many to list!
They serve excellent food at their family-friendly brew pub.

STRATHCONA SPIRITS DISTILLERY (SEE PAGE 76)

10122 81 Avenue NW | strathconaspirits.ca
⇒ Tours: Book online.
Favourite drink here: Badland Seaberry Gin.

TWO SERGEANTS BREWERY AND TAPHOUSE

510-10470 98 Avenue, Fort Saskatchewan | 780-912-9319 | twosergeantsbrewing.ca
Favourite beer here: Passion d'Ale Belgian Wit.
Taphouse on site.

YELLOWHEAD BREWING COMPANY

10229 105 Street NW | 780-423-3333 | yellowheadbrewery.com
⇒ Tours: Thursday through Saturday. Book online.
Favourite beer here: Premium Lager.
Check out all the local bands they sponsor on their website—so cool.

Facing page: photo courtesy of Edmonton Tourism
Following spread: photo courtesy of Neil Zeller Photography

CENTRAL ALBERTA

This is the land where most of Alberta's food has historically been grown. The lower reaches of boreal forest mean Parkland habitats of forests populated with hazelnuts, highbush cranberry, chokecherries, and saskatoon berries along with birch, poplar, pine, and spruce. Most of the land has been cleared and swaths of prairie, formerly populated with native grasses, are covered with a patchwork quilt of commodity crops like canola, wheat, and barley.

In the east, those native prairie grasslands and the species associated with them are protected by ranchers who are also conservationists, like Dylan and Colleen Biggs of TK Ranch (see page 135), Don Ruzicka of Ruzicka Sunrise Farm in Killam (see page 133), and Calvin Raessler of Top Grass Cattle Co. (see page 283). Only four percent of the world's native prairie grasslands still exist and this is where they can be found.

Along the western border of Central Alberta, the rugged high-elevation foothills of the Rockies run along the famous Cowboy Trail (Alberta Secondary Highway 22).

Darling towns like Didsbury and Caroline and hamlets like Bergen and Markerville are destinations worth the wander.

The Queen Elizabeth II Highway divides this intense farming and ranching zone east to west. A plethora of oil and gas derricks, gas plants, and refineries can be found off the highway here in any direction. Red Deer is a hub for the oilfield service companies but with each downturn in the economy, the people become more entrepreneurial. Perhaps one day we'll see as many breweries and distilleries as oil and gas plants.

Stop in Olds to visit the Olds College Brewery. Stop in Lacombe for a meal at Cilantro and Chive or coffee and cannoli at Sweet Capone's. Cozy up at Eco Café in Pigeon Lake for chef Tim Wood's (see page 102) renowned flavours.

Travel Tip

➤ To fully explore Central Alberta with year-round adventures, Pursuit Adventures offers hiking, snowshoeing, river rafting, skiing, and some farm and food tour experiences. Owners J.P. Fortin and Danielle Black Fortin have a base camp and café in Capstone at Riverlands in Red Deer. Check them out at pursuitadventures.ca.

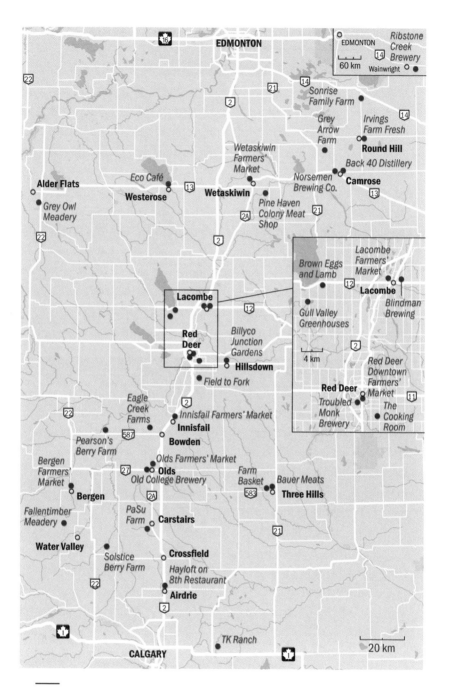

Note: Only artisans and producers who welcome visitors on site are shown on this map.

FOOD ARTISANS OF CENTRAL ALBERTA

Previous spread, left page: photo courtesy of The Jungle Farm

Mousse Cake Sally | Three Hills | 403-830-2253 | moussecakesally.ca

Leah Harvey in her schoolhouse home.
Photo by Karen Anderson.

Fine French pastries are not often (or ever) found along Alberta's dusty range and township roads. But when a search for commercial baking space in Calgary did not deliver, Leah Harvey began scouring the countryside within an hour's drive and that's how she found and fell in love with the renovated 1911 schoolhouse in Kneehill County that she now calls home. She designed and built the bakery of her dreams in her own backyard. She points out her auction deals and Kijiji finds including a grape-coloured KitchenAid stand mixer. "It was the cheapest colour!"

Once settled, she planted a huge garden complete with an array of hardy fruit trees and bushes, including some Lily Pond golden raspberries her dad mailed from Newfoundland. Though she's literally putting down roots in Alberta, her original home is the town of Carbonear, Newfoundland.

"I got an Easy-Bake oven when I was four and I was hooked." A grade eight trip to the nearby island of Saint Pierre, France, gave her the chance to taste French baking for the first time. "I spent all of my trip savings on raspberry tarts. There was no turning back after those tarts."

Harvey spent three years on Prince Edward Island where she completed both the culinary and pastry arts programs at the Culinary Institute of Canada. She also did a bachelor of commerce in entrepreneurship at Ryerson University in Toronto. Three and a half years in Fort Mac (Fort McMurray) doing auditing and finance for a construction company helped her save enough money to begin her entrepreneurial dream. "I took part in Open Farm Days in 2016 and met chef Judy Wood of Meez Cuisine (see page 172). She started buying my frozen pastries and then Gail Norton at the Cookbook Co. Cooks (see page 181) did too."

It's rare to meet someone so steadfast and true in her determination. "A car accident when I was 17 made me realize how precious life is. I want to constantly improve myself and help others. I've been given one of the greatest things in life—the chance to create."

Dancing Goats Farm | Acme | dancinggoatsfarm.com

Dancing Goats Farm owners Paul Chambers (left) and Craig Sanok with their herd. Photo by Karen Anderson.

When Craig Sanok and his partner Paul Chambers retired from successful careers in the ballet, they had no idea a short trip to see family in Washington state would change their lives forever. Prior to their visit, Sanok knew he wanted to work with animals and make good quality food, but he wasn't sure how to bring the two together. While Chambers took on an administrative position in the arts community, Sanok worked as a dog groomer and experimented, making cheese at home. Intrigued, he got a job with a local cheesemaker to fast-track his understanding of the craft.

Then, while visiting family in 2011 his purpose became clear. Chambers's sister got access to raw goat's milk, which she wanted to use to make yogurt. The catch was, she had to milk the goats herself. Knowing what an ardent animal lover Sanok was, she recruited his help. He was completely smitten by the goats and the experience. With the yogurt made, Sanok was invited to turn the rest of the milk into cheese. It was so delicious the idea of Dancing Goats Farm was set in motion.

Moving from a two-bedroom condo in downtown Calgary to their 128-acre farm near Acme in 2014, Chambers and Sanok built an artisanal creamery with a milking parlour, storage, and regularly inspected cheesemaking facility on site. "We don't want to produce food that people can't afford or have an operation we can't sustain."

Capping their herd at 50 nanny goats for now, Dancing Goats Farm produces small batches of five artisanal cheeses, including: the Waltz (fresh), Gavotte (surface ripened), Two Step (beer-washed, semi-firm), jitterbug (firm and mild with a natural rind), and Pavane (ash ripened). Find them on the menu at fine restaurants and retailers throughout Southern Alberta and watch for fun goat videos on their Instagram feed.

Rock Ridge Dairy | Ponoka | 403-783-4312 | rockridgedairy.com

Cherylynn and Patrick Bos.
Photo by Karen Anderson.

Patrick Bos knew at age five that he wanted to farm. He went to Olds College and wished to be a dairy farmer. Patrick spent a decade as a relief-milking farmhand. "If you told me when I was at Olds I'd be milking goats, I'd have knocked you flat. Goats were the lowest on the farm animal scale in terms of prestige."

Patrick and his wife Cherylynn now have over 700 snowy white goats. "They are smarter than cows, easier to manage and care for, and we absolutely love them."

Patrick is a talented welder, fabricator, and builder, skills that have allowed them to afford a state-of-the-art milking barn with rotating automated milking stalls that milk 60 goats at once. During their six-minute milking loop, the computerized system recognizes each goat's microchip and records the volume of milk produced. What took the Bos family nine hours every day now takes two and half.

In the milk processing facility, three steel drums tower in the first room. Organic Jersey milk is trucked over from a neighbour each week for exclusive processing under the Rock Ridge label. Goat's milk comes from their own farm and nine others nearby. Milk processing happens at one thirty in the morning Sunday and Monday nights. Patrick takes that shift until Cherylynn and her staff start at five thirty. He leaves then to put in a full day of milking and caring for the animals. Otherwise, his daily wakeup call is three thirty in the morning.

Cherylynn is in charge of cheese making with the goat's milk. She and their full-time cheesemaker handcraft fresh chevre and feta brined in whey and salt five days a week.

Rock Ridge Dairy and Vital Green Farms (see page 247) are the only independent milk processors left in Alberta. The milk in most grocery chains across the province is either trucked in from BC and sold in nostalgic glass bottles or processed by Montreal megacompany Saputo and sold under the Dairyland or Lucerne labels. Saputo buys the milk it processes from the Alberta Milk board. It also buys up anything unused at bargain basement prices. Grocers are allowed to buy only 10 percent of their milk from other dairies, like Rock Ridge and Vital Green Farms. The BC brands in those nostalgic glass bottles tend to win out. Our two micro dairies currently process only about 8,000 litres a week. It'd be nice to see demand for their product increase.

Sylvan Star Cheese Farm | Sylvan Lake | 403-340-1560
sylvanstarcheesefarm.ca

Janneke and Jan Schalkwijk at their factory in Sylvan Lake. Photo by Karen Anderson.

Jan Schalkwijk and his wife Janneke came to Canada in 1995 from their native Holland. Their son Jeroen had established himself as a Holstein dairy farmer on a piece of pastoral loveliness near Sylvan Lake and the senior Schalkwijks came along to help.

"We lived here for a few years and I couldn't find cheese that I liked so I had to start making it. I'd made cheese for 30 years in Holland. My family had always made cheese. My mother even won the medal for best Gouda in Holland in 1952 and Princess Wilhelmina awarded her the prize." That was in 1999.

Jeroen now has 300 milking cows. "It's very important to the taste of the cheese, what they eat. Alfalfa makes the tastiest milk." Though the dairy farm is right next door, the milk is held in tanks and trucked to the cheesemaking facility a few times per week. "I get up early. That's the life of a dairy farmer. But now, I only make cheese a few days a week." Janneke and Jan have stalls at several farmers' markets around the province and their own farm gate store. Many retailers and restaurants proudly sell their products.

Jan seems to win an award every time he enters the Canadian Cheese Grand Prix. "We've won for our Gouda, extra-aged Gouda, and smoked Gouda." At the World Championship Cheese Contest in Wisconsin, the smoked Gouda ranked number two in the world and more recently their extra-aged "Grizzly" Gouda ranked number four. It grates like Italian parmesan.

We tour the storage facility. There are thousands of wheels of cheese aging—and shrinking, as they do. Jan and Janneke's grandson Tom is finishing up some labelling. We take a few big rounds outside for a photo. Twenty years of cheesemaking in Alberta and a lifetime of knowledge from these two Dutch immigrants has delivered world-class artisan products for us all to enjoy. Of course, there was only one word for them to say while their photo was being taken—CHEESE!

Tim Wood | Eco Café | The Village at Pigeon Lake | 780-586-2627
ecocafepigeonlake.ca

Chef Tim Wood outside his Eco Café in Pigeon Lake.
Photo by Karen Anderson.

"My focus has always been to sustain a local food chain. It was a lot easier when I had my own supply 'forager' named Sharon Caswell. She would do the rounds to farms and pick up what I needed. Since she retired it's become much more challenging."

We are sitting with pots of mint tea at the back of Eco Café. Everything here is made from scratch by chef Tim Wood and his culinary apprentices. "Our signature dish was our game meat pies but since the elk rancher retired, we can no longer do them. I don't think people realize how fragile our food system is and how close we are to losing local food."

Wood started cooking professionally in 1971 at the Westin in Winnipeg. He stayed five years under chef Fred Zimmerman learning in a kitchen based on the principles of Auguste Escoffier, "King of Chefs, Chef of Kings."

In his own career Wood has cooked for Queen Elizabeth II and has been a culinary instructor at the Northern Alberta Institute of Technology, and before there was a Gordon Ramsay he was a restaurant rejuvenator hired specifically to breathe new life into food enterprises. "I was considered a radical because wherever I went, I urged management to switch their buying practices to *only* Alberta products. Finally, I realized the only way it would ever happen is if I had my own place." He opened Movable Feast in his hometown of Edmonton in 1981 and made *enRoute* magazine's top-restaurants list.

Now at Eco Café, the hub of its community, young apprentices come to learn from this master. "I'll retire when I find the one that wows me."

He gets up to go and pack for two weeks in Indonesia. Yoga and travel keep him grounded and inspired. A cup of lentil vegetable soup arrives and in just the first spoonful, there's more flavour coaxed out of the ingredients then most chefs can ever hope for. "It's the taste of Alberta. Our terroir is delicious. I just hope people understand that in time."

Jason Barton-Browne | Hayloft on 8th | 5101-403 Mackenzie Way SW, Airdrie | 403-980-8123 | haylofton8th.com

Chef Jason Barton-Browne at Hayloft on 8th.
Photo by Karen Anderson.

Southern Alberta Institute of Technology culinary grad chef Jason Barton-Browne has serious cooking chops. He built them working in Calgary's and the world's best restaurants. Now, being the executive chef at Hayloft gives him a chance to bring everything he learned at River Café and Teatro, California's Chez Panisse, London's Fat Duck, and some of Europe's best Michelin-starred restaurants to the small city of Airdrie, which he now calls home.

Barton-Browne and his wife, Eliese Watson (see page 158), live on a nearby acreage where she keeps bees and they are raising their daughter. Hayloft opened in June of 2016 and one of the biggest changes for this chef is adding to his list of suppliers. "Many of my suppliers are within a 20-minute radius of here. They are very small producers who have a personal relationship with whatever it is they are growing. We're a small enough restaurant at 55 seats that we don't need massive amounts of supply. Their size is a good fit for us and they love to see what we create with what they grow."

Some of the suppliers include fifth-generation cattleman Wayne Hansen, Didsbury's Shirley's Greenhouses, Blue Mountain Biodynamic Farms from Carstairs (see page 110), and Poplar Bluff in Strathmore (see page 267). "My neighbour Trisha Fehr grows haskaps, sour cherries, saskatoon, black currants, and herbs for us. I would love to see more small growers knocking on my door. It feels like there are many that are too shy to do that."

The menu is tweaked weekly in summer and monthly in winter. "Frequently when a menu says local it is just an overused marketing technique. To me, using local is about the economic cycle of keeping a community thriving. When I'm supporting farms 10 kilometres from here I'm feeding their family and when I ask for money for the food I cook I'm supporting my family. It's not about words on a menu," he says.

"I'd love to say 75 percent of my produce comes from Central Alberta—that'd be an accomplishment. I will welcome knocks on my door."

103

Patrick and Susan de Rosemond | PaSu Farm | Carstairs
1-800-679-7999 or 403-337-2800 | pasu.com

Patrick and Susan de Rosemond.
Photo by Matilde Sanchez-Turri.

Patrick and Susan de Rosemond started PaSu Farm on a parcel of land west of Carstairs in December of 1979. The couple had just immigrated from South Africa a couple of years before. "We were romanced by the idea of raising sheep and living off the land after reading *Harrowsmith* magazine." Only trouble was, Sue was a pharmacist and Pat, a business administrator, and neither had a stitch of experience farming or raising animals.

That didn't stop them though. Determined to live and raise their three children as close to nature as possible, the pair learned about livestock and pasture management at Olds College and then bought 300 sheep. "We chose to raise sheep over cattle so either of us could handle them and they produce so many things including meat, milk, pelts, leather, and wool."

As they entered the 1980s, land prices and mortgage rates soared and the price of lamb dipped, so the couple got creative and began offering farm tours and opened a small gift shop. "We'd explain the virtues and therapeutic uses of wool and natural fibres and sourced high-quality sheep and lamb-based goods that were well crafted, practical and affordable."

Before long, the tours and retail business created demand for a restaurant and Pat welcomed the opportunity to tie an apron on. Inspired by South African, French, and Mauritian cooking styles, Pat uses homegrown and organic ingredients as much as possible to create sumptuous country fare with an international twist. Since they have only one sitting per table, confirmed reservations are required in the restaurant, so call prior to arrival to avoid disappointment. "We want people to come and relax and eat and shop at their leisure and forget their troubles while we take care of them."

After almost 40 years on the farm, Pat and Sue still love their sheep and welcoming visitors. "We love it here and know others appreciate having a place to come and connect with nature. It is our deepest wish that this land forever be a place of restoration, where people can come to nourish their body, mind, and soul far away from the pressures of everyday life."

Bauer Meats and Farm Basket | 1041 2 Street, Three Hills
403-443-5607 | bauermeats.com

The Bauer family. Photo courtesy of the subjects.

Mike Bauer was born and raised on the Torrington, Alberta, farm he and his wife, Annette, and their two children live on. He took meat cutting at Olds College and started Bauer Meats in 1995 with a mobile abattoir, which he still operates. This means that as a butcher, he will go to the farm, kill and skin the animal, take it to the slaughterhouse, then custom cut and wrap the meat at his own provincially inspected facility and deliver it back to the farm (for personal use only—no off-farm resale).

"Mike can only manage two to four customers per week for this service and he would likely give it up completely if it were not so important to the community," says Annette. She was raised in the farming community of Provost near Wainwright and brings a career in food operations management to their business. The Bauers contract with specific ranchers that grow beef, bison, pork, and elk for their line of meats, jerky, and sausages. "Mike's passion is providing people with quality meat without fillers."

In 2007, the Bauers started going to farmers' markets to expand into retail and are now at the Calgary, Three Hills, and Symons Valley Ranch Farmers' Markets. "The other vendors at those markets have become family to us. We all support each other so now we've opened our Farm Basket store in Three Hills to sell our own plus many of our friends' products. We spearhead this store but also contribute to one called Olds Uptowne Market."

Pat's Greenhouse Jellies, Shirley's Greenhouse produce, Taste of Ukraine cabbage rolls, perogies, and borscht, and Mousse Cake Sally pastries (see page 98) are some of the purveyors you can find at this truly Alberta local store. It's the antithesis of everything big box. "It's good as long as we have the community support. We carry food people won't find in any grocery chain." It's a good point. With community support, together they'll breathe life back into rural Alberta.

The Cooking Room | 500-3020 22 Street, Red Deer | 403-872-2855
thecookingroom.com

Selena Hucal. Photo by Rachelle Scrase.

Though Selena Hucal has owned the Cooking Room cooking school for over a decade, its slightly out-of-the-way location means that people are still discovering it. Hucal practised as a registered dietician for 10 years before taking a break to have her family. She knew that when she returned to working outside the home she wanted to do more than talk to people about their diet. "The cooking school is my opportunity to help people gain the real skills they need to actually implement healthful eating.

"Recipes are available. The info is there. From my dietician practice, I saw people's need for the practical skills to turn a recipe into a meal for their family so we still do lots of classes that feature basic cooking skills like chopping an onion, sautéing, and stir-frying. That is the need we are meeting. Watching a TV show might inspire people to want to cook but we all still learn best by doing." The cooking school operates 10 months a year and offers at least two public classes a week along with many private events.

Calgary's Pierre Lamielle, Julie Van Rosendaal, Kevin Turner, and Mike Wrinch, along with Red Deer restaurateur Pete Sok and Chickadee Catering owner Nan Dell, are some of the local instructors who inspire guests to connect with local food.

Local ingredients are important to Hucal and she sources as many as possible from Alberta producers like Innisfail Growers (see page 116), Nixon Honey, Sylvan Star Cheese (see page 101), Troubled Monk (see page 140), and Big Bend for meats. She also spends time in Alberta's U-picks with her children each summer. "I'm decreasing the disconnect between food and where it comes from for my children. Besides, it's soul filling to go out to farms and pick for yourself."

Her advice for budding cooks? "Start with a whole local product and know what to do with it—it'll be fresher, taste better and you'll enjoy the quality."

Back 40 Distillery | 4701 36 Street, Camrose | 780-983-5167 or 780-271-2826 | back40distillery.com

Lorne Haugen (left) and Rick Lazaruik at the bar at Back 40 Distillery. Photo by Karen Anderson.

It used to be, if you didn't want anyone to know what you were up to, you took it to the back 40 acres of your property. Lorne Haugen and Rick Lazaruik never went that route but they like paying a bit of homage to that DIY spirit. They are self-taught distillers with a steely determination to go the long haul to making a profit doing what they love.

"We hunted together for 15 years. When we saw that the butcher just took our animals and combined them with everyone else's we decided to learn to make sausage ourselves," says Haugen, who was also motivated by a daughter with celiac disease. "I wanted to create something she could enjoy."

"We always enjoyed a cocktail while making sausages," says Lazaruik, "but we started to wonder about preservatives in the alcohol as well." The pair started making flavoured vodkas as Christmas gifts. They worked on the flavour profile and recipe for their Ol' Apple Betty for five years and went on to take a distilling course in Denver, Colorado. After learning that 80–90 percent of distillations are made from grain, they looked to create a gluten-free product. They use Rogers beet sugar from Taber and BC apples. There is nothing artificial in their formulations. The still was built in China; the bottles come from Italy.

Though they've been open only since May of 2017, they won the Judges Selection at the Alberta Beverage Awards. "This is our long-term vision of something to do when we retire," says Lazaruik. "We wanted to avoid the 'what now' question and I love bartending."

Back 40 Distillery has a licence to serve alcohol and is open on Fridays and Saturdays for tours and specialty cocktails. "We like to think of our WTF (Winter Time Frost) as a 'truth serum' and we love the stories we get to hear," says Haugen. "We hope to support ourselves doing this when we retire but as someone once said, 'Any fool can make alcohol but it takes a genius to sell it.'"

Fallentimber Meadery | Water Valley | 403-637-2667
fallentimbermeadery.ca

Part of the Fallentimber Meadery team (left to right): Dan Molyneux, Pat Ryan, and Nathan Ryan. Photo by Matilde Sanchez-Turri.

When you arrive at Ryan's Honey farm just off the Cowboy Trail between Cremona and Water Valley, there's a calm that washes over you. This is where Fallentimber Meadery resides. "It's a special place," says Dan Molyneux, co-owner and head of sales for the business.

He's been coming to his aunt and uncle's farm since he was a young boy. In 2010, when the opportunity came to help his cousins, Colin, Nathan, and Dustin Ryan sell their mead, he took it. "From the beginning, our goal has been to turn people's expectations of mead on their head."

Making mead more approachable and universal in appeal can be challenging, but Fallentimber has an ace up their sleeve: all of their meads are fermented solely from Ryan's Honey. Molyneux's uncle, Kevin Ryan, is a second-generation beekeeper. Ryan's Honey is renowned for its flavour and consistency, which exceeds the highest grades of colour, clarity, and moisture content set out by Canadian Food Inspection Agency.

"The placement of our hives is one of the reasons our honey is so special. The bees' nectar source determines the flavour. We put our hives in the foothills where the bees have access to wildflowers and clover."

Fallentimber makes a variety of meads ranging from sweet to dry. They have three traditional meads and four specialty varieties including: pyment, sacked mead, cinnamon, and saskatoon with berries from Solstice Berry Farm (see page 119).

They make four session meads, which are carbonated and have a lower alcohol content than their other meads. "The 'meadjito,' which is our take on a mojito, was developed by Nathan and I for a private event and people loved it." The pair spent two years refining it and released their creation in May of 2017. Fallentimber is barely able to keep up with demand.

Fallentimber Meadery hosts tours and tastings on weekends. Their honey and meads can be purchased in their farm store or in liquor stores across the province. Check their website for upcoming events—they are known for their celebrations.

Billyco Junction Gardens | 40110 Range Road 260, Lacombe
403-782-4263 | billycojunction.com

Bill and Edie Biel. Photo by Karen Anderson.

William (Bill) and Edie Biel have owned their quarter-section farm near Joffre since 1987. They originally ran it as a conventional hog operation but Bill, who was also a swine technician for the Alberta government, could see the changes in the market and they got out while they still had capital.

"We'd always grown our gardens organically so we continued and just increased how much we were growing," says Edie. "We've run a CSA (Community Supported Agriculture program) since 2000. It's 16 weeks and we give people a few weeks off throughout the season—back-to-school and Thanksgiving weeks are so hectic for people. We also offer a four-week fall share, which we augment with our homemade breads and preserves." For the past five years World Wide Opportunities on Organic Farms volunteers, or WWOOFers, have come to learn from the Biels and to lend vital help now that all but one of their own children have left the farm.

The property is surrounded by mature shelterbelts and during the conversion of the farm Bill got busy adding fruit trees, plants, and shrubs. "I never want to rely on one commodity again," he says. He also converted the pig barns to greenhouses. He practises seed saving and starts every plant that is grown on the farm from seed each spring. A former garage is their processing facility.

Starting in June, they open the farm as a U-pick with honeyberries, strawberries, rhubarb, sour cherries, raspberries, chokecherries, black currants, and sea buckthorn available in progression throughout the season. A great cook, Edie would like to mentor others with her skills. A cooking school in her small café space may be in the future. An upstairs suite has been added as a bed and breakfast option for guests and for the use of the wedding parties they host.

"I'm pleased with how far we've come," says Bill. "In the end, if we can make enough money to survive and leave something that someone can buy and carry on, then we'll have shown that more than just conventional crops and methods can thrive here." The Biels with their extraordinary flexibility and creativity have become farm-trepreneurs.

Blue Mountain Biodynamic Farms | Carstairs | 403-337-3321
bluemountainbiodynamicfarms.com

Kris and Tamara Vester. Photo by Karen Anderson.

"In 2018, we celebrate 20 years as a CSA (Community Supported Agriculture program)." Kris Vester and his wife Tamara enjoy a deep connection with their customers. "We've invested in relationships and the dividend is that we have an 80 percent retention rate. Our subscribers understand what it takes to grow biodynamically because they are part of our farm's seasons and cycles."

Blue Mountain is Demeter biodynamic certified. It meets international standards of biodiversity and ecosystem preservation, soil husbandry, livestock integration, and prohibition of genetically engineered organisms and chemicals of any kind. The farm is viewed as a living holistic organism.

Kris's parents came from Denmark and Germany, worked in Calgary, and saved to buy their quarter section near Carstairs in 1977. At age 44, Kris is the only one of eight children to farm. "I came back when my father was 73 years old. We farmed together until he passed at age 86. Now I will buy the farm, so the next few years will be challenging as we assume debt and update the infrastructure."

Blue Mountain is a diverse enterprise with pigs, laying chickens, vegetables, herbs, cut flowers, preserves, and seed cleaning and packaging. "The saving is important because with each passing year we are collecting the seeds of the plants that best tolerate the conditions here. We'll also add greenhouses so we can sell organic plant starts at the Seedy Saturdays in Calgary, Red Deer, and Edmonton.

"I do what I do because I love it. It challenges me to think on my feet and adapt. By and large, we take food for granted. I have serious concerns about the sustainability of the system we have. It doesn't serve the farmer. Consumers get lots of cheap calories but no dense nutrients. The planet suffers due to the massive use of herbicides and pesticides used. It's time to ask, what does cheap food really cost?"

Kris is also the president of the Slow Food Calgary convivium. He walks his talk.

Dirt Rich Farm | Bowden | 403-770-9555 | dirtrich.ca

Chrystal and Tyler Goertzen with a basket of organic kale at the Cochrane Farmers' Market. Photo by Karen Anderson.

Chrystal and Tyler Goertzen gave up careers as a nurse and aircraft mechanic for the richness of being able to raise their family on a patch of Central Alberta's fertile black dirt. The inspiration for change came when Chrystal's mother was diagnosed with a degenerative disease. It caused her to look at food as medicine. "I started buying organic everything."

Watching documentaries about the food system brought Tyler on board and one day the pair realized, "We need to stop complaining and do something about the food system ourselves." Despite childhood summers spent on their family's farms in Manitoba, neither had actually farmed until they bought their acreage near Bowden. "We saw it on Kijiji and Chrystal drove out from Ontario and bought it without me even stepping foot on it," says Tyler. That was in 2014.

The 2017 season was their official first market year at the Cochrane Farmers' Market where they sell salad greens, kale, Swiss chard, tomatoes, peppers, beans, peas, corn, zucchini, squash, carrots, beets, potatoes, and much more (check the website for their farmers' market schedule). They have an open-door farm policy and promise people before profits, community before self, and respect for the environment and their animals. "There will be no synthetic fertilizers, pesticides, herbicides, fungicides, hormones, antibiotics, steroids, or any other drug or chemical ever; just real food grown with integrity. Our focus is not on how appetizing food looks but rather on how nutrient rich and healthful it is."

Using permaculture principles, the Goertzens plan to add broiler chickens, pigs, and cattle over time. With a third child on the way, they'll spend one more winter renting in Bowden, with Tyler working aircraft maintenance contracts to make ends meet, before they move to living off grid at their farm. "We want sustainable living and farming. For us, fertilizer and glyphosates are not a part of that." The Goertzens are literally putting their money where their mouth is.

Eagle Creek Farms | 34532 Range Road 14, Bowden | 403 224 3995
eaglecreekfarms.ca

John Mills in the world's only organic sunflower maze. Photo by Karen Anderson.

Starting in 1921, four generations of the Mills family have farmed the land at Eagle Creek, near Bowden. John Mills returned to the farm in 2006 after attending the Nova Scotia Agricultural College (now part of Dalhousie University) where he specialized in organic growing methods.

He was chosen as a Youth Grower to represent Alberta at Slow Food International's Biennial Terra Madre in Turin, Italy, when he was 26 years old and has become known for his ingenuity and creativity. He has been working at converting the whole farm to organic status since 2008. After starting with 70 acres, he will soon have a whole section (640 acres) of land certified by Pro-Cert. "I'm doing it to take a stand. Synthetic fertilizers are not sustainable. I don't expect to change the world but I want to prove farming can be done differently."

Other factors in his success? "Diversification is key. Our seed potato business helps a lot. With the fruits and vegetables that we grow we now contribute to feeding 500 families through our CSA (Community Supported Agriculture) program. We have U-pick strawberries, vegetables, flowers, Alberta's only sunflower maze, a corn maze, and we grow garlic and pumpkins and have a farm-gate store from August 1 to October."

Mills is also known for attracting other youth to work with him. He employs 12 people full-time in summer and three year-round. "I'm grateful to have had Gert and Mads Lund of Lund's Organic Farm (see page 117) and Rosemary Wotske and Cam Beard of Poplar Bluff Organics (see page 267) as mentors."

Now Mills's mentorship has helped spawn nearby Country Thyme Farm, a 40-acre greens and vegetable operation owned by his former employee Daniel Chappell. "Along with Country Thyme, we are partnering with YYC Growers and Distributors in the first urban and rural agriculture CSA. The YYC Growers CSA has over 800 subscriptions. It's becoming a collaborative food hub.

"For me it was never a question of, Would I farm? It was only, What would I farm?" This 36-year-old food artisan is one to watch.

Fifth Gen Gardens | Wetaskiwin | 780-387-8876 | fifthgengardens.ca

Kristin Graves. Photo courtesy of Fifth Gen Gardens.

"This farm means everything to me and I want to find a way to continue our family's tradition. But, in my own way." These are the words of 28-year-old Kristin Graves. She's worked for 10 years as an X-ray technician in Edmonton but has had enough of the city. "I want the slower-paced life I grew up with. My dad took over this farm from his father when I was born. I'm the fifth generation and I can't stop wondering what will happen to this place if I'm the generation that doesn't come back."

Graves grew up helping her mom with her vegetable garden but her mom eventually gave up when the deer got to enjoy more of the crop than the family. The family still grow grains but gave up a herd of cattle that peaked at 900 animals to build and operate Northwinds Trout (see page 137). "One day I got the brainwave that I could convert our old cattle pens to a garden. They have really high reinforced fences to keep the deer out. I thought maybe I could sell my vegetables."

Friends who own a greenhouse gave advice. Graves started an Instagram account with great photography and had 15 to 20 customers in her first season—2017. "It was challenging but the reward is that I know where my food comes from, and it's *real* food, not processed. I love to cook and I share a recipe of my grandmother's in each week's delivery. I still use her pitchfork to dig my potatoes."

Graves saves her holidays to help her father and grandfather with the fish and grains at harvest time. "There are some things you can't learn from a book, like when they hold up a sample and say, 'When grain looks like this, it's ready.' It's the family aspect that drives me. It's *this* farm."

With date nights spent picking rocks, Graves's passion for farming better be contagious. "To farm, your heart has to be in it 100 percent. Then the hard work, long hours, and being covered in dirt just don't matter."

113

Grey Arrow Farm | 48037 Range Road 205, Camrose | 780-672-2142
greyarrowfarm.ca

Denis and Andrea Forstbauer at Grey Arrow Farm.
Photo courtesy of Andrea Forstbauer.

Denis and Andrea Forstbauer purchased their 35-acre market garden near Camrose in 2016. Denis had grown up in Chilliwack where his parents, Mary and Hans Forstbauer, were pioneers and leaders in organic and biodynamic farming since the late 1970s.

As a middle school teacher and photographer respectively, Denis and Andrea are realizing a long-held dream to own their own farm. Factors in their success include the fact that the former farm owners, Wayne and Karen Solliv, are great mentors. The farm has irrigation. Three hoop houses extend the season.

"Everything is planted in succession to fill the needs of our 70-plus CSA (Community Supported Agriculture) subscribers. We grow all the vegetables Denis grew as a child plus some peppers and onions. Our goal is to add unique offerings, things our customers can't get in a grocery store, to help them see the benefits of buying from us," says Andrea. Cucamelons and eggplants were a big hit in 2017.

"It's not just producing for the sake of it," says Denis. "I really enjoy this life and my parents instilled in me the desire to grow food in good soil. Fortunately, the previous owners never sprayed fertilizers or pesticides so we are in the midst of getting organic certification."

"We also hope to have a farm store on our property. We want to be people's source for local. We already partner with a local beef and chicken farm as well as a quail egg farm and a honey producer," says Andrea.

Summers are filled with lots of work but lots of time with their five children. "The oldest is already truly helpful," relates Denis. "We open the greenhouses early, have breakfast as a family, and then do chores. After the children are in bed, Andrea and I walk the farm again and make our next day's plan."

"I run all the social media and handle all the emails," says Andrea. "The internet has allowed us to gain customers and build community with other young family farms."

Denis finishes: "The goal is to get to a point where I can work on the farm and have it sustain our family. I believe it is possible."

Gull Valley Greenhouses | 40120 Range Road 283, Blackfalds
403-885-2242 | gullvalley.ca

Left to right: Jil and Scott Epple, Ava, Levi, Carmen, Ella, Carolyn, and Phil Tiemstra. Photo by Karen Anderson.

Phil Tiemstra grew up on a chicken farm in Barrhead, Alberta. "I could have stayed there but I was bored. I wanted to do something that was technologically challenging."

He went to Belgium and Holland to learn about hothouse growing. "They have a much milder climate. Our big challenge is that to grow the same produce we use five times the energy."

With his cousins (Doef's and S4 Greenhouses), Tiemstra started Pik-N-Pak but they soon realized they couldn't compete with the wholesale pricing of tomatoes coming out of Mexico. "We decided to concentrate on direct marketing to consumers since 1991."

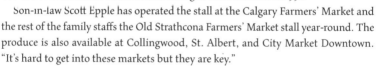

Son-in-law Scott Epple has operated the stall at the Calgary Farmers' Market and the rest of the family staffs the Old Strathcona Farmers' Market stall year-round. The produce is also available at Collingwood, St. Albert, and City Market Downtown. "It's hard to get into these markets but they are key."

Son Levi got a business diploma and returned to help diversify the offerings. Gull Valley now grows beefsteaks, Romas, orange, yellow, and red tomatoes on the vine, along with cocktail, cherry, grape, and heirloom Zebras. They also grow herbs, flat and round beans, butter lettuce, peppers, and eggplants.

The crops are grown hydroponically in coconut fibre husks. Bumblebees pollinate the plants. Good bugs eat the pests that are bothering the plants. CO_2 from their boilers is captured and fed back to the plants, water is recycled, and energy curtains have reduced their needs by 30 percent. "We'll lose a crop before we'd spray. We want to produce food you can pick and eat off the vine. Period.

"Ultimately, people can find cheaper produce but if we don't support Alberta growers, there won't be jobs and all that cheap produce will have just made us weaker in every way." Along with the markets you can enjoy Gull Valley produce at many of Alberta's finest restaurants.

Innisfail Growers Co-operative | innisfailgrowers.com

Left to right: Keri Graham, Leona Staples, Elna Edgar, Megan and Hanno Buyks, Carmen Fuentes, and Shelley Bradshaw. Photo by Karen Anderson.

In 1986, Shelley Bradshaw and her husband Rod bought Beck Farms from an uncle. They started growing carrots to sell at farmers' markets. Shelley quickly developed a loyal following who asked her to grow other produce. To lighten her load, she approached her neighbours, the Edgars, asking their daughters if they would grow peas and beans in exchange for the proceeds going to their college fund. Both girls paid for university with this money.

Edgar Farms is a centenarian homestead, with a grain and cattle operation that has been in the same family for over a century. Elna Edgar grew peas and beans but had a secret one-acre plot of asparagus along the back 40 that she tended over a three-year period. It wasn't until the plants matured and she was sure she had a winning hand that she told people about it. Edgar Farms now has over 30 acres of asparagus along with their original crops and cattle.

Down the road, Leona and Blaine Staples were growing spinach and strawberries so Bradshaw invited them to join the co-operative. They now teach jam and pickle making and have a hugely popular pumpkin patch and family activity centre on the farm.

The Buyks of Upper Green Farms grow potatoes for the group and, finally, a young farmer named Carmen Fuentes approached the growers to see if they would be interested in selling hothouse vegetables. She went to Olds College to study greenhouse growing so she could one day join the co-operative.

While the average age of farmers in Alberta is over 60, each of these farms has attracted the next generation back to the land. Through co-operation and collaboration, they produce, process, distribute, and market their own crops and they've given our province a winning formula for the survival of all family farms.

CO-OPERATIVE MEMBERS
Beck Farms | Rod & Shelley Bradshaw | 403-227-1020
Edgar Farms | Doug & Elna Edgar | 403-227-2443 | or Keri & Randy Graham | 403-227-5782
Upper Green Farms | Hanno & Megan Buyks | 403-227-4403
The Jungle Farm | Blaine & Leona Staples | 403-227-4231
Hillside Greenhouses | Carmen & Jose Fuentes | 403-559-9790

Lund's Organic Farm | Innisfail | 403-506-1903 | lundsorganic.com

Gert Lund and his crew weeding.
Photo by Karen Anderson.

Since 1981 Gert Lund has farmed organically in Alberta. "The significance of organic farming is in the care of the soil." Visiting with Lund is a chance to learn.

Though most of the exterior of our planet has been explored, its interior and the life in our soil remains largely uncharted territory. It's estimated that each teaspoon of soil has up to a billion bacteria, metres of fungal filaments, several thousand protozoa, and scores of nematodes, a.k.a. worms. "Chemical fertilizers change the pH of the soil to between one to two. It needs to be at seven to sustain the micro-organisms. When they die, the nutrients are locked in the soil. Soil needs organic life as the key to unlock and deliver nutrients to our food."

An immigrant from Denmark, Lund says, "In Europe, organics was already the way forward when I was leaving. We were fortunate to find virgin land here so that within a few years I could become certified organic."

Testing of food grown in Lund's soil has revealed 92 vitamins and minerals present. Vitamins and minerals are the taste we detect as humans, and that means the food he grows has big taste. Looking down the long rows covering these acres, there's a notable absence of weeds. Lund's son Mads and his grandsons, along with their loyal crew of Mexican temporary foreign workers, cultivate the rows by hand and hoe them daily to keep them weed-free. "A few weeds one year means plenty more the next, so none are acceptable to us."

With land this well cared for, it might shock you to learn that in 2007 the town of Innisfail annexed it for future development. Lund and his son, who has come home to farm the land for as long as it is possible, await the day when this fertile earth will be topped with asphalt for a new school and parking lot. For those of us used to enjoying the flavours of Lund's famous rainbow heritage and juicing carrots at the Calgary Farmers' Market, better enjoy them while they last. "We won't be able to start over."

As development encroaches on the vital food-producing lands along Alberta's QE2 highway between Calgary and Edmonton, Lund's words are ones to live by. "They aren't making more land."

117

Pearson's Berry Farm | Range Road 40, Bowden | 403-224-3011
pearsonsberryfarm.ca

Debbie and Duane Mertin, owners of Pearson's Berry Farm. Photo by Matilde Sanchez-Turri.

Before taking over Pearson's Berry Farm in 2004, Duane and Debbie Mertin were grain farmers in Saskatchewan. "If someone had told me that we'd be selling beverages, syrups, pies, and tarts for a living 30 years ago, I'd have told them they were off their rocker!"

When Len and Joyce Pearson were getting ready to retire, they were on the lookout for someone special to take over their farm. They needed a background in agriculture, integrity to uphold their legacy and to care for their customers as much as the Pearsons did. They found those qualities and more in the Mertins.

Choosing the right successors was critical because Pearson's Berry Farm has serious pedigree. Established in 1969, it was crowned the first commercial saskatoon berry orchard in the world. As pioneers and educators, Len and Joyce developed an extensive library of research on how to optimize saskatoon berry production on the prairies. There are approximately 300 saskatoon orchards in Alberta, Saskatchewan, and Manitoba thanks in part to Len and Joyce's hard work.

Pearson's Berry Farm currently turns 70–80,000 pounds of saskatoon berries per year into an array of delicious homemade products. Through Len's legacy, the Mertins are able to source a steady supply of saskatoon berries from a network of growers. "Our orchard is exclusively for our U-pick customers. We grow three varieties of saskatoon berries—Smoky, Northline, and Thiessen—because they ripen at different times, extending the picking season."

Duane and Debbie's ban on chemical use runs deep. "We don't use artificial flavours or colours in our products. As for the orchard, we parked the sprayer at the edge of the property 14 years ago and haven't applied any fungicides, pesticides, or fertilizers to our saskatoon berries since."

Made by hand and sold fresh (never frozen), Pearson's renowned baked goods along with their syrups, spreads, beverages, and lineup of Gordo's sauces and spices can be purchased year-round at their farm bakery or online. Look for their products at farmers' markets in Calgary and Red Deer and your favourite Christmas markets. (See website for details.)

Solstice Berry Farm | Range Road 2, Crossfield | 403-946-4759
solsticeberryfarm.com

Marsha and Rick Gelowitz on the porch of their cozy retail store. Photo by Matilde Sanchez-Turri.

Rick and Marsha Gelowitz always dreamed of having a piece of land big enough to make a living off and in 1994, they found it. Their dream quarter section offered views of the mountains, loamy soil, a mobile home, and pens and buildings for livestock. Before long, the couple had sheep and grew enough hay to feed their flock and sell the surplus.

In 2003, after their son Joey was born, Rick, who was still working full-time off the farm, decided to sell their sheep and convert their hay operation. "We had three saskatoon bushes that were flourishing in the garden. I had fond memories of picking saskatoons with my grandparents...so, you could say that between Marsha's green thumb and a little nostalgia, that's how Solstice Berry Farm came to be. We knew we didn't want to dabble."

If you visit Solstice Berry Farm, there's no way you would accuse the Gelowitzes of that. They dove into the world of saskatoon growing headfirst, learning as they went and planting 40,000 saskatoon bushes on 40 acres over five years. "We didn't open the U-pick until 2008 because it takes five years for the bushes to reach peak production."

While Rick still worked off the farm in information technology, Marsha earned her horticulture certification from Olds College and went to the Alberta Agriculture food processing centre in Leduc to learn how to handle the large quantities of fruit they'd be harvesting and processing. Guidance also came from some of the industry's best-known berry whisperers, Paul Hamer of the Saskatoon Farm (see page 270) and Len Pearson of Pearson's Berry Farm (see page 118).

Since saskatoon berries don't ripen off of the bush, the Gelowitzes invested in a state-of-the-art optical sorter. Lucy, as they call her, has a colour camera and lasers that scan the berries for ripeness and bruising and sorts them at a rate of 500 pounds per hour.

The annual harvest allows the Gelowitzes to create handmade products (from food to soap) for sale at their farm-gate store during U-pick season. Check their website for their farmers' market and Christmas show schedules.

Sonrise Family Farm | 52108 Range Road 190, Beaver County
780-910-1661 | sonrisefamilyfarm.ca

The Otto Family. Photo by Dawn LaBelle.

"I love dirt, and the feel of being outside all the time in the sunshine. It's part of my DNA. There's no other option." Shannon Otto grew up in Strathcona County and had a decade of what she describes as "obsessive gardening" before she and her husband Peter bought Sonrise Family Farm in 2016. "It was a big leap but I saw it on a real estate website and knew it was right for us."

The property in Beaver County had been a market garden and came with irrigation and a cooler. Peter Otto still works in the city of Edmonton. He grew up on a dairy farm and is used to long hours. "The ultimate goal is to have him here full-time."

The Ottos decided to offer a Community Supported Agriculture (CSA) program. Their soil had been resting for four years so they added mushroom compost and then planted two of their 10 acres. It's always fun to see how much will grow here in Alberta.

The Ottos grew a wide assortment: kale, spinach, arugula, Swiss chard, a variety of lettuces, fennel, cabbage, broccoli, cauliflower, kohlrabi, onions, scallions, cucumbers (English and pickling), tomatoes (heritage, plum, cherry, slicing, and coloured), peas, beans (yellow, green, dragon's tongue, and purple), Brussels sprouts, leeks, peppers, corn, winter squashes (pumpkins, Hubbard, acorn, butternut, buttercup, delicata, spaghetti, and Georgia Candy Roaster), summer squash (zucchini, gooseneck and pattypan), carrots (orange, yellow, red, white, and purple), radish, beets (red, yellow, white, and pink), turnips, a variety of potatoes, as well as herbs and dried flowers.

"We had the support of 13 CSA members in our first year. Facebook helped a lot. It might not sound like much but it is perfect for a mother of three young children. Plus, we have a Jersey cow named Valerie, 15 hogs, 50 laying hens—our members can order eggs from us." There are only a few reasons why a family would work this hard.

"We do this for food security and because freshness really matters. I like teaching my children to work hard and to grow up with capabilities. It's a deep-down, driven, crazy passion."

Steel Pony Farm | Tamara Ranch, Red Deer County | 403-506-3634
steelpony.ca

Mike Kozlowski farming at Tamara Ranch, near Red Deer, Alberta. Photo by Karen Anderson

"I love the physical work and the joy of knowing I'm feeding people." That's the immediate gratification for Mike Kozlowski but his mid- and long-range goals for becoming a farmer are all about connecting people with the earth again.

"I was in Africa and the people there asked me about my farm. They couldn't fathom that I didn't have one. I couldn't even tell them about one I'd been to in Canada because I grew up in Red Deer. To them, meat was something special that they only served to honoured guests. I was a self-righteous vegan then but they taught me I'd never be a well-rounded human being unless I knew about food production."

Kozlowski came back to Canada and immersed himself in learning how to grow food, doing internships on farms in Quebec and Ontario. Settling in Alberta in 2010, he leased land on three different farms but was frustrated to lose all the work he'd done to improve the soil with each move.

His brother-in-law, Blake Hall of Prairie Gold Pastured Meats (see page 131), had a similar struggle, so the two joined Tamara Ranch owner Tom Towers and a Holistic Management facilitator in a retreat to work out a plan where they could permanently rent land from Towers. Steel Pony, Prairie Gold, and their friend Sven Stave's Field to Fork (see page 124) all benefit in what they call the Tamara Ranch Project. They are next-gen farmers who simply cannot afford the $10,000 per acre that land sells for around Red Deer. Long-term renewable leases have given them an alternative way to fulfill their desire to grow food.

Kozlowski works full-time from March to November and employs a number of people in season. He runs a Community Supported Agriculture program and sells to restaurants, grocers, and Calgary's YYC Growers and Distributors collaborative as well.

"Part of our human composite is the land. Working with the land, connecting with it, it changes you." He's a self-professed soil worshipper.

Brown Eggs and Lamb | 40323 Woodynook Road, Lacombe
403-782-4095 | browneggsandlamb.com

Laura Siebenga with a few of her chickens in front of her store. Photo by Karen Anderson.

"My idea of local is food less travelled." Laura Siebenga and her husband Cal raised four children on this 17-acre parcel of land just west of Lacombe. She'd grown up on a farm near Ponoka and wanted her children to know something of that, so she bought them four chicks to raise.

"Chickens lay on average 0.8 eggs per day so pretty soon friends started asking if we'd sell eggs. I also got some sheep, just for fun. And pretty soon the demand was there as people started asking if we had lamb. We became sellers of brown eggs and lamb and it seemed a great name too."

Siebenga's been selling eggs for 20 years now. She is always well below the 300-laying chicken quota restriction. She's got 16 Suffolk ewes who lamb in May and three llamas to guard them from coyotes and stray dogs.

"Six years ago, I got my husband Cal to build me this mini farmers' market that we call Small Circle Store. It's fun for me. I get to connect with and meet different people all the time. I like good quality food and helping producers by giving them another outlet to sell their goods. Being on the way to Gull Lake keeps me busy in summer." On cue a local customer pops in to buy three dozen brown eggs.

A peek in the fridges, freezers, and shelves reveals local honey, wool products, and goods from Innisfail Growers (see page 116), Northwinds Trout (see page 137), and Rock Ridge Dairy (see page 100), along with her own lamb products. Stop in if you're in the area. If Siebenga's not in the store, there are always eggs available on the honour system.

Earth Works Farm | Alix | 403-742-9827 | earthworksfarm.ca

Brenda and Vance Barritt.
Photo by Amanda Hetchler.

Brenda Barritt's master's thesis turned into a self-fulfilling prophecy. Through the University of Plymouth in England she studied how nature is organized to be resilient and then compared that to how farms in Central Alberta are organized. "I ended my thesis by answering the question, If I were a farmer, what principles would I farm with?" And, with that clarity, a short time later, she and Vance Barritt married and moved back to his parents' farmland.

"Instead of feeling that humans are bad for the world, I wanted to find a way to become unapologetically human. Vance had taken his permaculture design certificate and we took a Holistic Management International course together. Now we know more about how to contribute to the regeneration of the land than we can currently implement. I'm impatient with our progress because I look at our young son and wonder what kind of world he will inherit. I feel an urgency."

The Barritts farm about five quarter sections in Alix (east of Red Deer) and at ages 39 and 43, they know they are fortunate. Unlike other farmers their age, they have worked out a succession plan with Vance's parents for gradually gaining full ownership of the land. Both still work off the farm part-time but since their wedding on the farm in 2011 they've gradually increased the numbers of cattle, pigs, chickens, and turkeys they are raising along with the market to sell it to.

"2017 was a year of partnerships and collaborations. We've spent five years building relationships and some things are starting to fall in place. We'll be supplying beef for YYC Growers and Distributors and we are open to other next-gen farmers using some of our land. We'd love to partner with an apiarist or someone who'd like to start a native species nursery."

The dream is that one day soon Vance will be able to farm full-time. Check the website for sales outlets. As Brenda says, "Every time we spend money on food, we are an investor creating the food system, our health, and our ecosystem."

Field to Fork | 27042 Township Road 372, Red Deer County
403-598-6955 | fieldtoforkalberta.com

Sven Stave. Photo by Emily Andres.

Sven Stave lived in Germany until he was 23. He came to Canada in June 2010 after spending two years travelling through New Zealand and Australia. Red Deer might seem like an odd choice for someone who loves surf and mild weather but a budding romance that's turned into a solid partnership provided the warmth to retain him. Stave applied for and got his permanent residence status.

In New Zealand, he had worked on a farm and loved it. In Alberta, during the winter of 2014, he took his Permaculture Design Certificate from Verge Permaculture (see page 186) in Calgary.

"I wanted to farm, but did not know where to begin. Rob Avis of Verge Permaculture introduced me to Blake Hall of Prairie Gold Pastured Meats (see page 131). At first I apprenticed with him and then Joel Salatin's course *Pastured Poultry Profits* helped me find a way to get involved."

Stave raised two batches of 400 birds his first summer. He built his own mobile chicken coops for about $600 each. "I had 800 birds and no customers," he groans at the learning curve. "Thank goodness for freezers."

Joining with Hall, who raises grass-finished cattle, and Mike Kozlowski of Steel Pony Farm (see page 121), who raises vegetables, the three have access to land from a benevolent farmer named Tom Towers on his Tamara Ranch. "Tom had converted his 400-acre farm to holistic management in the '90s. He's near retirement now but wants to help young farmers who can't afford land. We call ourselves the Tamara Ranch Project and the cross-marketing of our products has helped me gain customers.

"Pastured poultry is the fish of the prairies." Stave beams as he talks of research to support the claim—the positive omega profiles and linoleic acids that the chickens retain because of their natural diet on pasture. "My customers are the 10 percent of people who care to seek out non-conventional methods."

Grass Roots Family Farm | Ferintosh | 780-781-5929
grassrootsfamilyfarm.ca

*Michael, Laura, and Takota Coen with
Kolby Peterson. Photo by Jalene Mauws.*

Michael Coen bought the farm next door to his parents on the slopes of Red Deer Lake in 1984. He and wife, Laura, realized the chemicals they were pouring into the earth were not healthy for their family or the land. "Our belief is that we should leave the land in better condition than we found it.

"There's a lot of peer pressure for farmers to use synthetic pesticides and fertilizers. We are surrounded by people that want perfection—no weeds—and are driven by profit and yield at any cost. We'd like other farmers to have the same respect for the land that we have so we open our farm to the University of Alberta's Augustana campus in Camrose."

From going organic in 1988 to being a model for permaculture today, the Coens discovered that it takes more than not using chemicals to have a thriving farm. "We need to give back to the earth by increasing our biodiversity. We've added cattle and hogs and get up every morning to manage their grazing pattern so it is most beneficial to the land."

Takota, the Coens' son, originally left the family farm to learn carpentry but still helped out and eventually realized that he enjoyed farming more. "In 2012, I took a Permaculture Design Certification and have been working on scaling up the principles for an operation of our size."

That involves water management through swales, dugouts, and pipelines to pastures. Five years in they are seeing their pastures improving, rainwater is captured and there is less in the way of weeds, labour, and infrastructure money to put out. "One day we'll be able to sit back and manage but we're still in transition time in terms of labour." Takota has also been teaching courses with Verge Permaculture (see page 186) and Kolby Peterson, Young Agrarians apprenticeship coordinator, does workshops for Organic Alberta. They have taken the Holistic Management course and have found a supportive community.

"The best part is that we are now selling out of our beef. We've even converted a few vegetarians when they see how we are helping the earth," says Takota.

"It's nice to have someone to carry on," says Michael.

Honest Meat Co. | Caroline | 403-828-7971 | honestmeat.ca

Clayton and Sarah Berg. Photo by Honest Meat Co.

"Finding a partner that shares the same commitment to making it work is what keeps me going." Clayton Berg reflects on what it takes to start a farm in Alberta today. He grew up on an acreage in Caroline and loved taking care of their chickens and turkeys and helping out with his neighbour's steers. His parents added a quarter section to their acreage and he now rents two acres from them.

After completing a geomatics engineering degree at the University of Calgary Berg realized that while it had been fun to spend five years in the city, he missed the farming life. "I also realized that my farm dream couldn't happen without the right woman. Soon after, I met my wife Sarah—at a Valentine's party. We talked all night and it became obvious we shared the same goal of a simpler life."

Building a direct relationship with eaters seemed the path forward. The Bergs take orders for their pasture-raised birds based on a minimum of five per customer. Though they tripled their base to 30 families in 2017 their goal is to grow tenfold. "July harvest days on the farm are a chance for consumers to learn experientially how food is produced and to make informed decisions about how they spend their money."

The Bergs will add pork to future offerings and are looking at unconventional models for distributing the meat. Whole hogs may be slaughtered after being portioned and sold off in a crowdsourcing fashion. Clayton is currently gaining the necessary animal-finishing knowledge by raising a mixed breed of Duroc, Large Blacks and Berkshire. Lambs and goats are dreams on the horizon.

"We've been living on savings and are poor right now. I've taken a job off the farm for this fall and winter. Where we put our money really makes a difference. We've created the farming we've got now. If we put our money in the right places, the system will change."

Hoven Farms | Eckville | 403-302-2748 | hovenfarms.com

Tim and Lorianne Hoven at home on their farm.
Photo by Genevieve Renee.

Arriving at Hoven Farms near Eckville, an hour west of Red Deer, the land has changed from flat prairie to hills rolling up to forests on the shoulders of the Rockies. There's a lot of history for the Hovens here and Tim Hoven knows it all. He was born and raised on the land ranched by his father Cecil, grandfather Adolph, and great-grandfather Mathias. With his wife Lorianne and his family, he runs a cattle and grain operation, just like the Hovens before him.

"In the 1960s as everyone got caught up in the Green Revolution, my dad had large machines, silos, and diesel, but he's always been experimental and open-minded so when I came back to the farm in 1995, he'd taken a holistic management course and was switching back to the grass-finishing methods that my grandfather and his had always practised, only with more understanding of regenerative soil science that makes it all tick."

Hoven Farms became certified organic in 1997. "We now say we're in the business of grass and soil management. If we've got healthy soil, the grasses are full of nutrients and the cattle thrive. We manage their grazing putting large numbers on a small amount of land for a short duration of time."

The cattle spend anywhere from 24 to 32 months fattening in the pastures of this 2,000-acre spread. "This soil has sustained my family for 110 years. Lorianne and I are here to steward the soil so it is in better shape for our children and their children."

The Hovens direct market their beef from their website and sell it to Sunworks Farm (see page 134). Their use of social media to increase knowledge around what it takes to grow food is exemplary. Tim has a bachelor's in education and it shows in his collection of YouTube videos and Instagram posts. "I believe wonderful things can happen when you put people and soil together. You can improve the lives of many."

Irvings Farm Fresh | 18469 Township Road 484, Round Hill
780-672-2787 | irvingsfarmfresh.com

Nicola and Alan Irving in their Round Hill farm store. Photo by Karen Anderson.

The Irvings moved to Canada from England in July of 2005 and within a year Nicola was farming while Alan drove truck. "We couldn't find pork products we liked so we saw it as an opportunity. British sausages have a little bit more coarse texture and we didn't want any additives or preservatives. We started with chickens and made sausages to practise but then got stuck with pigs," says Nicola. "We knew what to do with pork meat and we started to make the British bits we missed like back bacon rashers, Cumberland and Lincolnshire sausages, and black and white puddings."

"The Cumberland is our bestseller. Nicola did months of research to get the recipe just right," says Alan. "I found an old-fashioned English cookery book from the Women's Institute. I learned to look at the ingredients in ratios and at least got a list of ingredients this way. We love it when our British customers say how much nostalgia our foods create for them. You know you've got the recipe right when that happens," says Nicola.

"In 2007 and 2008, *Edmonton Journal* writer Judy Schultz wrote us up a couple of times and each time she did our business doubled," says Alan. "We were doing about 10 markets a week then."

In 2008 the Irvings moved to Round Hill, population 70. They do so much processing now that they can't grow all their own pork anymore but are pleased to source some from Pine Haven Colony (see page 130). "They share our approach to how animals should be raised. We are authentic and honest. Our quality and customer service are high and we believe in making food that's whole, simple, and basic again," says Alan.

Check the website for farmers' markets and retail outlets or shop online.

Nature's Green Acres | Beaver County | 780-336-2265
naturesgreenacres.com

(Back to front) Danny, Shannon, Madalynne, Joshua, and Molly (Amelia) Ruzicka. Photo by Karen Anderson.

Danny Ruzicka's delivery truck breaks down and his wife Shannon goes to fetch him. Their three home-schooled children, Madalynne, Joshua, and Molly, offer themselves as farm tour guides. The hogs are first. They are Tamworth, Large Black, Mulefoot, and Berkshire and they live on pasture and in a fenced-off area of forest. They are heritage breeds that don't do well in confinement. We watch them root and wallow and luxuriate in their freedom.

Next, we stroll to the chicken coop, the farm dogs patrolling our path at all times. We pause at a couple of sheep that come to the children for scratches. The cattle are in a far pasture, barely visible across a creek. They spend their entire lives on grass.

The property is a half section of land purchased in 2001. Danny works full-time (or more) as a farrier to afford the land. Only 80 acres were ever tilled and they've been returned to grass. There are archeological findings of teepee rings, and buffalo bones were hauled away by the truckload from an area that was a buffalo jump.

Danny and Shannon pull up. A Scotch mist of rain chases them into the house. A fire is built and mugs of hot tea appear. We sit and talk a bit.

"We took a Holistic Management International course in 2010 but we'd started direct marketing in '09. We dropped off samples to Blair Lebsack (see page 69) and he happened to need product for a Gold Medal Plates competition he was entering. We butchered 23 animals so that he could have the cuts he wanted and that pushed us to get busy and sell the rest of the animals," says Shannon. "After that we started marketing half and whole animals and have been selling out. Blair takes about 24 cattle a year and lots and lots of our pigs. He uses the whole animals now."

"Every year we move towards our goal of greener pastures and year-round grazing. We've just bought 65 calves and have Black Simmental, South Devon, and Braunvieh bulls. We fenced off the creek this year and will get to bale feeding this winter," says Danny. He has to go back out to shoe a few horses after dinner. "On a farm, we measure progress in seasons and years. Our happiness comes from being on the land."

Pine Haven Colony Meat Shop | 454037 Range Road 234, Wetaskiwin
780-352-6328 | phmeatshop.ca

Pine Haven Colony Meat Shop manager Tim Hofer.
Photo by Karen Anderson.

The Pine Haven Hutterite Colony farms 7,000 acres in total and was established in 1994. There are 109 members who live communally with elders mentoring youth in values and best practices to uphold their way of life. "We have three priorities—God, people, and the land."

Tim Hofer is a member of the management team at the colony and runs the abattoir, processing facility, and wholesale retail meat shop. The colony processes 15 cattle and 60 hogs per week and exactly 6,000 chickens per year. They do their own distribution as well. The animals at Pine Haven are all raised on pasture and grass-finished.

"Getting animals back on pasture for their whole lives increases the health of our soils. Enriching the biological life of the soil helps us raise nutrient-dense food for our people. Synthetic NPK fertilizers grow volume but the plants they produce lack the necessary nutrient density that sustains life. Conventional farms get paid by volume. Things would be different if the emphasis was instead on nutrients."

Not every colony operates this way. "This farm has these ideas. This is what works best for us. From an early age, my parents and grandparents leaned towards natural methods and working with nature. I developed a dislike for conventional methods without even realizing it. When I became of age to manage here, I had the opportunity to change our trajectory."

Many in the Alberta food system have noticed that change. Pine Haven supplies brands like Irvings Farm Fresh (see page 128), TK Ranch (see page 135), and Acme Meat Market (see page 84) because of their commitment to transparency and the alignment between values. Business is good enough that they will double the size of their facilities in the next year.

"I never grew up with much technology but when I discovered the educational assets available on YouTube and the internet, I was open to utilizing them. I've learned a great deal from Dr. Christine Jones of amazingcarbon.com and Gabe Brown of brownsranch.us. The system needs to be bucked for the sake of our future generations."

There are approximately 600 Hutterite colonies in Alberta. Hutterites first arrived here in 1918. Since the 16th century they have upheld the ways of their founder, Jakob Hutter, who did not believe in war or taxes but instead believed that communal living brings one closer to God.

Prairie Gold Pastured Meats | Red Deer County | 587-876-5736
prairiegoldmeats.ca

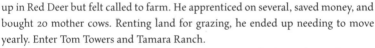

Left to right: Hawksley, Angela, Blake, and Rosie Hall. Photo courtesy of Prairie Gold Pastured Meats.

"My grandpa could sell 50 head of cattle in the fall, buy a new truck and support his family on what he made. Now he'd have to sell 300 to do the same. Only one in six of those farmers made it. There's been a massive brain drain as they and their children left farming."

Blake Hall sees the big picture. "We are entering a time when the most massive transfer of land in North America's history will happen as baby boomer farmers retire. Will they be selling to foreigners who will rent our land back to us or will we find creative ways for youth to get back into farming?"

Hall was not born on a farm. He grew up in Red Deer but felt called to farm. He apprenticed on several, saved money, and bought 20 mother cows. Renting land for grazing, he ended up needing to move yearly. Enter Tom Towers and Tamara Ranch.

Towers had been holistically managing Tamara since the '90s. The ranch is surrounded by conventional grain growers. He knew if he sold, there'd be a good chance all the soil building he'd done would be lost. He also wanted to stay on his ranch and not have to move off with retirement. When he saw Hall selling grass-finished beef stock on Kijiji, he got to know his story. The two worked out a stable tenure agreement that gives Towers rental income and Hall an annually renewing five-year lease. Towers gets to stay on the land he stewarded, and Hall has the security of a permanent place to breed and grow pasture-raised, nutrient-dense food.

"The precedent of a business owner renting a storefront is there." Hall's business just happens to be cattle and the ranch and a website are the storefront where he sells herd shares in beef, pork, and fresh eggs, all grass-finished.

"Farming gives my life purpose. There's a lot of meaning to raising a family here, to growing food that makes people healthy, and to preserving the watershed and building the soil. It feels important to show it can actually be done."

Redtail Farms | Castor | 403-430-0160 | redtailfarms.ca

Dana Blume with Ian, Coen, and Fynn Griebel. Photo by Karen Anderson.

Ian Griebel's extended cab truck bounces through the broken sod of a pasture he's rejuvenating as we drive out to check on his mixed-breed Angus, Medicine River Luings, and Belted Galloway yearling cattle. They're smaller in stature than most breeds ranched and have black, red, brown, and beige hides that are thick and shaggy. "Our genetics are about finding the animals that will fatten while being finished on grass only. They'll stay on the ranch two to two and a half years and have plenty of fat on them before slaughter."

A blue heron flies over as we drive past a faded grey corral that was once a feedlot. "My dad did things the conventional way until he took a holistic management course that helped him have the confidence to change. This land has been free of sprays for over 20 years."

It's been one of the driest years on record and yet large segments of the pastures here in these 2,000 acres of East Central Alberta Parkland meets Prairie are green and lush. There's water in the dugouts and resilience in the soil.

Griebel and his wife Dana Blume live on the family's home quarter and operate on 11 more. "We like to think not about how much land we have but instead how healthy it is. I'm reaping the benefits of trees my grandfather planted. I want to do the same for my grandchildren."

It's dusk and a great horned owl swoops from a light standard as we arrive back at the home Griebel's grandfather built. Dinner is barbecued steaks with crisp yellow fat curling around each portion, fresh garden vegetables, and salad. "I like to think we are creating the fine wine of beef. Ours is tender, marbled, and has the flavour of this land. The meat was recently tested and had an omega fatty acid ratio equal to salmon."

After dinner, we scrape the leftovers in a bucket for the Berkshire pigs raised on pasture and in the trees. The Griebels sell quarter, half, and whole beef and pork from their website.

Ruzicka Sunrise Farm | Killam | 780-385-2474 | sunrisefarm.ca

Don Ruzicka checking on the farm in his vintage truck. Photo by Karen Anderson.

"Our goal is quality food, not quantity." We're driving to a cabin at the heart of Don and Marie Ruzicka's 640 acres (a full section) of land near Killam. As the baby-blue vintage "four on the floor" stick-shift truck pulls to a stop alongside a long narrow lake, Don explains that 97 different bird species have been counted here. "We have a partnership with nature." He smiles with his eyes.

Don has planted 105,000 trees on this land since taking ownership in 1983. He worked with Ducks Unlimited to build a dam and create the 11-acre lake we gaze at as we sip mint tea with honey. Across the fields we can see his brother's farm, the family's homestead since 1905.

At one point, Don owned seven sections of land. Then he read E.F. Schumacher's *Small Is Beautiful* and realized that "industrial agriculture has taken us places we never should have been." He became an organic farmer and delved deeply into holistic management. Today, with his commitment to care for nature and its sacred balance, his farming practices are beyond organic.

"When we started out, we went to some farmers' markets with photos. Marie wanted to show people why our food costs more than the grocer. We put a sign up—all are welcome—at our farm. We had over 300 guests last year." Students from University of Alberta's Augustana campus in Camrose and its Spirit of the Land course are regulars. "My advice to them is that change happens one person at a time and to not be shy—take risks."

Finishing animals on pasture only was a radical change. Don knew it was healthier for the animals and thanks to a University of Toronto researcher named Dr. Richard Bazinet, his meat has now been tested and found to have the same omega profile as cold-water fish. "There's satisfaction in knowing it is healthy for the land and for people."

By the time we are done our pot of tea and heading back to the farmhouse, it's hard to leave the company of this sage, artisan, observer, and contributor to life.

Sunworks Farm | 1-877-393-3133 | sunworksfarm.com

Ron and Sheila Hamilton at home on their farm in Armena. Photo by Karen Anderson.

In 1997, Ron and Sheila Hamilton packed up their family and moved to a quarter-section farm in Armena, near Camrose. Neither of them had ever farmed a day in their lives. Ron laughs when he thinks of it. "It wasn't so cool to farm back then. Most people were leaving farms to move to cities."

The Hamiltons went against the grain because they were convinced that the food they'd been eating was making them ill. Their daughters had a plethora of allergies. Sheila lived with the pain of fibromyalgia and arthritis and was told she'd be wheelchair bound as she aged. They decided that if food could make them that ill it could also be their medicine.

They found a like-minded community when they attended a holistic farm management workshop. They found a mentor in Virginian polymath, farmer, and writer Joel Salatin. They read up on organic, regenerative, and humane farming practices. Then, they put it all into practice.

The first year they raised 80 chickens in outdoor mobile chicken coops. Now they raise over 130,000 annually in mobile coops. They have 4,000 laying hens, raise 1,500 turkeys per year, and process about 30 head of grass-finished cattle each month. They collaborate with Serben Farms (see page 41) to grow ethically raised free-range pork.

Few producers undertake what the Hamiltons do. Now with 400 acres total, they've built their own processing facility so their animals won't have the stress of being transported. They're part of every slaughter to personally ensure it is done as humanely as possible and have been certified humane since 2005. They have their own smokehouse run by master butcher Carlos Lopez, who, along with farm manager Isaac Fergoso, is among a half dozen Mexican families the Hamiltons have helped become Canadian citizens—a legacy they are thrilled with.

Anyone who visits Old Strathcona Farmers' Market in Edmonton will know that Ron loves offering samples of their products for the chance to talk to his customers. Check Sunworks Farm's website for retail and seasonal farmers' market locations.

TK Ranch | Spondin in Special Areas 2 and 270197 Inverlake Road, Langdon | 403-854-8532 | tkranch.com

Dylan and Colleen Biggs. Photo by Karen Anderson.

Thomas Koehler (TK) Biggs was an MIT grad from New York who landed in Alberta's Special Areas in the winter of 1956. Nobody thought he'd make it through his first particularly snowy winter. Biggs thought that's how Canadian winters were supposed to be. He also didn't know about the devastating droughts of the Depression era. He had a bumper crop of brome grass and paid off the mortgage on his four sections in the first year.

"Marrying a pioneer rancher's daughter, Mary Hallet, saved him." Dylan and Colleen Biggs, the current owners of TK, laugh as they share the story of Dylan's father's early years.

Dylan was the one, of TK and Mary's five children, to carry on. He went to Olds College and the University of Lethbridge but taking a holistic management course in 1985 changed his management style to measuring the triple bottom line of people, planet, and profit. He met Colleen, who had taken environmental studies at the University of Alberta, and their marriage is a good fit to this day.

"Because my father was not steeped in traditional thinking, he was open to trying new ideas. When there was a 'normal' market crash in '95 due to a surplus of beef, he wanted to take control and get rid of hormones and antibiotics. Colleen did the research and we started direct marketing in '97," says Dylan.

"I remember putting packs of beef in a cooler, getting our daughters into car seats and driving for hours to restaurants to see if they'd try it. Chef Simon Dunn was the first to take it. I worked on Community Natural Foods for three years. We've been there over 20 years now," says Colleen.

As independent abattoirs disappeared across Alberta, the Biggses had to drive their cattle farther for slaughter and processing. They've taken on debt now to build an abattoir on the ranch and a meat processing facility 20 minutes from Calgary. "Now I'd like to have an education centre so people can come and learn about our ethically treated humane grass-fed animals," says Colleen. With her determination, it will happen. Check their website for retail locations or to shop their online store.

YR Bison Ranch | Red Deer | 403-343-0683 | yrranch.ca

Yvonne and Rod Mills with their sons Cody and Reese. Photo by Karen Anderson.

Rod Mills is a heavy-duty mechanic and millwright. Yvonne Mills was a realtor who loved horses. She scoured the countryside around Red Deer to find an acreage for her horses and was surprised to find a place completely fenced for and housing bison up for sale. Neither of the Millses had ever ranched a day in their lives but when the previous owner asked if he could leave some animals on the land, they agreed. He cared for them and they got used to having bison around. They became fascinated. When the rancher was ready to move them, they asked if they could keep eight. They bought a bull in 2006.

"At first we bought feed from neighbours. Then we bought more land for hay. Rod got a new tractor with a cutting rake and baler. His first attempts at baling were pretty amusing," says Yvonne.

Over a decade into bison ranching they've got two distinct herds and 80 animals. One herd is 100 percent pure plains bison from the grasslands of Theodore Roosevelt National Park in North Dakota and the other is 100 percent pure wood bison from Elk Island National Park. The Millses have immersed themselves in soil health, rotational grazing, and breeding coursework. They've built a farm-gate store, overhauled their website, and added social media.

"We do this because we think biodiversity is important. We love our customers—some of them drive from Smoky Lake and Edmonton—and we love these animals and want to contribute to keeping them pure (no beef crosses). They will only eat grasses—no grain ever," says Rod.

"Our customers have always been there for us. We've doubled in the last two to three years. We're both really proud of what we've accomplished," says Yvonne. Out in the paddock the bison stop and suck back gallons of water from a special watering box. It's the end of a long and dusty day. The Millses are making a list of things to do as we drive. They are definitely ranchers now.

Northwinds Trout Ltd. | Ponoka | 780-352-8592
northwindstrout@hotmail.com

Richard Graves with cedar-planked trout.
Photo by Karen Anderson.

"What's one more job?" Richard Graves chuckles as we talk about what's involved in the daily work of this former cattle operator, still grain farmer and now fish farmer. Rainbow trout open aquaculture is possible on this 1,000-acre ranch near Ponoka because huge gravel deposits were discovered in the early '90s. "After the gravel is removed, the pits fill up with water naturally. I plant bulrushes and grasses around them and then stock them with triploid (sexless) rainbow trout."

The first pond was for his own recreation, but as Graves added ponds (he now has five), stocking and feeding the trout, some of which can weigh 30 pounds, became expensive. "I converted my old calving barn into a food safety–inspected processing facility. Then I started developing recipes for value-added products that I sell to cover the cost of feed." That was in 2012.

Graves now makes 21 different products including whole fish, burger patties, marinated fillets, lox, smoked trout kippers, pepperoni sticks, and a garlic and cranberry sausage. He brings a cedar-planked tasting of crab- and shrimp-stuffed fillets straight from a huge smoker and trout kippers from the walk-in cooler. The meat is cleanly cut with no bruising or unwanted bones. Graves's ability to devise recipes to complement the trout's gentle flavour is duly noted.

On a damp and rainy fall day we climb into a sturdy jeep and go to check the ponds. White pelicans sit in a line along the far shore of the first. A cormorant does a low bombing run. Bears, foxes, big cats, raccoons, eagles, osprey, and even the odd egret are attracted to these open waters teeming with fish. Graves curses softly—there's always a loss for the farmer.

We cross the Battle River at a couple of low-water marks and wind through Parkland forests of golden-leafed native hazelnuts and highbush cranberries, chokecherries, poplars, aspens, and spruce. A doe and her twins wander across the path. "I love this land and want my children to be able to make a living here." That's the why and the one more job this man really cares about.

FARMERS' MARKETS
Check the website for current hours prior to your visit.

BERGEN FARMERS' MARKET
Bergen Community Hall, 10 kilometres south of Sundre on Highway 760 or 10 km west of Highway 22 on the Bergen Road. Follow the signs.
Saturdays 10:00 A.M.–1:00 P.M., June to September | thebergenmarket.ca

INNISFAIL FARMERS' MARKET
Innisfail Arena, 5804 42 Street | Thursdays 10:00 A.M.–1:00 P.M., May to September albertafarmersmarket.com/farmers-market/innisfail-farmers-market

LACOMBE FARMERS' MARKET
Lacombe Arena (parking lot), 5429 53 Street | 403-782-4772 | Fridays 9:00 A.M.–1:00 P.M., May to October | facebook.com/LacombeFarmersMarket

OLDS FARMERS' MARKET
Cow Palace, 5116 54 Street | 403-556-3770 | Thursdays 3:30 P.M.–6:30 P.M., May to October | oldsregionalexhibition.com

RED DEER DOWNTOWN FARMERS' MARKET
4900 block of 50 Avenue | 403-340-8696 | Wednesdays 3:30 P.M.–6:30 P.M., May to October | facebook.com/reddeerdowntownmarket

WETASKIWIN FARMERS' MARKET
Wetaskiwin Mall, 3725 56 Street | 780-360-1110 | Wednesdays 10:00 A.M.–2:00 P.M., January to December | Saturdays noon–4:00 P.M., January to December facebook.com/groups/154597307916211/about

WATERING HOLES

Check the website for current hours prior to your visit.

BACK 40 DISTILLERY (SEE PAGE 107)

4701 36 Street, Camrose | 780-983-5167 or 780-271-2826 | back40distillery.com
⇒ Tours: Friday and Saturday.
Favourite drink here: Ol' Apple Betty—it's so original.

BLINDMAN BREWING

Bay F, 3413 53 Avenue, Lacombe | 403-786-2337 | blindmanbrewing.com
⇒ Tours: By appointment.
Favourite beer here: Long Shadows Pale Ale.

FALLENTIMBER MEADERY (SEE PAGE 108)

Water Valley | 403-637-2667 | fallentimbermeadery.ca
⇒ Tours: Saturdays and Sundays year-round, or by appointment.
Favourite mead here: Meadjito.

GREY OWL MEADERY

452036 Highway 22, Alder Flats | 780-542-1413 | greyowlmeadery.com
⇒ Tours: By appointment.
Favourite mead here: Apple Honey Wine (Cyser).

NORSEMEN BREWING CO.

6505 48 Avenue, Camrose | 780-672-9171 | norsemenbrewing.com
⇒ Tours: During open hours by request.
Favourite beer here: Who wouldn't love a beer named Eric the Red?

OLD COLLEGE BREWERY

4601 46 Street, Olds | 403-556-8258 | oldscollege.ca
⇒ Tours: By appointment.
Favourite beer here: Hay City—it's available year-round.
Home of the Olds College Brewmaster program. Easy access off Highway 2.

RIBSTONE CREEK BREWERY

4924 51 Street, Edgerton | 780-755-3008 | ribstonecreekbrewery.ca
⇒ Tours: By appointment.
Favourite beer here: Great White Combine.
Taproom is open Fridays and Saturdays.

TROUBLED MONK BREWERY

1-5551 45 Street, Red Deer | 403-348-2378 | troubledmonk.com

⇒ **Tours: By request.**

Favourite beer here: Pesky Pig Pale Ale—it has a great story to go with the name.

Snack on cheese from Sylvan Star and meats from nearby Viva Deli as you sip your suds.

Facing page: photo courtesy of Edmonton Tourism

CALGARY

Fort Calgary was founded in 1875 and the City of Calgary was incorporated in 1884 with 4,000 hardy inhabitants. Originally known as the Sandstone City, for the many buildings made from locally quarried Paskapoo sandstone, it's also been called Oil Town and Boom and Bust Town. But, the stickiest name of all is Cowtown, and that has a lot to do with a certain event held here each year.

In 1912, a cowboy-cum-impresario named Guy Weadick approached four prominent businessmen—A. E. Cross, Patrick Burns, Archibald McLean, and George Lane—to fund the Calgary Stampede. For 10 days in July, every year since, the city has hosted the world's largest outdoor rodeo, exhibition, grandstand show, and music festival.

During Stampede, the city abounds with free pancake breakfasts and barbecue events. It's a great chance to experience Alberta's authentic western culture as everyone is decked out in their cowboy best and hospitality is foremost on our minds. People eat a lot of Alberta beef during that time but there's a lot more on the menu during Stampede—and the other 355 days of the year.

Slow Food Calgary, a convivium of Slow Food International, has worked since 2002 to promote good, clean, and fair food from local producers. The Southern Alberta Institute of Technology culinary program has attracted world-class culinary instructors that are producing young chefs who've started dozens of independent restaurants celebrating and using local produce. Immigrants have come to Calgary from the four corners of the globe, and that is also reflected in the city's numerous ethnic restaurants and grocery stores.

There are close to 500 backyard beekeepers in the city and hundreds of community gardens. Outside of the downtown core, livable, walkable neighbourhoods like Inglewood, Kensington, Mount Royal, Mission, and Marda Loop are food-centric places to explore.

While many visitors to the province land at Calgary International Airport and drive straight to Banff, for those who add a little more

Previous spread and facing page: photos courtesy of Tourism Calgary

time to their itineraries, Calgary's attractions like the National Music Centre, the Glenbow Museum, WinSport, Heritage Park, the Calgary Zoo, Telus Spark science centre, Arts Commons, and over 1,000 kilometres of cycling trails will be a great reward. The city's food scene will fuel your explorations and satisfy any appetite.

Travel Tip

> Check calgaryfoodtours.com for walking tours of the city's best food-centric neighbourhoods or hop on calgarybrewerytours.beer to ride your way to the best craft brews and spirits in town and along the Bow Valley to Banff.

Facing page: photo courtesy of Tourism Calgary

MARKET
RESH PRODUCE
100%
GUARANTEED
FORNIA
EEN
IONS
69 / EACH BUNCH

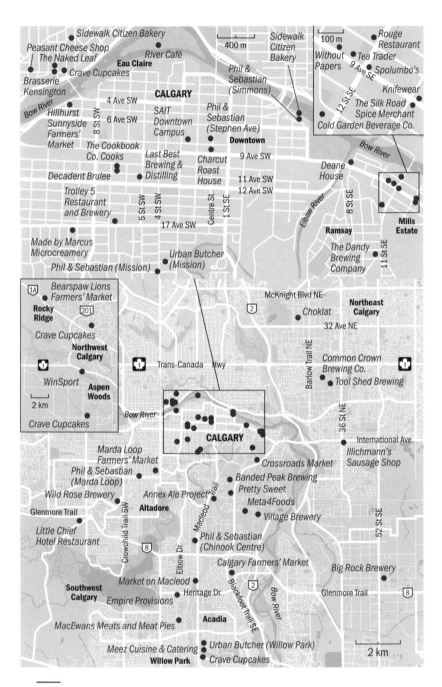

Peasant Cheese Shop
The Naked Leaf
Sidewalk Citizen Bakery
River Café
Eau Claire
Phil & Sebastian (Simmons)
Sidewalk Citizen Bakery
Rouge Restaurant
Without Papers
Tea Trader
9 Ave SE
Spolumbo's
Knifewear
Brasserie Kensington
Crave Cupcakes
CALGARY
The Silk Road Spice Merchant
Cold Garden Beverage Co.
12 St SE
Bow River
Hillhurst
Sunnyside Farmers' Market
4 Ave SW
6 Ave SW
SAIT Downtown Campus
Phil & Sebastian (Stephen Ave)
Downtown
8 St SW
The Cookbook Co. Cooks
Last Best Brewing & Distilling
Charcut Roast House
9 Ave SW
Bow River
Deane House
Decadent Brulee
11 Ave SW
12 Ave SW
8 St SE
Trolley 5 Restaurant and Brewery
5 St SW
4 St SW
Centre St
1 St SE
Elbow River
Mills Estate
17 Ave SW
Ramsay
11 St SE
Made by Marcus Microcreamery
Urban Butcher (Mission)
The Dandy Brewing Company
Phil & Sebastian (Mission)
1A
Bearspaw Lions Farmers' Market
McKnight Blvd NE
Northeast Calgary
Rocky Ridge
201
Choklat
32 Ave NE
Crave Cupcakes
Northwest Calgary
Barlow Trail NE
Common Crown Brewing Co.
Tool Shed Brewing
WinSport
Aspen Woods
Trans-Canada Hwy
2 km
Bow River
CALGARY
36 St NE
Crave Cupcakes
International Ave
Illichmann's Sausage Shop
Marda Loop Farmers' Market
Crossroads Market
Phil & Sebastian (Marda Loop)
Banded Peak Brewing
Pretty Sweet
Wild Rose Brewery
Annex Ale Project
Meta4Foods
52 St SE
Glenmore Trail
Crowchild Trail SW
Altadore
Village Brewery
Little Chief Hotel Restaurant
8
Macleod Trail
Phil & Sebastian (Chinook Centre)
Southwest Calgary
Market on Macleod
Elbow Dr
Calgary Farmers' Market
Big Rock Brewery
Empire Provisions
Heritage Dr
2
Blackfoot Trail SE
Bow River
Glenmore Trail
8
MacEwans Meats and Meat Pies
Acadia
Meez Cuisine & Catering
Urban Butcher (Willow Park)
Crave Cupcakes
2 km
Willow Park

Note: Only artisans and producers who welcome visitors on site are shown on this map.

FOOD ARTISANS OF CALGARY

Brassica Mustard | 403-277-3301 | brassicamustard.com

Desmond Johnston and Karen Davis.
Photo by Karen Anderson.

If you've ever seen blazing yellow mustard blooms swaying under an Alberta blue sky, chances are you'll never forget it—it's that beautiful. Canada is one of the world's leading producers of mustard seed and most of it is grown right here, on the Alberta and Saskatchewan prairies. While the lion's share of Canada's yield is exported and processed elsewhere, Brassica Mustard is bucking that trend.

After graduating from the Southern Alberta Institute of Technology as a Red Seal chef in 1991, Desmond Johnston and his wife and co-founder Karen Davis had the know-how and access to locally grown mustard seed so they began making the condiment and gifted it to family and friends for Christmas in 1995. The following year when they moved out of province and took a break from making it, their inner circle was not pleased. "They were pretty vocal about it, so we've been making it ever since."

The decision to make flavoured mustards was a simple one. Most home cooks and chefs have plain mustard in their kitchen. "We wanted to take a versatile ingredient people are familiar with and add some intrigue." With a groundswell of support from the local culinary community and growing popularity at markets and craft shows, the time was right and Brassica Mustard officially launched in 2001. They started with two signature mustard flavours: Brassica Roasted Garlic and Cranberry Honey. Their Horseradish and Dill mustard soon followed. For their 10th anniversary, they added Black Pepper and Whole Grain mustard, made in a traditional European style.

Upholding the highest quality and their motto "Prairie grown, prairie made," Brassica uses only Alberta mustard seed, local honey and naturally flavoured vinegars. "The beauty of our mustard lies in its simplicity. We use premium ingredients that produce clean flavours. That's why our mustard doesn't taste like anything else out there."

Brassica Mustard is available at select retailers province-wide and through their online retail shop.

Note: *Brassica* is the genus name of the mustard family. Other plants from this genus include cabbage, kale, Brussels sprouts, and canola.

Crave Cupcakes | cravecupcakes.ca

Jodi Willoughby (left) and Carolyne McIntyre Jackson. Photo courtesy of Crave Cupcakes.

Real butter, freshly milled Alberta flour, and eggs cracked by hand. While many of us resort to cake mixes from a box, we all know that when it comes to baking, real ingredients prepared from scratch taste better. This is the ethic that sisters Carolyne McIntyre Jackson and Jodi Willoughby brought to their business, Crave Cupcakes, when they started it in a small shop in Calgary's Kensington district in 2004.

"We grew up on a ranch outside of High River. Our mother Helen and our grandmothers were great bakers. Neighbours were always popping in for coffee and some of our mom's baking. We wanted to bring the care that it takes to bake like that to more people," says McIntyre Jackson.

"We go through about 400 pounds of Foothills Creamery butter per week per store," says Willoughby. "Our bakers crack about a quarter million eggs by hand each year and use a whopping 70 tons of flour. We shop at Innisfail Growers (see page 116) for Beck's carrots to make our carrot cakes and we use Jungle Farm's zucchini to make our chocolate zucchini cakes. We try to feature something local in each of our cupcakes of the month."

For their 10th anniversary, they renovated the original store and added a classroom that they named the 7D Quarter Circle Kitchen after their family's brand and in recognition of the place that started it all for them. Though the company name speaks only of cupcakes, they've also become quite famous for cakes, pies, cookies, and that very Canadian sweet known simply as "squares."

"At busy times like Christmas, if you see a little white-haired woman in one of the shops, that's our mom, Helen. She's always there for us and pitches in to this day, helping with our children, baking, or packaging. She's still such an inspiration for us," says McIntyre Jackson.

Crave only sells goods that are baked fresh each day. Day-old products are donated to charities throughout the province. Their caring goes beyond what comes out of their ovens. Check the website for Crave's five Alberta locations and phone numbers.

Decadent Brulee | 722 11 Avenue SW | 403-245-5535 | decadentbrulee.ca

Pam Fortier, Decadent Brulee owner.
Photo by Karen Anderson.

Travel opened Pam Fortier's eyes to the inherent possibilities of food, especially her time spent in France and Spain. From a young age, she read *Bon Appétit* magazine and would make everything in it, refining and changing recipes as she read her way through.

She originally completed the Southern Alberta Institute of Technology culinary program because she was contemplating opening a restaurant on Denman Island. When that fell through, she followed her natural inclination to the sweeter side of life and attended Dubrulle Pastry School in Vancouver. "Both of my grandmothers were amazing bakers and I've always had a sweet tooth."

Fortier returned to Calgary in 1997 and bought Decadent Desserts, a business established in 1983 that was famous for having the city's first cappuccino machine. "I told my instructors that I would only ever use real ingredients in my baking and they told me I'd never last. People wouldn't pay for it." Twenty-plus years later, Fortier has proven them wrong.

While most bakeries use prepackaged mixes, powdered eggs, milk solids, and inexpensive oils, Fortier makes all of the sweets in her shop from scratch using real butter, eggs, flour, and sugar, all from Alberta. Cakes are her specialty.

"I believe each element of the cake needs to be delicious and that the sum adds up to more than its parts." Her coconut cake must be the most photographed and recommended cake in Calgary. Other favourites are her 14-Karat Cake, Lemon Poppyseed, and Chocolate Obsession.

"I don't bake at home anymore so we make amazing meals. I live, eat, and breathe food and analyze everything I make with the question, Could it be better?"

In 2016, Fortier bought Brûlée Pâtisserie, which specialized in artfully decorated, lighter classic French genoise cakes. She's now merged the two businesses to become Decadent Brulee. "We've learned a lot and upped our game in the decoration of our cakes but to me, taste will always come before looks."

The Naked Leaf | 4-1126 Kensington Road NW | 403-283-3555
thenakedleaf.ca

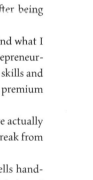

Jonathan Kane at the Naked Leaf.
Photo by Kevin Kwan.

While attending dance school in Salzburg, Austria, Jonathan Kane discovered he couldn't drink coffee. "It made me so physically ill, I stopped drinking it and began exploring the world of tea."

As a professional dancer, Kane found himself on the road a lot, training and performing throughout Europe. With access to some of the best teas in the world, his knowledge and appreciation deepened quickly. Not only did tea give him the energy to keep pace with a gruelling schedule, it offered numerous restorative benefits too.

In 2004, after a 13-year career in dance, Kane accepted a teaching position in the Fine Arts department at the University of Calgary. Three years later, after being steeped in the world of dance most of his life, he needed a change.

"I'd spent years looking for my favourite teas in Calgary but couldn't find what I wanted, so I decided it was time to build it myself." Kane enrolled in the entrepreneurship program at Mount Royal University to learn some important business skills and then opened the Naked Leaf in 2008. He specializes in sourcing all-natural, premium whole-leaf teas and he carries 13 custom blends.

"We source teas that are beautiful and of exceptional quality but what we actually sell here is the pleasure of tea. We show people the importance of taking a break from their routine to savour and enjoy their tea."

Supporting artists in the community is important as well. The shop sells handcrafted tea wares by local ceramists and features local artists' work on tea labels and tins. Working with chocolatier Albert Kurylo they've created more than 12 unique tea-chocolate bars exclusively sold at the Naked Leaf.

"We've also collaborated with local businesses like the Beehive who make chai spice body wash and lotion for us and we've supplied TrueBuch Kombucha (makers of fermented tea) since they started in 2014."

The Naked Leaf takes telephone orders and you'll also find their teas on the menus of select restaurants, bed and breakfasts, and bakeries in Calgary, Red Deer, and as far away as Saskatoon.

Phil & Sebastian Coffee Roasters | philsebastian.com

Sebastian Sztabzyb (left) and Phil Robertson.
Photo courtesy of Phil & Sebastian Coffee Roasters.

Phil Robertson and Sebastian Sztabzyb, who started their eponymous coffee-roasting company in Calgary in 2007, have sourced coffee beans directly from Kenya, Ethiopia, Burundi, Colombia, Bolivia, Panama, Costa Rica, Guatemala, Honduras, and El Salvador.

The first wave of coffee innovation started when Tim Hortons promised "always fresh" percolated drip. Automatic espresso machines were a second wave. Starbucks and their handmade barista-driven java started a third wave. Phil & Sebastian (P&S) are driving the fourth wave by sourcing single-estate "boutique beans," which they then develop individual roasting profiles for so that the terroir of the land is expressed in your cup. To do this, they often microfinance farmers so they can afford better seeds and fermenting storage facilities.

"Now we've even bought a farm," says Sztabzyb. "We've partnered with Margarito Herrera in Honduras and we'll start planting there in 2017. It will be a model farm, a learning facility for us and eventually for our producing partners in other countries." Robertson and Sztabzyb, both engineers, have exacting standards and bring all the beans from country of origin in their green unroasted state.

Each bean gets its own roasting profile. To do this they purchased from Russia a Probat 45 roaster that was made in Germany in 1961. Robertson spent two years designing the combustion, gas, electrical, and electronics systems as well as writing the control software.

"I worked with welders, machinists, millwrights, electricians, and gas fitters to put it all together," he says. "Off-the-shelf roasters are built by people who are very capable at building machines but they're not actually coffee roasters themselves, so the control systems they implement simply don't make sense for the way we roast."

"We really do this because we're tired of watching people drink bad coffee—not because they choose to, but because they don't know better," says Sztabzyb. P&S are doing something about that. Their coffee can be found at over 200 retailers as far away as New York City, but it all started here in Alberta. Check the website for café and retail locations.

154

Pretty Sweet | 536 42 Avenue SE (in the Manchester Business Centre)
prettysweetco.com

Vicki Manness, owner of Pretty Sweet bakeshop.
Photo by Justine Milton.

Vicki Manness always knew she'd work with food. Watching her grandmothers dance their way around the kitchen preparing dinner or a batch of cookies really left an impression on her.

When Manness was young, her family moved from Domain, a small hamlet outside of Winnipeg, to Calgary. Following high school, she enrolled in the Southern Alberta Institute of Technology's culinary program. Midway through, she realized she enjoyed making sweets a lot more, so she signed up for the baking and pastry program and earned her Red Seal certification in both cooking and baking.

Before starting Pretty Sweet in 2009, Manness worked in the kitchens of some of Calgary's best bakeries including former sweet hot spot Nectar, River Café, Urban Baker, and Jelly Modern Doughnuts, to name a few. "I love what I do. Never once have I thought, 'Why am I doing this?'"

When you see and taste Manness's baked goods, you realize how passionate she really is about her craft. "It's important that everything we make looks and tastes its absolute best. Having culinary training has given me a great foundation for my baking. I have an exceptional palate and understand complex flavours and pairings because of it."

Passion, creativity, and experience count for a lot but so do her recipes. "Most of them—a good 80 percent—are from my grandmothers. We've adapted them to give them a modern twist."

From custom wedding cakes to sticky buns, squares, baked doughnuts, and cookie sandwiches, you'll find something pretty and sweet to ease any craving at this bakeshop.

Place your custom orders online or stop by the bakery (check the website for hours) to see what's on deck. You can find Pretty Sweet's goodies at select retailers around Calgary like Greater Goods, Distilled Beauty Bar, and Market Collective.

Sidewalk Citizen Bakery | 618 Confluence Way SE and 338 10 Street NW
403-457-2245 | sidewalkcitizenbakery.com

Michal Lavi and Aviv Fried, owners of Sidewalk Citizen Bakery. Photo by Matilde Sanchez-Turri.

After graduating from the University of Calgary with a physics degree and working as a biomedical engineer, Aviv Fried and his partner, Michal Lavi, a geologist, came to a crossroads. Fried had been offered a lucrative job in Toronto, but he didn't want to go. "I wanted to stay so I could make things with my hands and we could live according to our values."

Fried realized the niche for great bread in Calgary still needed to be filled. So, he studied with the best: Tartine in San Francisco and Poilâne in Paris. A tattered copy of *Bread* by Jeffrey Hamelman became his bible and a big swoop of flour dust permanently marked his forehead.

Taking the scientific rigour he knew as an engineer and applying it to the art of bread making enabled Fried to preserve the food values and traditions from his homeland and create a sourdough bread that was uniquely his. Now people come to study with him.

Both from the same part of Israel, Fried and Lavi grew up in a bread culture and their need to feed people was ingrained early on. "For us making food and sharing it is an important way of showing love."

Wanting to feed a diverse group of customers, they expanded to have two cafés and a catering division. Inspired by a *stage* at fellow Tel Aviv native Yotam Ottolenghi's restaurants in London, their menu features Middle Eastern and Mediterranean-inspired street food with plenty of options for carnivores and vegetarians and gluten-free options too. "To make really delicious, high-quality food like ours, you can't cut corners. We use ethically raised, hormone- and antibiotic-free meats in salads and sandwiches and free-range eggs and organic flour for our baked goods."

Since starting their business in 2010, Fried and Lavi have shown numerous charities and the Calgary food and arts communities a lot of love by giving back as invested citizens.

Tea Trader | 1228A 9 Avenue SE | 1-888-676-2939 | teatrader.com

Ted Jones, owner of Tea Trader, has been "selling tea since 1993." Photo by Matilde Sanchez-Turri.

"The first thing that touches my lips in the morning is a cup of Darjeeling. Black. No milk." Ted Jones grew up in Norwich, England, and has fond memories ·of waiting for the local tea merchant, Mr. Maxey, to pop by the house with their tea order. It was common for most families to have their staples arrive through doorstep deliveries, but somehow Mr. Maxey's visit was always a little more special.

In the 1980s, Jones moved to London and worked as a commodities trader, but longed to be self-employed. He considered a number of options but kept landing back on tea. "My great-grandfather was a tea merchant in Wales. It's a business with a lot of history and traditions associated with it...and it's a highly sought-after product. Tea is an integral part of many people's lives." Jones follows up his morning cuppa with about five more, weaving them in throughout the day while working as a business consultant in Calgary's energy sector.

After immigrating to Canada, Jones and his wife Colleen officially established Tea Trader in Toronto in 1991. In 1992, they came west and settled in Calgary. A year later, they ramped up the business and opened their doors. "I'm happy to have a business that sells something people enjoy and is self-supporting so it can be successful without me. I can use the connections I've made over the years to acquire the best teas possible."

As an old-fashioned tea merchant, Tea Trader sells a wide range of traditional and high-quality loose-leaf teas locally and throughout the world through their mail-order business. They have several custom blends (try Eight Bells or Persian Nights), tea wares, and accessories, and are the exclusive supplier of local Wolf and Willow honey.

Visit this hidden-gem tea shop in person or check out their website for their online catalogue.

Apiaries & Bees for Communities (ABC Bees) | abcbees.ca

Eliese Watson. Photo courtesy of ABCBees.

Eliese Watson grew up in rural Alberta and enjoyed a life connected to the land. When she left home to attend university, she felt displaced. She looked to urban beekeeping as the antidote to her big-city blues.

Attending a beekeeper conference, she met the director of Honey Care Africa, an organization that microfinances, trains, and finds a market for an extensive community of beekeepers in East Africa. He encouraged Watson to become a community connector in Alberta and she's been queen bee of a steadily growing hive since starting ABC Bees in 2010.

Locally, she found a mentor in Patti Milligan of Edmonton's Lola Canola Bee School education programs. Watson started teaching workshops and organizing collective bee and equipment purchasing because it was difficult for new beekeepers to access what they needed.

Watson has certified over 2,000 level-one and level-two beekeepers. Her influence is undeniable with 80 percent of beekeepers in Alberta now having fewer than 100 colonies and most having fewer than five. "ABC Bees has offered a service that has quadrupled the number of hobbyist beekeepers here and the variety and volume of honey for sale has also increased from both rural and urban producers."

Through a program called Bees for Communities she runs beekeeping mentorship programs sponsored by corporate partners with the goal of involving local socially responsible businesses in showcasing the importance of ecological stewardship for pollinator conservation in urban habitats. There are now 13 partners in Calgary.

Working in a hive with Watson, she seems at one with the bees, picking them up with ease to examine their health. She is a walking encyclopedia of bee behaviour and teaches at both the Northern Alberta Institute of Technology and the College of the Rockies. She is triumphant that after she was asked to advise Canada's Senate on the role of urban beekeeping, they enacted two of her recommendations.

Watson has 100 hives of her own and says, "There's nothing better than biting into a still-warm, fresh-from-the-hive piece of honeycomb." Her golden reward seems well deserved.

Mob Honey | 587-435-1854 | mobhoney.com

Amber Yano. Photo by Alyssa Howland.

Beekeeper Amber Yano of Mob Honey has a life-threatening allergy to bee venom. She went through venom immunotherapy so that she can safely be around her hives but she still carries an EpiPen, just in case. She loves bees that much.

Yano originally started beekeeping in 2011 with no experience, just a deep-seated love for the buzzing insects and their important role in nature. "Honeybees are a barometer for the health of the planet. If they die, it's a clear sign the planet is sick."

Her business model is to supply unpasteurized wildflower honey from urban hives to local businesses, families, and individuals that sponsor a hive for $350 per season. Yano sets up, tends, and houses the hives throughout the season, ensuring the bees are happy, healthy, and productive. She'll also harvest and deliver the honey. Sponsors can buy up to 100 pounds from their hive at a wholesale rate and either give it as gifts or sell it under their own label. "We provide a high-quality, sustainable honey to people who care about bees and the planet."

Each year, Mob Honey increases its hive count, providing more opportunities for people to become involved. "This year we are up to 60 hives. We'll split the strong colonies and this winter, I'll be learning how to rear my own queens. There's always something new to learn, which I love." The end goal is to gradually expand to 500 hives.

Some of Mob's current sponsors include Spolumbo's (see page 162), Kloiber's Meats, OEB Breakfast Co., and Red's Diner. You can find the honey in some of these stores or you can order it through the YYC Growers and Distributors' Community Supported Agriculture program. "They buy half of my honey every year and put jars of it in their harvest boxes." Yano is a beekeeping hobbyist who has taken her passion and turned it into a green-collar small business that's good for Calgary and good for the planet.

Empire Provisions | 8409 Elbow Drive SW | 403-244-0570
empireprovisions.com

David Sturies and Karen Kho, owners of Empire Provisions. Photo by Matilde Sanchez-Turri.

Though from different cultures, Dave Sturies and Karen Kho smile when they recall childhood memories of large family feasts. Those memories, along with a shared passion for recreating their favourite meals from their travels, inspired the couple to reconsider their career paths. "Sometimes we do what we're trained for, but that doesn't mean it's what we were really meant to be doing," says Kho.

This realization prompted Sturies to leave a career in environmental science to immerse himself in the world of butchery, meat cutting, and curing. He worked first at Second to None Meats, which is now the Urban Butcher (see page 190), and then at Teatro Restaurant where Kho worked as operations manager.

Empire Provisions began with a few pop-ups and catering events to showcase the couple's recipes for sausages, charcuterie, and pâtés. Word spread quickly of the quality and flavour of their products. In May of 2016, Jayme McFayden and Kelly Black, the owners of Una Pizza + Wine, offered them space in their prep kitchens to launch and the business took off from there.

"We take pride in amplifying the natural flavours of the meat and we give credit where it is due, to the farmers who raise the animals." They source pasture-raised pork from Alberta producers. Broek Pork Acres (see page 275), Bear and the Flower, and Redtail Farms (see page 132) are all key suppliers who raise their animals without added hormones or unnecessary antibiotics. They source lamb from Ewe-Nique Farms for their merguez sausage.

Kho and Sturies break down and use the entire animal to prevent waste. They make all their products by hand and have developed all of their own recipes together. "I am Filipino and Dave's family is from Calabria in Italy. We draw on our family's recipes, our travels and memories for the inspiration for our products."

Empire Provisions now has their own location in Calgary's Haysboro neighbourhood complete with a storefront and café. You can check their website for the list of restaurants and retailers that feature their products. Kho and Sturies's work now encompasses everything they are passionate about: great food, travel, and bringing people together.

Illichmann's Sausage Shop Ltd. | 1840 36 Street SE | 403-272-1673
illichmannscalgary.com

Dana and Ken Meissinger, owners of Illichmann's Sausage Shop. Photo by Matilde Sanchez-Turri.

In 1999, as seamless as a sunrise, Dana and Ken Meissinger took over the family business, Illichmann's Sausage Shop, from Ken's parents, Joe and Rose, who were looking to retire. Joe and Rose Meissinger bought the shop shortly after immigrating to Canada and spent 30 years building a reputation for making high-quality artisanal cured meats and sausage.

From a very young age, Ken worked alongside his father, a master butcher and sausage maker in his native Austria, and learned butchery and the art of curing meat in the German tradition. "There's no school that can teach you everything Ken knows. He's been doing this his whole life. He can look at a sausage and know instantly if it'll be good or not."

While butchery and the art of curing meats have seen a resurgence lately, very few Albertans have the experience, know-how, dedication, and patience to make as many Old World European-style meats and sausage varieties as well as Illichmann's does.

The shop is a meat lover's paradise with 100 types of deli meat, specialty bacon, sausages, and smoke-cured meats without fillers or artificial flavours. "All of the meat we use is sourced locally from suppliers we've had since we started. We cut, cure, blend, and smoke everything right here using the same recipes and methods Joe and Rose did."

Illichmann's Sausage Shop also processes wild game for hunters and sells fine cuts of local beef, pork, lamb, and bison. You'll find European import items including cheese and condiments (with a focus on German goods) and they offer catering as well.

While the succession of Illichmann's spans generations, so does their customer base. "We know our customers by name and their orders by heart." Their loyal customers are the main reason the business celebrated their 50th anniversary on October 28, 2017. "What we love most is seeing our customers bring their kids in. So many have grown up on our food. We feel good about the part we play in helping each generation keep their family traditions and culture alive."

Spolumbo's | 1308 9 Avenue SE | 403-264-6452 | spolumbos.com

Left to right: Mike Palumbo with Tony and Tom Spoletini. Put their surnames together and you've got Spolumbo's. Photo by Darcy Sorochan.

While helping Joe Tudda (his father-in-law) build Villa Firenze restaurant, Tom Spoletini and his friend Mike Palumbo were talking about their future. The pair, along with Tom's cousin Tony Spoletini, were transitioning from careers in the Canadian Football League. They thought about going into the construction business, but Tudda suggested they make sausage instead.

Armed with his mother-in-law Teresa's spicy Italian sausage recipe, Tom with Tony and Mike began making sausage in the kitchen of Villa Firenze during the night. Their first machine made four sausages per minute (now they have two that make 300 per minute).

"Our sausage is not an afterthought that uses up trim and leftover meat. We've built every one of our sausages carefully, using premium cuts from the animal." If you want to know what's in any of their products, all you have to do is ask. "We have 30-plus types of pork, chicken, turkey, lamb, beef, and game sausages. There's nothing but meat and spices in them. No binders, fillers, MSG, or preservatives. They're simple and fresh. We're not scientists. We like to know where our food comes from and exactly what's in it."

Spolumbo's is a powerful case study for food's power in re-gentrifying a neighbourhood. "Inglewood was a very tough part of town when we moved here in 1992. We wouldn't let our families come to the shop, it was that bad."

The first storefront was a 10-seat deli only blocks away from their current location. Being ex-football players had its advantages. People naturally gravitated to the trio at the cozy deli. But they maintain it's the quality and taste of their sausages that won people over. They opened their current 100-seat deli with a federally inspected sausage factory in August of 1998.

Tom, Tony, and Mike are generous supporters of hundreds of community charities every year. Most people never hear about their good work, which is just how the Spolumbo's crew likes it.

You can buy their sausages at their deli, at any Calgary Co-op grocery store, or at the Millarville Farmers' Market in summer.

VDG Salumi | 514 17 Avenue SW | 403-990-6690 | vdgsalumi.com

Chef Stuart Kirton (left) and Ivo Andric.
Photo by Matilde Sanchez-Turri.

Chef Stuart Kirton and Ivo Andric, founders of VDG Salumi, became friends while working at the Living Room Restaurant. Both had a passion for great food, especially artisanal cured meats, but it wasn't until Andric was laid off from his day job as an analyst that the two got serious about making and selling their own traditional Italian salumi. (Salumi is the Italian word for cured meat, like charcuterie is in French.)

VDG Salumi launched in 2016. The name is an acronym for *volto di guanciale*. *Guanciale* refers to pork cheeks, which were the first thing chef Kirton ever cured. He went to the Southern Alberta Institute of Technology and George Brown College for culinary training. "I was still in high school and living in Toronto when I bought Michael Ruhlman's book on charcuterie. I read every page and started experimenting. There was lots of trial and error but I learned a lot."

He learned even more during his four-month externship at La Scuola Internazionale di Cucina in Sicily. After his coursework, he went north to cook for Massimo Spigaroli of Antica Corte Pallavicina near Parma. "We would tie and hang 500 pieces of coppa each night, it was amazing." After returning to Canada, Kirton worked in Toronto with his mentor, chef Gabriele Paganelli, whose curing techniques Kirton relies on to this day.

VDG makes six types of salami in small batches by hand with the freshest local pork. "Ivo oversees the aging process daily, so we are able to consistently recreate all of our products. The fermentation process extends the life of perishable products. Mould is what adds flavour and preserves the meat. As people understand the process and their palates expand, we'll be able to keep more of Alberta's delicious meats here to enjoy."

VDG Salumi is available in over 60 restaurants in Calgary and Canmore as well as grocery stores and supermarkets across the province. Check the website for retailers.

Cultured Butter | | 403-650-8571 | cultured-butter.com

Kristie Lee. Photo by Laurie Brown of Laurie Mac Brown Photography.

After a trip to France with her daughter, Kristie Lee couldn't get over how delicious the butter tasted. The following year, before she decided to leave her sales job in the oil and gas sector, Lee asked everyone she met what their passions were. What she didn't realize at the time was she already knew hers and it would eventually turn into a tasty new venture.

"One day, I remember arriving home to see my husband (Korey Conroy) busy in the kitchen making cultured butter by hand. When we tasted it, I was instantly reminded of the butter I had eaten in France . . . and that's how it all began."

Back before refrigeration, all butter was cultured to keep it from spoiling. In France, this tradition has been maintained and it's the main reason French butter is so delicious. The secret: cultured cream.

Cultured butter consists of fermenting the cream before the butter is churned. By introducing some dairy-friendly bacteria to the fresh cream, the sugars in the cream are converted to lactic acid. This thickens it and produces additional aroma compounds that make for a more concentrated buttery taste with a slight tang.

After adapting an original recipe, Lee now handcrafts 140 packages of fresh, homemade cultured butter each week in small batches. She uses only grass-fed cream from farms like Rock Ridge Dairy (see page 100) and as many seasonal ingredients as she can source from local farmers' markets. With her cream delivered on Monday, left to ripen for two days, then churned, washed, hand pressed, packaged, and delivered to fine food retailers on Thursday, it's hard to find a fresher product. Lee currently sells seven flavours. Visit her website to find a retailer near you.

Made by Marcus Microcreamery | 121-1013 17 Avenue SW
403-452-1692 | madebymarcus.ca

*Marcus Purtzki in front of his microcreamery.
Photo by Karen Anderson.*

"Our creativity comes from incorporating local ingredients, seasonally." In a rare moment of quiet, Marcus Purtzki sits on a bench in front of his microcreamery to talk shop. "In spring, we roast strawberries for two hours to bring out their flavour. This summer we shucked 120 ears of Taber corn for each batch of that flavour. The raspberry beet soft serve was a big hit too. Now we are morphing to all things pumpkin, roasting them first to extract the most flavour. For Thanksgiving, there will be a sweet potato ice cream with toasted marshmallows." He smiles at the thought.

Purtzki is as seriously committed to the science of ice cream as he is to the flavours. He has a B.Sc. in food science (dairy was his focus) and an M.Sc. in nutrition.

"I didn't intend on becoming a cook. I was hired in a Michelin-starred restaurant in New York City as a nutritionist but before long I was in the kitchen." He also worked in Vancouver's fine dining scene, but when his wife accepted a job as a pediatrician in Calgary, Purtzki switched back to his passion for developing food product lines. Having always wanted to have his own business, he used the commercial kitchen where he worked to develop his own line of Made by Marcus Macarons during off hours. Not wanting to waste the egg yolks (macarons use only the whites), he began making small batches of ice cream. Four years later, he was churning out hundreds of litres daily and happily moved to his current spot with a full production facility in the back.

"The ice cream takes three days to make. We use Vital Green Farms (see page 247) organic milk and just bought our own homogenizer to perfect the fat distribution needed for our product. With aging, churning, and a couple of trips through special freezers we achieve a consistency people just can't get at home." That explains the lineup down the block most evenings.

Peasant Cheese Shop | 1249 Kensington Road NW | 587-353-3599
peasantcheese.com

Crystal McKenzie. Photo by Karen Anderson.

Crystal McKenzie, owner of Peasant Cheese Shop, admits she hadn't tasted fine cheese until she trained as a chef while in her 20s. She always thought she would open a restaurant but her love of cheese led her to open a specialty shop instead. "If you stop and think about it, cheese is one of the most miraculous foods on earth."

She's right. Most cheeses have fewer than six ingredients and there's more than a thousand varieties available globally, each with its own special aroma, taste, and texture. Cheese lovers fantasize about trying them all.

Cheesemaking has been traced back 4,000 years. Artisanal styles and varieties have emerged through efforts to overcome environmental and geographic constraints affecting the balance of water, acid, and salt during the cheesemaking process. Achieving the right balance in these areas is key to encouraging certain microbes to flourish, so that each cheese ripens into its intended form.

Training in France and with several artisans in North America, McKenzie tried her hand at the craft of cheesemaking but prefers being a cheesemonger. "I enjoyed learning how to make cheese but sourcing and selling it means I get to explore new varieties all the time and, in turn, help my patrons discover them as well."

From bloomy (soft ripe) to washed rinds, to high alpine and Goudas, Peasant Cheese Shop has a rotating selection of 100 cheeses including several made in Alberta. McKenzie's mindset as a chef has her rounding out the offerings with house-made and imported crackers, pickles, jellies, charcuterie, and fresh rustic breads, along with chic serving pieces. The shop staff prepare cheese and charcuterie boards for events, host regular cheese tastings, and sell memberships to their own cheese club, a monthly program for fromage lovers to experience newly acquired varieties.

Note: Check out Crystal's Cheez Whuz, her delicious all-natural twist on the tasty classic by a slightly different name.

Chef Cam Dobranski | Brasserie Kensington | 1131 Kensington Road NW
403-457-4148 | brasseriekensington.com

Serial entrepreneur and chef Cam Dobranski.
Photo by Matilde Sanchez-Turri.

At one point, chef Cam Dobranski entertained the idea of becoming a marine biologist. Luckily, his love of food and hunger for challenges won out. He got started in the industry as a line cook in his uncle's restaurant in Edmonton and went on to earn his Red Seal from the Northern Alberta Institute of Technology before beginning his professional career at Hardware Grill working under the watchful eye of chef/owner Larry Stewart (see page 67).

Dobranski went on to cook all over the world, including Switzerland where he stayed for two years. Since coming back to Canada, he's found time to get a business diploma and set up several businesses including his three restaurants and a chef's apparel company called Medium Rare.

Cooking for over 25 years now, he admits he's in the kitchen less than he'd like. Still, his staff are aligned with his food philosophy, which is inherently tied to the land and the people who forage and grow the ingredients they cook with every day. "I love that I am able to use my businesses to support local producers and the important work they do."

No matter which of Dobranski's restaurants you dine at, everything is made in-house, from scratch. He is known for his nose-to-tail butchery skills and creativity in using every part of the animal. His food honours the animals and pleases his customers' palates. He sources lamb from Driview Farms (see page 278) and beef from several local suppliers. Most of his produce comes from Galimax Trading (see page 250), but he tops up his supply with wild foods in spring and summer from independent foragers and trips to the farmers' market.

In 2015, Dobranski was recognized for his commitment to developing Alberta's food culture and was selected to participate in the Cook It Raw Alberta consortium with 14 Alberta chefs and seven international superstar chefs.

Connie DeSousa and John Jackson | Charcut Roast House | 101-899 Centre Street SW | 403-984-2180 | charcut.com

The inseparable duo and co-owners of Charcut, John Jackson and Connie DeSousa. Photo courtesy of Charbar.

The Caesar, a drink that put Calgary on the map, was invented at the Owl's Nest restaurant. This is also the place chefs John Jackson and Connie DeSousa met in 1999. Much like the drink, the pair have helped bring renown to Calgary's burgeoning culinary scene.

After their stint at the Owl's Nest, the two set out on their own, travelling throughout the UK, United States, and Europe, donning aprons in some of the best restaurants in the world. They also cooked their way through international culinary competitions. Before long, their paths converged again, this time in San Francisco, where they opened the prestigious Mobil five-star St. Regis Hotel in 2005 to much acclaim. Inspired by the established farm-to-table culture in San Francisco, Jackson and DeSousa returned to Calgary with their families to establish a similar concept here.

Unlike California, Alberta lacked a formal infrastructure between chefs and producers and the farm-to-fork movement was still being established. So, before opening Charcut Roast House in 2010, Jackson and DeSousa travelled to 40 farms in 40 days across Alberta to find farmers and artisans they could rely on to supply their new restaurant. "We broke bread with everyone we visited and many of those farmers still supply our restaurants to this day." The duo were amazed by the diversity of products and were excited to discover the ingredients growing throughout the province. "We set out to build more than a restaurant; the goal was to build a community and to make food producers the stars."

Charcut's chef-driven menu with a big emphasis on local meat and produce caught the attention of Alessandro Porcelli, founder and director of Cook It Raw. He was interested in their style and approach so he invited them to Cook It Raw in Charleston. DeSousa and Jackson then introduced Porcelli to the Alberta Culinary Tourism Alliance (ACTA) and ACTA sent several Alberta chefs to the Terroir Symposium in Toronto. Jackson and DeSousa were instrumental in bringing Cook It Raw to the province and creating international interest in Alberta's food culture and cuisine.

The pair continue to evolve simple ingredients and shape Alberta's food identity through their cooking advocacy work.

Glen Manzer | Creative Restaurants Group | creativeri.com

Glen Manzer, executive chef for the Creative Restaurants Group. Photo by Matilde Sanchez-Turri.

"Growing up, everyone always knew I'd become a chef." Born and raised in Winnipeg, Glen Manzer's first food memory was at a horseshoe tournament and long-table dinner at Lac du Bonnet. "I was about 13 years old and I was cooking with the ladies. We put about a half pound of butter in each side of spaghetti squash and that was the first thing I made. It tasted so good."

Manzer graduated from the culinary program at Red River College in Manitoba in 1989. He came west in 1996 after working at hyperlocal Prairie Oyster Café. He was head chef at River Café and then joined the Creative Restaurants Group. His food philosophy and cooking style have always been heavily influenced by the Mediterranean. "Rustic, simple, bold flavours with lots of meat and gluten. Did I mention how much I love the last two?" he says with a smile.

Sourcing the best ingredients from as close to his kitchen as possible is what Manzer does best. Favourite producers include Broek Pork Acres (see page 275), Hog Wild Specialties (see page 37), Highwood Crossing (see page 274), and Driview Farms (see page 278).

Using local ingredients while maintaining an authentic menu at the group's Italian-inspired outlets like Bonterra Trattoria, Scopa, Cibo, and Posto Pizzeria can be challenging. "Local tastes better but there's no substitute for some of the authentic Italian ingredients so we stay focused on buying the highest quality in everything and make up for it where we can."

After surviving a battle with cancer over a decade ago, Manzer still loves being in the kitchen. "I couldn't and wouldn't want to do anything else but this. It's fun! I can't think of a more rewarding career. We welcome people into our world and then it's our job to make their meal and experience special." The Creative Restaurants Group is not a chain per se. They develop restaurants that fit with the neighbourhoods in which they are located, and that formula has made for some unique contributions to Alberta's food culture. See the website for restaurant locations and details.

Chef Bill Alexander | Little Chief Hotel Restaurant at Grey Eagle Resort and Casino | 587-390-1400 | greyeagleresortandcasino.ca/dining

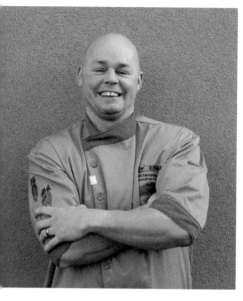

Executive chef Bill Alexander.
Photo by Matilde Sanchez-Turri.

When you meet chef Bill Alexander—"the smiling chef"—you'll understand exactly how he got his nickname. He never stops smiling, or moving, for that matter. Alexander joined the culinary team at Grey Eagle Resort and Casino on the Tsuut'ina Nation in March of 2016 as the executive chef of Little Chief Restaurant and food services.

Alexander grew up on a horse ranch in Quebec where he and his family lived off the land. "We did some hunting, raised livestock, and had a huge garden, almost as big as this restaurant." After his parents divorced, Alexander and his mom and brothers moved to Ontario where he took over the cooking duties since his mom worked full-time. "My brothers were my first customers and they were very picky. They taught me something really important though, that my cooking shouldn't be about me."

At 17, Alexander had a career-defining moment. The general manager at the restaurant where he was working part-time as a line cook pulled him aside just as he was leaving for his other job. "I'd been working for him for six months and he said he saw a lot of potential in me. Then he asked me to quit my other job. I hadn't considered cooking as a career until then but within six months, I was in charge of the kitchen."

The menu at Little Chief Restaurant puts a modern twist on traditional First Nations food. "We're proud of this menu because we're able to showcase First Nations cuisine with some of the best ingredients in the world, grown right here in Alberta."

An example? Applewood smoked elk chops with beetroot rhubarb compote, potato stuffed fry bread, and pickled carrots with carrot top pesto, which won Alexander and his team first place in the culinary challenge at the Canmore Uncorked food festival in 2017. While this Cordon Bleu–trained chef will make people rethink indigenous-inspired cuisine, if you ask him what the biggest factor is in making delicious food, he'll tell you, "Being a good person. There's no separating the two."

Barb Sheldon-Thomas | Love2Eat | 519-741-5176 | love2eat.ca

Barb Sheldon-Thomas. Photo by Karen Anderson.

Barb Sheldon-Thomas is a chef and certified holistic nutritional practitioner, but that's not enough. "Funding agencies need proof that cooking changes health and improves life expectancy. I want to be part of the solution and help move us there."

Sheldon-Thomas is also a professional speaker, wellness retreat leader, private chef, and culinary instructor who teaches in the school system. "As a nutritionist, I decided I can't tell people, I need to show them. After 24 weeks with me, in the school system I work in, those children can cook anything. I like to say knife skills equal life skills."

Food literacy—knowledge of whole foods and how to prepare them—is Sheldon-Thomas's passion. "I've just started my master's degree at Royal Roads University. I'll spend the next two years assessing how cooking and food literacy change health with concrete health outcomes as the measurements of success."

Sheldon-Thomas supports Alberta food producers at every opportunity. When we met she was one of the chefs preparing a dinner for 400 people at Rootstock, an annual event organized by the Food Water Wellness Foundation to promote regenerative farming practices. It will be exciting to watch this chef's impact on our food system and we can't help wondering if health care would cost less in Alberta if every school had a culinary instruction program.

You can book Sheldon-Thomas for wellness retreats or speaking engagements through jennifer@shepherdmanagementgroup.ca.

Judy Wood | Meez Cuisine & Catering | 216-10816 Macleod Trail South
403-264-6336 | meezcuisine.com

Chef Judy Wood. Photo by Danielle Paetz.

Chef Judy Wood's first food memory goes all the way back to the age of three, making pie at her mother's side. "Mom taught herself how to cook. She had a great palate and could fix any dish with butter, cream, or booze. She got me hooked on cooking."

Her father did his part too. He was an international banker and travelled a lot, but when he was home they entertained guests and clients from all over the world. Wood and her mother made all the food, receiving high praise.

"When my dad travelled for work, he would bring each of us a book from the place he visited. When he came back from a trip to Paris, he brought me the *La Varenne Cookery* book. After trying every recipe in it, I told him that's where I wanted to go to school."

Being trained at the famous L'École de Cuisine La Varenne in Paris was very intense but Wood met Anne Willan, who established the school, and even had Julia Child and Paul Bocuse (food royalty) visit her class. After receiving her Grand Diplôme, Wood held a string of head chef and executive positions at premier restaurants and food establishments in both Calgary and Toronto. She then worked as a personal chef, opened her own café, entertained throngs of viewers as the Saturday-morning chef on Global TV for over a decade, and taught cooking classes in Calgary, France, and Italy.

While cooking and mentoring other chefs is Wood's lifeblood, educating and connecting people with local producers is her passion. "I love cooking because I believe food is life. I want to do my part to ensure the farm-to-fork movement becomes a part of everyday life again because our future depends on it."

Visit Meez Cuisine for prepared meals or cooking classes or to plan your next event.

Sal Howell | River Café | 403-261-7670 | river-cafe.com | Deane House 403-264-0595 | deanehouse.com

Sal Howell at River Café. Photo courtesy of River Café.

Sal Howell was born in Wales and raised in the Channel Islands and throughout Europe. Her parents were an architect and an artist who would buy old homes and "do them up." Howell learned early about the value of fine food and also of curated spaces and experiences.

After attending Mount Allison University in Sackville, New Brunswick, Howell arrived in Alberta to work at Lake Louise in 1988. There she admired what restaurant designer Witold Twardowski and the O'Connor family had done with Deer Lodge, Emerald Lake Lodge and Buffalo Mountain Lodge. "They were really the first to showcase what is uniquely Albertan by serving indigenous game meats like bison, elk, and venison."

In Calgary, Twardowski helped Howell create a setting that would also be an experience. They took River Café from a city park kiosk to the grand old fishing lodge it is now. "People have the experience of a walk in the park and arrival at this completely different space right in the heart of the city.

"Since 1991, we keep asking how local we can be. At first it was hard to find the producers but we started with one and it led to more. Curating it can be tricky but when you have such a clear path, it really drives you."

Starting with Dwayne Ennest at the helm, other chefs have included Glen Manzer (see page 169), Scott Pohorelic, Andrew Winfield, and now Matthias Fong. Jamie Harling is the inaugural chef at sister restaurant Deane House.

"Every chef takes our food to another level. They are all mentored and then they mentor others. We've put systems in place to allow creativity and collaboration. We get them out to forage and explore local producers each year.

"We'll keep championing local. We are losing productive land that could be used to produce food so I think we'll see strategic alignments between conservancy groups and food producers. The food community has grown so much. I think it's getting stronger and more interesting all the time." After 30 years in the industry, she should know.

Paul Rogalski | Rouge Restaurant | 1240 8 Avenue SE | 403-531-2767
rougecalgary.com

Paul Rogalski in the garden at Rouge Restaurant.
Photo by Karen Anderson.

Whether he is setting sail to cook for a Canada 150 celebration of our nation's culture on an icebreaker in the Arctic or duking it out on the set of *Iron Chef America* with his celebrity chef friend Michael Smith, Paul Rogalski is always an ambassador for Alberta's food, travel, and restaurant scene. A Calgary native, he graduated from the Southern Alberta Institute of Technology culinary program in 1986.

The early years of his career were spent in fine dining with mentors like Klaus Wockinger at Calgary's iconic La Chaumiere restaurant and Vince Parkinson at the Delta Bow Valley between work and travel stints in Southeast Asia and Grand Cayman. He and business partner Olivier Reynaud took over the lease of A.E. Cross House restaurant in 2001. They painted the historic building red, turned the menu to French-inspired locally sourced food, and in 2002 Rouge Restaurant was born. In 2010, they placed at number 60 on San Pellegrino's top 100 restaurants in the world and are still the highest-ranking Canadian restaurant to ever make that list.

Rogalski says it all started when the Monterey Bay Aquarium recognized Rouge for its sustainable seafood program in 2009 and he was invited to a workshop with culinary luminaries like Thomas Keller, Sam Choy, Alton Brown, and John Ash, whom he credits as one of his biggest influences. Rogalski was asked to cook for the 2010 Vancouver Olympic Village athletes and he continues to collaborate, returning to Cayman for an annual "cookout" with Eric Ripert and to Mexico's six-star resort Le Chique with his friend Jonathan Gomez Luna. At home, Rouge hosted a dozen years of Slow Food International Feast of Fields festivals to help promote the connection between Alberta's farmers and consumers and Rogalski was one of 14 Alberta chefs chosen for Cook It Raw, a project that gave Alberta cuisine a narrative with seven signature foods.

As we stand in Rouge's immaculately tended garden with two hives of bees busy pollinating the plant life, Rogalski says, "The future of food must be sustainable to be relevant." He also sees that while the techniques chefs use may be born of fine dining, diners themselves are just looking for a chance to break bread together in a casual, comfortable way. He thinks there's no place better to do that than Alberta.

Andrew Hewson | Southern Alberta Institute of Technology (SAIT) School of Hospitality and Tourism–Professional Culinary Program | sait.ca

Chef Andrew Hewson picks an apple from his espaliered apple trees. Photo by Karen Anderson.

Growing up in Calgary and with a grandmother in nearby High River, Andrew Hewson was always happy to help in the kitchen. He liked it. He did not like his university life at the University of British Columbia and when he really thought about what he wanted to do, cooking was always the answer. He attended Dubrulle French Culinary School in Vancouver. "From the first day, I was hooked and I've never looked back."

Cooking took him to prestigious posts in New York City and to England where he had the chance to travel frequently to France and Italy. Wherever he went, he soaked up the food culture. After opening the Ritz Carlton in Philadelphia and running the kitchen there for five years, 9/11 and a pregnant wife made him rethink his situation. When the opportunity came to work with chef Michael Noble at Catch (a former high-end sustainable seafood restaurant at Calgary's Hyatt Hotel), Hewson returned to Calgary. In 2005, Hewson started as a culinary instructor at SAIT and after noticing a disconnect between his students and their knowledge of whole food ingredients, he spearheaded efforts to build a culinary garden.

"I used the term 'culinary agro-literacy' to describe what the garden (called Jackson's Garden) had to offer and in 2010–11 I took a sabbatical as the Cadmus Trades Teaching Chair to expand on that concept and to look at how we could build content on issues like food sustainability, nutrition, and knowledge of farming practices into our program."

Jackson's Garden is currently uprooted as SAIT expands but no sooner was it removed than approval and planning were launched for a new and improved garden. "In just eight years, the impact the garden has created is tremendous. Through every block of training the students get reinforcement about local food. Senior chefs share their experiences of gardening and picking food. The culinary garden has completely permeated the culture around here and I think they graduate with greater respect for food and what it takes to grow it." Seems like a lasting legacy—and a good one for Alberta's food system.

Michael Allemeier | Southern Alberta Institute of Technology (SAIT) School of Hospitality and Tourism–Professional Culinary Program | sait.ca

Michael Allemeier, certified master chef.
Photo courtesy of the subject.

"The shortest route from the producer to the stove makes food taste—and look—better." Michael Allemeier's family left his native South Africa for Hong Kong when he was a teen. Once settled, his mother adopted the local custom of going to the market to shop only for what she needed that day. "This is where I fell in love with food. Everything had to be of the highest quality. The Chinese culture mandated it. Keeping food to eat later was repulsive to them. This art of eating fresh and local became ingrained in me at that time."

Next Allemeier's family immigrated to Winnipeg. He trained at Red River College's culinary program at an exciting time when mentors like Simon Smotkowicz and Takashi Murakami were competing for Team Canada in global events. He moved to Vancouver to be close to great ingredients and cites John Bishop as his greatest influence.

In 2003, Allemeier came to Calgary to run Teatro and remembers being the first chef to buy from local farmer Rosemary Wotske at Poplar Bluff Organics (see page 267). As executive chef at Mission Hill in Kelowna for five years, he had over 50 local growers that would fax him Sunday evening what they were going to bring him that week. "My message to farmers was always, 'If you grow it and it's delicious, I'll buy it.'" Those ingredients helped him build Okanagan's Cuisine de Terroir.

The culinary garden at SAIT sealed the deal for Allemeier to come and teach. Recently he spent four years to become one of only three certified master chefs in Canada. "I worked hard to hone my skills and show the students that learning never ends."

Advice to young Alberta chefs? "Know the flavours of the local food. They really have to love this approach because it is a lot more work but to me it always seemed the path of least resistance. Besides, how can I call myself a pro if I have access to wonderful produce and I turn my back on it? Inspiration comes when you let the ingredients speak to you."

Angelo Contrada | Without Papers | 1216 9 Avenue SE | 403-457-1154
wopizza.ca

Chef Angelo Contrada.
Photo by Matilde Sanchez-Turri.

Born to Italian immigrant parents, Angelo Contrada always knew he'd make a living cooking for people. He made it official at the age of 12 when he started as a dishwasher in the restaurant that his mom was cooking at. When he was 19, Contrada was in charge of that kitchen and then went on to work in several Italian restaurants before opening his own, Gnocchi's, in 1995.

In 2001, Contrada and his childhood friend Jesse Johnson partnered to open Sugo in Inglewood. Here the duo helped shape Calgary's food scene by proving a garden-to-table food philosophy was possible in our climate. Though Sugo is now closed they still grow their own herbs and produce for its sister restaurant, Without Papers Pizza.

"What my dad (Michelangelo) or Jesse and our families aren't able to grow, we buy from local producers who come to the kitchen's back door to sell to us. In winter, I source my produce from Galimax Trading (see page 250). If I'm short on anything after that, I go to the farmers' market."

While it'd be a whole lot easier to order vegetables from the big-brand restaurant suppliers, Contrada can't stomach the idea. "My whole life, we've had a garden. This is how my family eats and I only feel good if I feed our guests the same way."

Contrada has a way of creating a family atmosphere. "I've mentored a lot of kids who were around the same age as I was when I started. They keep me young and I love it."

Contrada considers his mother, Antoinetta, to be his greatest mentor. "My parents and family were my first teachers. I read and studied books and watched every chef I worked with to learn as much as I could and I'm still learning."

After more than 40 years in the kitchen, Contrada is set to receive an honorary Red Seal in cooking from the Southern Alberta Institute of Technology. Look for him in one of his signature hats at Without Papers or out dining at Anju, his favourite restaurant in town.

Liana Robberecht | WinSport | 88 Canada Olympic Road SW
403-247-4542 | winsport.ca

Liana Robberecht, executive chef at WinSport, in her signature pink chef's coat. Photo by Phil Crozier.

Chef Liana Robberecht got her first taste of farm-to-table cuisine while growing up in Smithers, BC. Her best friend's parents had a huge garden along with chickens and cattle on their farm. Together, she and her friend would cook delicious food with whatever they had on hand. Little did she know those memories would fuel a way of life and translate into a successful 25-year culinary career.

"Whether I am making the best sandwich ever or a dish for a white-linen dinner, I take tremendous pride in understanding the ingredients I bring together so that I enhance their flavours and texture to make every bite delicious."

Robberecht's skills as a chef have layers and depth like her food. She has a Red Seal in cooking from the Northern Alberta Institute of Technology and a professional pastry diploma from Vancouver's Dubrulle French Culinary School. Renowned for her plating and food presentations that are visual feasts, she credits spending her spare time painting as inspiration for her creations.

Robberecht became the executive chef at WinSport in June 2015 after spending 18 years at the prestigious Calgary Petroleum Club. "WinSport is a massive operation. It's very easy to source all local ingredients for a small restaurant, but this facility is entirely different because it is a high-volume, multi-outlet operation. The key to making important changes is to remember slow and steady wins the race. I am lucky that my director and the executive team of WinSport share and support my vision—and we've already begun to increase the amount we source locally."

Robberecht is an avid traveller and active volunteer within Alberta's food community. She's deeply involved with Slow Food Calgary and Women Chefs and Restaurateurs, and is a great supporter of Alberta's Open Farm Days. In 2011, she was crowned Chef of the Year by the Alberta Foodservice Expo and *Canadian Restaurant & Foodservice News* magazine. In 2015, she was one of 14 chefs chosen to participate in Cook It Raw Alberta and to contribute to a culinary narrative for the province.

Choklat | 3601B 21 Street NE | 403-457-1419 | www.chokolat.com

Brad Churchill. Photo by Matilde Sanchez-Turri.

Cacao beans are found in the heart of cacao pods, football-shaped fruit that grow on trees located plus or minus 10 degrees from the equator. Turning cacao beans into chocolate that reveals the cacao fruit's subtle terroir in a silky melt-in-your-mouth way is an art that chocolate maker Brad Churchill excels at.

First, it takes access to the best cacao beans in the world. When 90 percent of the world's chocolate is controlled by a few companies, that's not as easy as it sounds, but when he set out on his quest to make bean-to-bar chocolate in 2005, Churchill had a family member in the import/export business and was able to secure a shipment of cacao beans from one small estate in Central America.

Cacao beans from one estate are known as single origin and they've become highly sought after because—just like grapes and coffee beans—depending on the place they are grown, they express different flavours. Connoisseurs of chocolate love the taste profiles and have helped bean-to-bar become a rapidly growing trend.

Churchill was Alberta's first and is one of Canada's finest bean-to-bar chocolate makers. He opened Choklat in Calgary in August of 2008 after spending thousands of hours doing research, speaking with world-renowned chocolate scientists, and testing hundreds of recipes in his home kitchen.

Now, with a steady supply of cacao beans from estates in Mexico, Costa Rica, Brazil, and Venezuela and a state-of-the-art chocolate factory, he's able to ship his products across the country, hold a variety of chocolate making and appreciation classes, and sell direct to customers and wholesalers. "Artisanal products being sold at a premium price must be of the quality that they claim, and I'm happy to offer complete transparency and inclusion for people who are as passionate about chocolate as I am." Stopping by the factory for a fix of Churchill's incomparable sipping chocolate is one of our favourite indulgences year-round.

cōchu chocolatier | cochu.ca

Anne Sellmer, confectioner and owner of cōchu. Photo by Janet Pliszka of Visual Hues Photography.

Known in her family and community for creating elaborate cakes (her Yoda cake is legendary), Anne Sellmer has always loved working with food. A stay-at-home mom for 12 years, Sellmer and her husband encouraged their three sons to discover and do what they were passionate about.

Taking her own advice, she enrolled in a chocolate-making class at the Southern Alberta Institute of Technology. She loved it. Next, she took an online course with Ecole Chocolat. She apprenticed for a short time with world-famous confectioner Bernard Callebaut in Calgary before completing a master-level chocolatier program in BC.

In 2016, she expanded the commercial kitchen in her home and by spring of 2017, cōchu (named after her three boys: Cole, Charlie, and Hugo) was open for business. The response to her chocolate has been overwhelmingly positive from near and far.

Sellmer has entered her creations in several North American and international chocolate competitions and has won 26 awards (and counting) since November 2016. She's also been recognized as one of the Top 10 Confectioners and Chocolatiers in North America.

Sellmer loves food, art, and science and considers chocolate to be the ultimate vessel for bringing her passions together. "I'm always looking for new ways to evolve the entire chocolate-tasting experience because when we really enjoy our food, we pause and enjoy life too."

The recipes for her bright, bold flavours have been developed by Sellmer and every chocolate is made by hand in small batches. Some of her local collaborators and ingredients include: coffee from Phil & Sebastian (see page 154), gin from Eau Claire Distillery (see page 254), sea salt butter from Cultured Butter (see page 164), and honey from Drizzle. The cōchu chocolate line is a mix of contemporary and classic flavours that meld global and local ingredients together. Check the website for retailers or to order online.

The Cookbook Co. Cooks | 722 11 Avenue SW | 403-265-6066
cookbookcooks.com

Gail Norton at the Cookbook Co. Cooks.
Photo by Matilde Sanchez-Turri.

Economic recessions don't often spawn great things, but the teacher hiring freeze of 1984 did. With her freshly inked degree in hand, Gail Norton looked for work as a special-education teacher. "One person in our graduating class was hired, that was it." With prospects so grim, Norton went on a road trip across Canada and ended up at the Cookbook Store in Toronto. "As soon as I walked in and looked around, my skin began to tingle."

With her abiding love of food, voracious appetite for books, and affinity for shopping, the spark of opening something similar back in Calgary was ignited. Without capital, Norton approached her mother, Jean, a talented home cook, and together with one other investor, opened the Cookbook Co. Cooks in August of 1984.

They moved to Mount Royal Village in 1989 and then to their current location in 1996 after Norton's high school friend Richard Harvey, a passionate local sommelier, approached her with the idea of creating a culinary hub for food lovers. The space now houses Harvey's MetroVino Wines and the Calgary Wine Academy, Decadent Brulee bakery (see page 152), and Norton's store with all things culinary—cooking classes, catering, culinary escapes, and a carefully curated supply of kitchen and specialty ingredients for home cooks and chefs.

While Norton has hosted hundreds of internationally renowned chefs and cookbook authors since 1984, she's most proud of our local food culture. "Our store has always been a stepping stone for Alberta's food artisans, producers, and chefs—often serving as their first point of entry to the marketplace. We've given people the chance they needed."

Norton shrugs off any praise and says instead that it's been her good fortune to be able to create a life around all the things she's interested in. Today, the Cookbook Co. Cooks continues to demystify the cooking process and inspire anyone who stops by to gather great ingredients, have fun in the kitchen, and make real food to share with family and friends.

The Silk Road Spice Merchant | 403-261-1955 | silkroadspices.ca

Colin Leach and Kelci Hind in their Inglewood store in Calgary. Photo by Karen Anderson.

When you love to cook, access to great ingredients is vital. Fresh and rare spices can be especially tricky to source. Kelci Hind and Colin Leach love to create in the kitchen and saw their own difficulties in sourcing the spices they needed to make their favourite Indian and Mexican recipes as an opportunity. They found only one store in all of Canada that made one-stop shopping for spices possible. So they decided to create a business that could deliver the quality they desired.

That was in 2008. They now have three stores in the province and ship spices across North America from their online store. While candied ginger, cinnamon, and Chicago Steak Spice continue to be their best sellers, they've started to incorporate a taste of this place too.

"Sharples Ranch near Drumheller is a place that we'd go to kick back, throw horseshoes, and grill up some Alberta beef over a wood fire. We created a rub to enhance the flavours of the beef and remind us of those good times," says Leach.

"I grew up fishing with my dad in the Bow River," says Hind. "Our Bow River Fish Blend is my salute to those memories. It's just black pepper, dill, parsley, chives, and freeze-dried shallots, but add a little butter and salt and you've got an unforgettable taste of this place."

The Silk Road Spice Merchant sells over 250 spices from around the world and has created over 100 of their own blends. Mixologists rely on their extensive stock of botanicals and bitters. They've collaborated to create DIY gin and root beer kits with those botanicals. There have also been collaborations for a camping spice kit and a masala daba Indian spice box to go with the locally published *A Spicy Touch: Family Favourites from Noorbanu Nimji's Kitchen,* which our own Karen Anderson co-authored with her mentor Noorbanu Nimji.

"You don't have to be a trained chef to play with spices," says Hind. "Just get to know the flavours and have fun."

Check the website for locations or to shop from their online store.

Deepwater Farms | 610-600 6 Avenue SW | 403-836-0939
deepwaterfarms.com

Left to right: Paul Shumlich, Jane Richert, and Kevin Daniels. Photo by Matilde Sanchez-Turri.

In 2014, Paul Shumlich and Kevin Daniels were busy running successful businesses to put themselves through school. Shumlich was enrolled in the Economics and Entrepreneurship program at Mount Royal University and Daniels was pursuing an environmental science degree. When they stopped in at the grocery store to pick up a few things, they noticed the organic produce was coming from California and Mexico. It was expensive and looked terrible.

They had heard about aquaponics and were intrigued by it, so that summer they built—on a shoestring budget—a 100-square-foot prototype. "We wanted to invest our time and energy into a social enterprise, one that was sustainable, allowed us to grow food responsibly, and would have a positive long-term impact," says Shumlich. Deepwater Farms was born.

This unconventional farming method combines aquaculture (fish farming) and hydroponics (growing plants in water) in a single, closed system. Fish are kept in ponds and produce waste that is broken down into nitrites and then nitrates by micro-organisms. The waste water is sent to the plants, which absorb the nitrates and, in the process, clean the water, which is then sent back to the fish. Recirculation means the system uses approximately 95 percent less water than conventional farming. It's completely organic and it grows plants at incredible rates.

Soon the operation was teeming with produce so they cold-called local chefs and found a market hungry for their quality greens. Scaling up to reach commercial production proved to be more challenging because of the complexity and interconnected nature of the system and Calgary's cold winters, but they did it.

From February of 2018 on, they'll have the ability to produce 72 tons of organic leafy greens as well as 10,000 pounds of edible fish (barramundi, also known as Australian sea bass) annually in their 10,000-square-foot facility. Produce is delivered the same day it's harvested. "There are no shortcuts in long-run thinking. Every choice matters. When people buy our products, they are doing good and helping us advance and improve the way we produce our food."

Dirt Boys Urban Farming | Sunnyside | 403-606-9007 | dirtboys.ca

Dennis Scanland beside a garden box he built.
Photo by Matilde Sanchez-Turri.

Dennis Scanland of the Dirt Boys is on a mission to change Calgary, one yard at a time. He became an urban farmer after working in IT for a large multinational company for most of his career. "My wife and I wanted to be the ones raising our sons, not someone else." This reasoning led him to look for part-time work, something he could involve his kids in. He discovered Small Plot INtensive (SPIN) farming and launched his business, Dirt Boys, on Seedy Saturday (a local seed exchange forum), March 1, 2013.

Along with their SPIN farm, Dirt Boys offers a range of services including yard conversions for those who want to grow their own food. For those who don't want to get their hands dirty but still want some tasty vegetables, Dirt Boys will farm your yard, give you some of the bounty, and sell the rest.

The Dirt Boys are very passionate about urban farming and can be hired to present on a wide range of topics including food security, soil health, and the benefits of growing your own food.

They currently farm a quarter acre of land and apply permaculture principles to their methods focusing on soil health and restoration. Most of the yards they farm are in the communities of Sunnyside and Bridgeland. While Scanland loves selling his produce to people right in the community where it's grown, most of his organic produce is sold through YYC Growers and Distributors' Community Supported Agriculture (CSA) harvest box program and at the Hillhurst Sunnyside Market.

YYC Growers and Distributors is a co-operative composed of 18 farms and producers operating within 100 miles of the city's core. It provides a vital support to small urban farmers like Dirt Boys who have limited storage, refrigeration, and time to market their highly perishable produce. The harvest box program was the brainchild of Rod Olson of Leaf & Lyre (see page 185), Dennis Scanland of Dirt Boys, Jerremie Clyde of Little Loaves Farm, and Dave Carlton from the Leaf Ninjas, back in the winter of 2013. The CSA program started with 65 families in 2014 and grew to 820 families by 2017. "We always have room to feed more people. I feel like Johnny Appleseed. It's so rewarding being able to grow food for families in my community and feed that many people."

Leaf & Lyre Urban Farms | 403-703-3217 | leafandlyre.net

Rod Olson in a field of his famous kale.
Photo by Jeremy Klager Photography.

Small Plot INtensive or SPIN farming was started in Saskatoon by a market gardener named Wally Satzewich. He realized that there was more yield and profit in farming small amounts of land intensively with high-value crops in warm urban settings with access to water and proximity to markets than in farming less intensively in a rural setting. In 2008, he shared his model through online modules so others could benefit from his expertise.

Rod Olson grew up on a farm and though he lived in Calgary he longed for a way to grow food as he had done with his family. Recovering from back surgery in 2008, he happened upon Satzewich's website and convinced his brother-in-law Chad Kile to join him as the back and the brawn while he would be in charge of business planning and marketing.

In March of 2010, their story was picked up by CBC Radio and listeners called in to donate their backyards for the duo to begin their business: Leaf & Lyre Urban Farms. Homeowners get a share of the produce raised in return for the use of their land and water.

Olson has been running Leaf & Lyre alone since 2013 with most of his land base in his home community of Bowness. He has rehabilitated soil that was "addicted" to and damaged by chemical fertilizers by increasing the total organic carbon in the soil to grow more nutritious, flavourful food. "Good soil holds carbon in it. It's the building block of life and it belongs in the soil, not the atmosphere."

Not only was Olson the first urban farmer in Calgary, he's also the biggest and his dream of being known as the Bowness Urban Farmer is becoming a reality. You can find Olson's hyperlocal produce at the Bownesian Grocer in Bowness and through YYC Growers and Distributors, Summer Harvest Box Community Supported Agriculture program, an urban and rural farmers' co-operative he helped establish. Chances are if you order the kale salad at UNA Pizza + Wine, Olson grew the kale.

Verge Permaculture | 227 Fonda Way SE | 403-770-9789
vergepermaculture.ca

The Avis family. Photo by Gavin Young.

"Permaculture is a design system centred around meeting human needs by improving natural ecosystems. Its intention is to give back more than is taken," says Michelle Avis. Michelle and her husband Rob are owners of Verge Permaculture in Calgary.

Short for permanent agriculture, permaculture's designs mimic nature's principles to create soils, farms, architecture, and cultures that are sustainable and self-sufficient. The late Bill Mollison founded the movement in the late '70s and was named by the *Guardian* as one of 50 people most likely to save the world.

The Avises are engineers and global leaders in teaching Permaculture Design Certificate courses and consulting on the applications of the principles. They've certified over 1,000 people and are helping to create entrepreneurial green-collar careers for Albertans.

Their own journey began after seeing a documentary called *Greening the Desert*. It featured renowned permaculture expert Geoff Lawton, who along with his team transformed one of the most arid places on earth—desert near the Dead Sea—into a lush 10-acre garden using permaculture principles of water management and soil regeneration. They were inspired and travelled the world to study and gain the expertise they needed to bring permaculture to Alberta and Canada.

"It's really all about water management," says Rob, "whether you are growing food for your family or running a large-scale farm." Grads from the program have started soil health, composting, edible landscapes, food distribution systems, agrihoods, chicken farms, and large-scale farming businesses as well as community gardens. Over 500 grads are profiled on their website.

The Avises' own home is a model of sustainability. They grow most of their own food, have planted a food forest in their front yard, designed water-harvesting features, built a passive solar greenhouse in the backyard, and put energy retrofits on the house. "Lasting change can't take hold unless business and regenerative practices come together," says Michelle. "Permaculture teaches us that humans can have a positive effect on the world."

Last Best Brewing & Distilling | 607 11 Avenue SW | 587-353-7387
lastbestbrewing.com

Bryce Parsons, master distiller at Last Best.
Photo by Leah Schwantz.

Last Best Brewing & Distilling opened in 2015. It's the fourth location for the Bear Hill Brewing family of breweries and pubs. The company was founded in Jasper in 2005 by childhood friends Brett Ireland, Socrates Korogonas, and Alex Derksen. They named Last Best after the Canadian government's 1890s marketing campaign promoting the Prairies as the last best chance for homesteaders to own their own land. Using the world-class grains that grow here, Last Best and Bear Hill are pioneering craft brewing and distilling in Alberta.

Bryce Parsons, head of Last Best's distilling program, describes his need to become a distiller as an "itch that needed to be scratched." The only place to get your master's in distilling and brewing is in Edinburgh, Scotland, at Heriot-Watt University. Parsons left a career in nursing to attend and took over Last Best's distilling program in 2014.

Parsons makes a barrel of whisky every week with Alberta's world-class grains. While the whisky ages in wood barrels for three years he makes other spirits like gin, rum, and vodka. "I use traditional techniques and artisanal methods in my distilling. I draw on brewing and distilling practices from other countries and the culinary arts to develop different expressions (of the grains) in the spirits I make."

Creativity, initiative, and variety abound in Alberta's distilling community. Stirring and shaking up preconceived ideas about whisky and other spirits is high on everyone's agenda, particularly Parsons's. "Constant innovation is vital. We see it as an essential part of establishing whisky making in Canada, putting Alberta on the map, and broadening the appeal of distilled liquors worldwide."

Whether you prefer craft beer or spirits or both, visit Last Best for a brewery and distillery tour. Tastings, lunch, and dinner are available daily at the brew pub. The menu features dishes made from Alberta ingredients that pair extremely well with their beers.

Knifewear | knifewear.com

Kevin Kent, founder and owner of Knifewear, in his original Calgary store. Photo courtesy of Knifewear.

Kevin Kent graduated from the Southern Alberta Institute of Technology culinary program and worked with Fergus Henderson at St. John Restaurant in London, England. On a day off, he attended a trade show and discovered how sharp Japanese knives were.

"The rep said, 'You should really experience how sharp these are.' I thought I did a pretty hot job of keeping my blades sharp but when I went to slice with my usual amount of pressure, I stuck the knife so deeply into the cutting board, we had a hard time getting it out. I was blown away. I very quickly realized I was working way harder than I needed to be. When you are chopping hundreds of pounds of vegetables in a day, if you can cut your work in half, it only makes sense to do so."

Soon Kent was spending all his disposable income on Japanese knives. While he was working at Calgary's River Café on his return to Alberta, friends that tried his knives wanted some of their own. "I sourced some in Japan and started selling them out of my backpack, getting around town on a bicycle."

He graduated to a counter in a specialty shop and then opened his first store in Calgary's Inglewood community in 2008. Kelowna was next and though that store is now closed, there are four more in Edmonton, Ottawa, Vancouver, and the Calgary Farmers' Market (check the website for addresses and contact information). Knifewear also does brisk domestic and international business online.

Kent now has relationships with about 30 blacksmith families in Japan who hand forge the knives he sells. With filmmaker Kevin Kossowan (see page 75) he's made two documentaries about their artistry. Along with his entrepreneurial bent, Kent is a serial philanthropist giving to many Alberta and international charities.

With the knives, slicing is believing. They are carbon steel, hand-sharpened masterpieces that feel as effortless as a hot knife cutting through butter, even on a thick-skinned tomato. Each of the stores offers knife skills classes. As Kent says, "These knives help cooks work smarter, and that's awesome."

MacEwans Meats and Meat Pies | 17-9620 Elbow Drive SW
403-228-9999 | macewansmeats.com

Gordon Robertson, butcher and owner of MacEwans Meats and Meat Pies. Photo by Matilde Sanchez-Turri.

"Honour and integrity serve as the ethos of my life. I get up every day to do my very best to make others happy." For Gordon Robertson, owner of MacEwans Meats and Meat Pies, those values underpin every career he has had from butcher to soldier to emergency medical technician (EMT) to musician and back to butcher. "My life has literally come full circle."

From a young age Robertson wanted to be a soldier, but his father suggested he learn a profession first. "In Britain, butchery is a recognized trade so you can specialize in it in high school. I apprenticed with a butcher who had a High Street shop and thick stripes on his apron."

Robertson earned his stripes working six days a week at the butcher shop while going to school to learn theory. Once a certified butcher, he joined the army and was a soldier from 1993 to 2005. While in military training at the Canadian Forces Base in Suffield in 2004, he grew fond of Alberta and decided to leave the army after honoured service and settle in Calgary. He still longed to make a difference in people's lives so he became an EMT in 2009. On Easter weekend in 2013, he noticed MacEwans Meats was up for sale, and decided to buy it.

For 30 years, MacEwans Meats has specialized in providing traditional British "fayre" and Scottish heritage foods. From fresh cuts of local meat (beef, pork, lamb, and chicken) to British cheeses and grocery items to meat pies and their renowned haggis, Brits will find a taste of home throughout the shop. "All of the pasties, bangers, puddings, and haggis are made by hand using traditional recipes inherited from Ian 'John' Hopkins who started the shop."

Quality is everything to Robertson. All of the meat he uses is locally sourced from Alberta producers and his preferred vendors are those who put a priority on environmental and social sustainability. "I take great pride turning these amazing ingredients into delicious food. I think it's very important to embrace Canadian culture but you don't have to forget your identity and traditions, and our food can help you with that."

Between January 2 and January 25 (Robbie Burns Day) MacEwans Meats makes and sells 3,500 pounds of haggis.

Urban Butcher | urbanbutcher.ca

Lancelot Monteiro, executive chef for Cilantro restaurant. Photo courtesy of CRMR.

Urban Butcher is part of the Canadian Rocky Mountain Resorts (CRMR) family of companies, which includes restaurants, mountain lodges, a bakery, a game ranch, and, now, butcher shops.

By reimagining the butcher shop and making it relevant in today's busy world, the Urban Butcher offers meat lovers and home cooks the inspiration to get back in the kitchen. Executive chef Lancelot Monteiro and master butcher Bob Choquette work together to supply customers with access to the best local cuts of meat and recipes to cook their favourite meals at home. "Cooking at home isn't hard if you have access to the right ingredients."

The Urban Butcher sells the finest-quality meats, raised ethically and naturally, including Alberta beef, pasture-raised pork, free-range, free-run, organic poultry products, various deli products fresh from their smokehouse, pasture-fed lamb, and grass-fed bison from CRMR's own game ranch.

For many, traceability and transparency surrounding where their meat comes from, how the animals were raised, and whether they were handled humanely matters. "We source our meat and poultry from local farms whose practices prioritize the animal's health and quality of life from beginning to end." This is a very different approach from most grocery stores, who purchase their meat and poultry in huge volumes and distribute it to their stores for sale. This means they're sourcing from massive farms or multiple farms with different rearing practices.

Accessing game meats, particularly bison, and knowing how to cook it can be challenging. "Our bison meat comes from our game ranch from animals that were grass fed their whole life and raised just beyond the city limits. There isn't another butcher shop who offers that." Urban Butcher has locations in Mission, Willow Park, and Granary Road; check the website for details.

Pennybun's Mushrooms | 4528 14 Street NE | 403-629-5301
pennybunsmushrooms.ca

Dirk McCabe holding some of his fresh grown mushrooms. Photo by Karen Anderson.

The French call it a cep, the Italians a porcino. Also known as the penny-bun bolete, all these names refer to the king of mushrooms. Since it is so highly prized, Pennybun's Mushrooms makes a great name for this company in Calgary that grows and sources mushrooms to enhance Albertans' eating experiences.

Co-founder Dirk McCabe was raised in Colorado on a cattle ranch. The family grew most of their own food and spent a lot of time outdoors, which suited him perfectly. His mom was of Italian heritage and a chef. "She was a gem. When I was little she'd let me help her—I'd get to crack the eggs. She showed love for others with food."

McCabe fell into the food scene quite naturally with such an influence in his life. He learned authentic Japanese cuisine from a local family, worked in a barbecue restaurant and smoked every type of meat imaginable before moving to Ottawa to attend Le Cordon Bleu Culinary Arts Institute. While in culinary school and after he finished, McCabe worked at Beckta Dining and Wine Bar—a stalwart of fine dining in Canada's capital city. After six years, McCabe moved to Calgary for a change of pace.

"Mushrooms are very nutritious and no one was foraging for them here or growing them so I thought I should. I've always been fascinated with the wild side of food." Without any prior experience, McCabe started Pennybun's Mushrooms with the help of his old mushroom supplier back in Ontario. He learned early on that conditions have to be perfect in order to grow mushrooms. "All of my mushrooms are grown on wood. Depending on the variety, each one takes a different amount of time to colonize and bear fruit."

All of Pennybun's foraged ingredients are harvested from the wild by foragers with 40–50 years of experience. For wild or tame mushrooms that you can't find at the supermarket, contact Pennybun's directly to place your order or stop by McCabe's stall at the Hillhurst Sunnyside Community Farmers' Market Wednesdays, year-round.

Meta4Foods/OysterTribe | 903B 48 Avenue SE | 403-214-1478
meta4foods.com and oystertribe.com

Of course Eric Giesbrecht has a fish tank and a couple of comfy chairs to welcome his "OysterTribe" in his Meta4Foods headquarters. Photo by Karen Anderson.

What do you get when you cross a chef with a philosopher, oyster dealer, Slow Food board member, and calendar model who has a fondness for biohacking to improve his performance? You get Eric Giesbrecht, OysterTribe ringleader, owner of Meta4Foods and its dynamic lineup of premium products from the land and the sea.

Meta4Foods is a food distribution company and OysterTribe is its heart. Specializing in the sale of premium Canadian shellfish, both companies showcase the power of relationships. By promoting transparency and authentic connections between food lovers and food producers, Giesbrecht has built a business and tribe at the same time. The result is a diverse offering of high-quality ingredients that both food lovers and restaurant chefs can feel good about buying. "I think like a cook and buy ingredients like one too. Everything I sell is directly sourced from small operators and people I know who value the same things I do: quality, sustainability, and community."

While Giesbrecht's career path from chef to entrepreneur wasn't as extreme as the shifting waters of the intertidal zone his favourite oysters come from, it wasn't a gentle ebb and flow either. In 2005, he morphed from chef to oyster shucker and began delivering shellfish for the original Oyster Man, close friend Brent Petkau. In 2009, Giesbrecht returned to cooking and worked as a personal chef and caterer while still delivering shellfish. As his OysterTribe community grew, and with it a local appetite for oysters and other shellfish, the tides turned once more in 2012 and Giesbrecht opened a retail shop in the front of his warehouse.

Meta4Foods carries more than 20 varieties of East and West Coast oysters, other shellfish and seafood including hand-harvested seaweed from Haida Gwaii, Canadian caviar and sturgeon, sashimi-grade fish from the South Pacific, and line-caught fish from the Northwest. Other fresh ingredients include wild foraged mushrooms, fiddleheads, and longhorn beef from 7K Ranch in Millarville. A menagerie of other local artisanal specialty foods can only be found on site. Shop in person for wholesale or retail quantities and get free cooking tips and other pearls of wisdom at the same time.

FARMERS' MARKETS

Check the website for current hours prior to your visit.

BEARSPAW LIONS FARMERS' MARKET
25240 Nagway Road | Sundays 10:00 A.M.–2:00 P.M., June to October
403-239-0201 | bearspawlions.com

CALGARY FARMERS' MARKET
510 77 Avenue SE | Thursday–Sunday 9:00 A.M.–5:00 P.M., year-round
403-240-9113 | calgaryfarmersmarket.ca

CROSSROADS MARKET
1235 26 Avenue SE | Friday–Sunday 9:00 A.M.–5:00 P.M., year-round | 403-291-5208
crossroadsmarket.ca

HILLHURST SUNNYSIDE FARMERS' MARKET
1320 5 Avenue SW | Wednesdays 3:00 P.M.–7:00 P.M., year-round | 403-283-0554 ext.
228 | farmersmarket.hillhurstsunnyside.org

MARDA LOOP FARMERS' MARKET
3130 16 Street SW | Saturdays 9:00 A.M.–1:00 P.M., June to October | 403-244-5411
mardaloop.com/farmers-market/farmers-market

MARKET ON MACLEOD
7711 Macleod Trail SE | Thursday–Sundays 9:00 A.M.–5:00 P.M., year-round
587-354-1120 | marketonmacleod.com

WATERING HOLES

Check the website for current hours prior to your visit.

ANNEX ALE PROJECT

4323 1 Street SE | 403-475-4412 | annexales.com
⇒ **Tours: By request.**
Favourite beer here: Metes & Bounds and their all-natural root beer.
Taproom available and pints, flights, bottles, and growler fills.

BANDED PEAK BREWING

119-519 34 Avenue SE | 403-700-3941 | bandedpeakbrewing.com
⇒ **Tours: By request.**
Favourite beer here: Summit Seeker.
Growler fills and flight tastings on site.

BIG ROCK BREWERY

5555 76 Avenue SE | 403-720-3239 | bigrockbeer.com
⇒ **Tours: Regularly scheduled. Book online.**
Favourite beer here: We still love Grasshopper with a twist of lemon.
Alberta's first microbrewery.

COLD GARDEN BEVERAGE COMPANY

1100 11 Street SE | 403-305-6288 | coldgarden.ca
⇒ **Tours: By appointment.**
Favourite beer here: Red Smashed In Buffalo Jump, an Irish Red Ale.

COMMON CROWN BREWING CO.

943 28 St NE | 587-356-4275 | commoncrown.ca
⇒ **Tours: By request, contact carley@commoncrown.ca.**
Favourite beer here: Journeyman IPA.

THE DANDY BREWING COMPANY

11-1826 25 Avenue NE | 403-769-9399 | thedandybrewingcompany.com
⇒ **Tours: By appointment.**
Favourite beer here: Donald Sutherland as Hawkeye Pierce (aren't they great at naming their beers?).

LAST BEST BREWING & DISTILLING (SEE PAGE 187)

607 11 Avenue SW | 587-353-7387 | lastbestbrewing.com

⇒ Tours: By appointment.

Favourite drink here: Amazing beer and cocktails. Last Best Beer Caesar combines both!

Part of the Bear Hill Brewing family of breweries, this fourth location has a distillery as well as a brewery and pub.

TOOL SHED BREWING

9-801 30 Street NE | 403-775-1749 | toolshedbrewing.com

⇒ Tours: Saturdays, book online.

Favourite beer here: People Skills—this cream ale smooths the way.

TROLLEY 5 RESTAURANT AND BREWERY

728 17 Avenue SW | 403-993-7227 | trolley5.com

⇒ Tours: By appointment through laurab@trolley5.com.

Favourite beer here: High Five with five kinds of hops.

Get the smokehouse poutine with any of their beers.

VILLAGE BREWERY

5000 12A Street SE | 403-243-3327 | villagebrewery.com

⇒ Tours: Twice on Saturday, book online.

Favourite beer here: It's a tie between the Blonde and the Wit.

WILD ROSE BREWERY

2-4580 Quesnay Wood Drive SW | 403-720-2733 | wildrosebrewery.com

⇒ Tours: Wednesdays, 7:00 P.M.

Favourite beer here: Velvet Fog—need we say more?

THE ROCKY MOUNTAINS

- BANFF
- BOTTREL
- CANMORE
- COCHRANE
- JASPER
- LAKE LOUISE

The Rocky Mountains in Alberta are home to two of Canada's oldest national parks—Banff and Jasper. Banff was Canada's first, created in 1885, and Jasper followed in 1907. Together they provide a wildlife refuge for indigenous grizzly bears, elk, moose, deer, coyotes, wolves, bighorn sheep, and mountain lions.

Between 2 million and 5 million people visit the parks each year to enjoy the jagged glacier-capped peaks, the crystal-clear lakes, and the rivers that flow through the land like ribbons of emerald and jade. A hiker could spend a lifetime and never trek the same trail. Backcountry lodges and front-country resorts and iconic castles and hotels welcome the world.

Canmore has established an annual food and drink festival, Canmore Uncorked, that was named best event by Tourism Canada. Many of the Bow Valley's best chefs live in this town, which serves as the gateway to the Rockies, and several have launched their own restaurants and bars. There are two breweries, along with a number of distilleries and several food processors in the town as well.

Canmore, Banff, and Jasper all have weekly farmers' markets. Because it is difficult to grow produce in this region, the residents appreciate the vendors who make the trek to supply them from other parts of Alberta.

Banff's iconic Fairmont Banff Springs Hotel makes 1.5 million meals each year and has 20–30 chefs in its culinary apprenticeship program. It's a culinary institute and will have a profound impact as it continues to fulfill its mandate to provide guests with as many authentically local experiences and foods as possible.

Locals and visitors can stroll Banff Avenue or take a gondola to the top of towering Sulphur Mountain—now home to another great fine dining establishment thanks to recent renovations. Seasonal food festivals are yet another draw for the town along with its nightlife and hidden-gem picnic spots. The Trans-Canada Legacy cycling trail that

Previous spread: photo courtesy of Banff Lake Louise Tourism
Facing page: photo by Karen Anderson

connects Banff and Canmore is a great way to work up an appetite for either town's culinary delights.

Lake Louise has its share of iconic hospitality outlets. Canadian Rocky Mountain Resorts' Deer Lodge (see page 211) is notable for forging and maintaining a cuisine as iconic as the surroundings.

Jasper is five hours from Calgary and four hours from Edmonton but always worth the drive. The Icefields Parkway is one of the world's most scenic drives.

Travel Tips

➤ Check albertafoodtours.ca to explore Canmore and Banff's food scene with local guides.

➤ For backcountry trail rides and your own camp cook, the Guinn family has been guiding and outfitting their guests since the 1930s. Check out their offerings at boundaryranch.com.

Facing page: photo courtesy of Banff Lake Louise Tourism

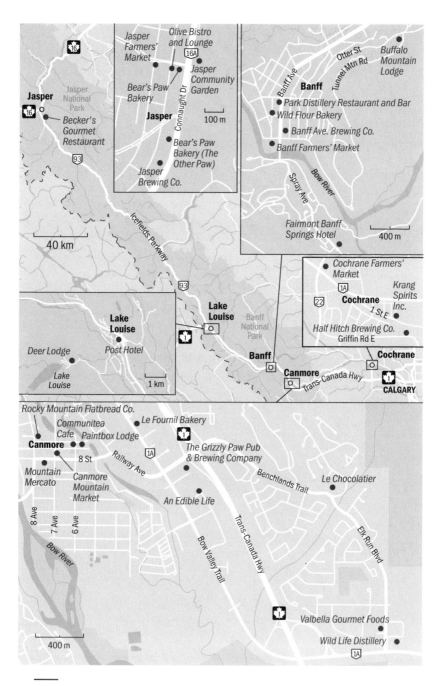

Jasper

Jasper Farmers' Market
Olive Bistro and Lounge
16A
Bear's Paw Bakery
Jasper Community Garden
Connaught Dr
Jasper
100 m
Bear's Paw Bakery (The Other Paw)
Jasper Brewing Co.

16
Jasper
Jasper National Park
16
Becker's Gourmet Restaurant
93

40 km

Icefields Parkway

93

Banff

Otter St
Tunnel Mtn Rd
Buffalo Mountain Lodge
Banff Ave
Park Distillery Restaurant and Bar
Wild Flour Bakery
Banff Ave. Brewing Co.
Banff Farmers' Market
Spray Ave
Bow River
Fairmont Banff Springs Hotel
400 m

Cochrane Farmers' Market
1A
Krang Spirits Inc.
22
Cochrane
1 St E
Half Hitch Brewing Co.
Griffin Rd E
Cochrane

Lake Louise

Lake Louise
Banff National Park
Deer Lodge
Post Hotel
Lake Louise
1 km

Lake Louise

Banff
Canmore
Trans-Canada Hwy
CALGARY

Rocky Mountain Flatbread Co.
Le Fournil Bakery
Communitea Cafe
Paintbox Lodge
Canmore
1A
The Grizzly Paw Pub & Brewing Company
8 St
Railway Ave
Benchlands Trail
Le Chocolatier
Mountain Mercato
Canmore Mountain Market
An Edible Life
8 Ave
7 Ave
6 Ave
Bow River
Bow Valley Trail
Trans-Canada Hwy
Elk Run Blvd
Valbella Gourmet Foods
Wild Life Distillery
1A
400 m

Note: Only artisans and producers who welcome visitors on site are shown on this map.

FOOD ARTISANS OF THE ROCKY MOUNTAINS

Bear's Paw Bakery | 4 Pyramid Lake Road and 610 Connaught Drive, Jasper | 780-852-3233 | bearspawbakery.com

Kimberley Stark. Photo by Karen Anderson.

When Kimberley Stark bought Bear's Paw Bakery in 1997 she thought, "How hard could it be?" She'd never owned a business but, mercifully, had youth and determination on her side. Stark is originally from Winnipeg but with a father in the RCMP, the family moved often throughout the Prairies. "I came to Jasper to work for three months with some friends, went back to university but then, after travelling for a while, Jasper was the place where I had felt everything clicked for me so I came back. I pumped gas and drove taxi for three years to save money. I knew that if I wanted to stay in Jasper and own my own home I'd have to own my own small business. Turns out owning a business is tough! There were times where I did both the day and night baking and just laid my head down for five-minute naps to keep going."

Mental and physical toughness are traits Stark has also fostered with her life goals outside of work. "I set the goal to run a marathon on every continent and I've done that now. I even got to be a sponsor for the one in Antarctica."

Along with her famous white chocolate and raspberry scones, which garnered a mention in *O, The Oprah Magazine* in 2008, Stark makes custom cakes and does anywhere from 40 to 85 wedding cakes per year. "I love the architecture behind it and have travelled to New York, Boston, and Los Angeles for coursework."

Stark is sensitive to her loyal local patrons as well as the tourists who visit Jasper from all over the world each hectic summer season. "Last year we renovated to add a sidewalk express window for the locals. They can come there, order their usual, and not have to deal with the lineups of people who might be struggling with language or with knowing what coffee is like theirs back home." Locals and visitors alike love walking into the cozy original bakery, seeing the glass display cabinets stacked high with sticky buns, bear's paws, cookies, squares, and sandwiches, and heading out on the trails with a special treat to enjoy at the summit of their hike.

Communitea Cafe | 117-1001 6 Avenue, Canmore | 403-688-2233
thecommunitea.com

Marnie Dansereau.
Photo courtesy of Communitea Cafe.

Marnie Dansereau is celebrating 20 years of living in the Rockies in 2018. Born in Edmonton, she attended the University of Calgary and moved to Canmore as a personal fitness coach specializing in yoga and cycling.

One day in 2006, after morning yoga, she went out for a walk and her life changed. She was listening to a Deepak Chopra talk about the importance of community. "I had an epiphany that the world was becoming disconnected and that the most important thing I could do with my life was to find a way to bring people together. Every time Chopra said the word *community* in his talk, my mind saw the word *communiTEA*. Always a tea fanatic, I knew I had the name for a business."

On her way home, Dansereau walked past a new mall with a "for lease" sign on the corner unit. She went in, signed the agreement, and, with only a name as her business plan, opened Communitea Cafe six months later.

Dansereau used her personal-trainer background to design the food program, which features vegetables, eggs, and dairy products sourced from Southern Alberta farms and distributed by Galimax Trading (see page 250). "Pilot Coffee from Toronto are our roasters and we have 84 different loose-leaf teas and blends sourced from Canadian tea suppliers who specialize in unique, organic, and fair-trade teas. The peppermint and rosehip teas are from Alberta.

"I present food the way that I eat. Little things like throwing a pile of spinach in the bottom of a bowl help get more fruits and vegetables into people's diets. We're not vegan or fully vegetarian. We have free-run chicken, eggs, and prawns so people can add the proteins they want. We also have high-calorie, high-quality foods for people who are fuelling up after 40-to-50-kilometre bike rides."

Regular yoga classes and a fall, winter, and spring lineup of Canadian musical groups round out the offerings of this bustling gathering space. "We're more of a restaurant now but it's good. We're helping to create a culture of joy." Expect a renovation in 2018.

Le Fournil Bakery | 101-1205 Bow Valley Trail, Canmore | 403-675-5005
fournil.ca

Pascale Tétreault. Photo by Karen Anderson.

"A goal without a plan is just a dream." Sitting on the patio of her bakery facing the towering east end of the Mount Rundle range, Pascale Tétreault is paraphrasing Antoine de Saint-Exupéry, greeting her regular clientele—in both French and English—and sharing the story of how she left behind a career in IT and administration to open a *très française* bakery in Canmore. The brisk mountain air is softened with each bite of billowy laminated Chocolatine pastry and sip of crema-capped coffee.

Raised in Montreal, Tétreault came of age when great French baking emerged in her city. Her parents took her to shops like Pâtisserie De Gascogne and Tour Eiffel and her palate became acquainted with excellence—especially in bread. During her 30s, she experienced eating completely local ingredients on a trip through the Charlevoix region of Quebec. She felt a joy that led her to think she'd missed her calling in life. Divorced and living in Canmore, she decided to develop a business plan that would help her realize her goal of bringing great bread—the food she missed the most from her former home—to the place she has now chosen as home.

She attended bread-making school at the San Francisco Baking Institute with a focus on the most difficult bread of all, the baguette. Using only *levain* (French for sourdough) and freshly milled flours from Alberta, the bakers at Le Fournil take three days of feeding, forming, and proofing to perfect each loaf on offer.

Back inside, the minimalist white and grey decor of the café pulls all eyes to the cases of colourful *pâtisseries* and *viennoiseries*. Le Fournil's website supplies a glossary of French baking terminology so you'll know the difference. Tétreault is educating our palates one customer at a time. A *fournil*, she explains, refers to the village bakehouse where the *boulanger* baked off each person's loaves.

"Some regulars drive from BC, Edmonton, and Calgary, others save up to come once a week for a treat. We love that with our *fournil* we've become their *boulanger*."

Wild Flour Bakery | 101-211 Bear Street, Banff | 403-760-5074
wildflourbakery.ca

Liana Groten. Photo by Karen Anderson.

"I'm proud of the quality we achieve. People come for our organic breads and all the vegan offerings we create." Liana Groten graduated from the Southern Alberta Institute of Technology culinary program as a pastry chef and has been a baker at Wild Flour Bakery in Banff for a few years now. "When people think of Alberta, they might not realize that vegan is a thing here. There's a really large market for it actually."

Wild Flour, which opened in 2004, uses sourdough from Peter Poole, the owner, that is 40 years old. Sourdough is important in the history of Canadian pioneers. That simple mix of flour, water, and ambient bacteria and yeast is what kept a lot of them alive. "We have three different sourdoughs on the go at all times and take two to three days to make our breads. Every day there are a few different breads, pastries, and savoury treats made with those doughs."

Wild Flour Bakery sits on land adjacent to the building that housed Banff's first bakery, the Old Crag Cabin. A young baker named Athanase Laurendeau used the log cabin as both his home and bakery from 1888 to 1890. During the construction of Wild Flour, a sign for Kwong Lee Restaurant, Bakery and Fruit was found between two walls. Kwong Lee means "expansive profit" and the Chinese baker and owner was known by the same name. He was believed to have originally come to Canada as a Canadian Pacific Railway worker. He ran his business on Bear Street from 1905 to 1912, then sold his building to Banff icon Norman Luxton and returned to China where he died in 1918. The sign now hangs in Wild Flour as a reminder of the international heritage that has shaped Banff's community.

In another throwback to the way things once were, Wild Flour bakes all its breads on a stone hearth. When you've wandered through the candy shops of Banff Avenue, which are really fun too, it's nice to take a stroll down Bear Street to find this hidden gem.

Valbella Gourmet Foods | 104 Elk Run Boulevard, Canmore
403-678-4109 | valbellagourmetfoods.ca

Left to right: Chantal, Jeff, Walter, and Leonie von Rotz. Photo by Karen Anderson.

It was a tough go for Walter and Leonie von Rotz when they opened their tiny Alpine Meat Shop in Canmore in 1978. "The mines had just closed so all the people could afford was ground beef. We lived above the shop and made ends meet," says Leonie. The pair are both from central Switzerland but met in Banff in 1974 when Walter was working as a sausage maker and Leonie as a server.

"Our goal was to build a wholesale business. We had no salesperson so I decided to get a knife-sharpening machine and offer that to all the chefs in the valley. Canadian Mountain Holidays was our first account. By 1982 we'd built a 3,000-square-foot processing facility. Today we have 40,000 square feet," says Walter.

"Dad is a social butterfly," jokes daughter Chantal. "He knew every chef and our growth was built on those friendships." Both the von Rotz children have joined the family business. Jeff went to Switzerland for seven years to hotel management school and to Zurich to work in meat processing facilities and learn the craft. Chantal went to the University of Calgary and now manages the deli operation in their storefront that serves about 500 customers per day.

Valbella, which means "beautiful valley," makes air-dried smoked bison, bundnerfleisch, coppa, prosciutto, chimney sticks, landjaeger, and smoked bacon and hams. They also prepare numerous ready-to-cook products like beef Wellington and tourtières. There are no colours, additives or MSG in any of the foods. Smoking is done with natural birchwood. "Charcuterie needs good mountain air," says Walter.

"Logistically it might make more sense for us to be in Airdrie or Cochrane," says Jeff, "but our brand is synonymous with the Rockies. We've decided to stay, increase our specialization and access to our products across Alberta."

"By the time a product made out east hits the stores here, our products that were made on the same date are long since consumed," says Walter. "If the freshness is there, the product sells."

Valbella Gourmet Foods' products can be found across Alberta; check the website for retailers.

Carole Beaton | An Edible Life | 109-112 Kananaskis Way, Canmore
403-609-9957 | anediblelife.ca

An Edible Life chef/owner Carole Beaton is the picture of Canmore's healthy mountain lifestyle. Photo courtesy of An Edible Life.

"I love coming to work every day." When she's not creating whole-foods dishes like her famous goji energy balls, cashew chicken curry, or yam and kale stew, you'll find Carole Beaton riding the ridges of Alberta's rugged Rockies or bombing along the hills of Basque country in Spain on her mountain bike. Born with a genetic kidney disease, she turned to a life of fitness and food as medicine to prolong her chances at a longer life.

Beaton came to the Bow Valley for a winter and decided she needed to find a way to stay permanently. She worked as a mountain biking instructor, started her own tiling company, and then after over a decade in the construction industry, she took a holistic nutrition certificate and realized she'd found her true path. Longing to make a true impact on people's nutrition, she decided that instead of becoming a nutrition counsellor and just talking about how to eat better, she would actually prepare healthy meals for those who don't have time to do so.

Her cozy little kitchen and retail shop just off Railway Avenue in Canmore is a bustling hub for fit folks who'd rather spend their days hiking or skiing than cooking. With products like grass-finished beef from Top Grass Cattle Company (see page 283) and cage-free pork products from Spragg's Meat Shop (see page 281), her ingredients speak to the quality of her offerings. An Edible Life has doubled its sales and staffing since opening in 2014 and Beaton was recently voted Canmore's Entrepreneur of the Year.

"I like being part of the local food movement, supporting food producers, and just having the chance to talk to people about how they eat when they pop into my shop to pick up food." Beaton has found her place and her people, and along with her own goal of living longer, she has a good chance of helping others do so as well.

Kami Cochrane | Becker's Gourmet Restaurant | Icefields Parkway, Jasper
780-852-3779 | beckerschalets.com

Chef Kami Cochrane by the Athabasca River.
Photo by Karen Anderson.

Wedged between Lake Huron and Lake Erie in Ontario lies a village called Newbury. Kami Cochrane was raised here and got a job at age 14 in a family-run grocery store. She made cakes, worked in the deli, and was a meat cutter. She went on to complete the three-year culinary administration program at Canadore College in North Bay and did practicums at both the Fairmont Banff Springs and Jasper Park Lodge (JPL) before graduating in 2002. She worked at Becker's Chalets in Jasper in the summer of 2003.

"One of my great JPL mentors, Patrick McClary, asked me to work with him back in Ontario. I got my Red Seal as a chef and pastry chef but when I heard Becker's was looking for an executive chef in 2011, I applied. The owners, Lina and Claudio Venchiarutti, flew me out to cook for them and I got the job just before my 30th birthday."

W. Fay Becker originally built Becker's Chalets in 1937. The Beckers were the only owners until the Venchiarutti family purchased the property in 1978. In 1953, Marilyn Monroe stayed in cabin 33 during the making of *River of No Return*.

"We have guests that have returned every year for decades. The first thing they order is Becker's famous baked brie. Then they want Alberta game. Fortunately, Rocky Mountain Game Meats ships to us. I keep money in my budget to go to the weekly farmers' market in town to buy fresh produce for daily specials. I'm limited on how much I can buy there but it keeps my creative juices flowing."

Cochrane will finish her Chef de Cuisine designation by the 2018 season. She's started training apprentices at Becker's Gourmet Restaurant and loves giving back to her profession. Sitting in the dining room, eating her smoked Hog Wild Specialties (see page 37) boar chop and watching the sparkling waters of the Athabasca flow by with Mount Kerkeslin towering in the distance, it's easy to see why Becker's is a perennial favourite.

Alistair Barnes | Canadian Rocky Mountain Resorts | 403-410-7417
crmr.com

CRMR executive chef Alistair Barnes at Buffalo Mountain Lodge in Banff. Photo courtesy of CRMR.

"We are a tight-knit community all striving for the same thing, to make Alberta a destination for quality dining. Naturally the hiking and skiing are here but after enjoying the outdoors everyone wants to sit down and have a fabulous meal."

Alistair Barnes was born on the Channel Island of Jersey, where he began cooking at age 15 in a high-end hotel. He moved to Switzerland for further training. "In the fall, game was just what you ate. It was the season. When I came to the Rockies, I expected the same but all we got were some dried-up bits from back east."

Barnes was hired by Pat and Connie O'Connor in 1986 to run their newly opened Deer Lodge in Lake Louise and then Buffalo Mountain Lodge in Banff. "They were so passionate about outdoor pursuits and great hospitality that they wanted to create special places for people to experience Alberta. When I told them my product woes they said, 'We've got the land, let's start raising our own.'"

The O'Connors hired Dr. Terry Church, a veterinarian who worked closely with Alberta Agriculture's research station in Lacombe, to raise wild game to chef Barnes's specifications. "That was in the late '80s. Today elk and bison are still 50 percent of sales in our restaurants and we still raise our own."

As executive chef for what has become Canadian Rocky Mountain Resorts (CRMR), Barnes oversees his colleagues. In Calgary, there is Ken Canavan at their production facility, Thomas Neukom at the Lake House, and Lance Monteiro at Cilantro and Urban Butcher (see page 190). Valerie Morrison is at Emerald Lake Lodge, Tyler Tays at Deer Lodge, and Kelly Strutt at Buffalo Mountain Lodge (see CRMR's website for information on all its hotels and restaurants). "Chefs stay with us a long time because they are treated as professionals. They keep their costs in line and have some flexibility for free time with family. They know guests come first and grumpy chefs need not apply." He laughs as he says it.

Barnes is indeed happy to still practise his art. "They still call me in to do chef's tastings of game meats from the farm. Cooking is still my favourite thing to do and I cook every night at home."

jW Foster | Fairmont Banff Springs Hotel | 405 Spray Avenue, Banff
403-762-2211 | fairmont.com/banff-springs

jW Foster, executive chef at the Fairmont Banff Springs. Photo by Karen Anderson.

With 30 apprentices spending two to three years in the kitchens of the Banff Springs, jW Foster had dreamed of coming to Banff as executive chef, not only to be responsible for the 1.5 million meals made in this "Castle of the Rockies" every year but to influence the next generation of chefs.

Raised in one of Canada's agricultural hubs, Foster began his cooking career in Guelph, inspired by his grandmother's love of the art and time spent in her kitchen. He spent a season at the Fairmont Chateau Lake Louise in 1992 and went on to work in high-end country inns across Ontario before becoming a sous chef at Toronto's Royal York where he led the apprenticeship program. Tenures at Fairmont hotels in Dallas, San Francisco, and China gave him a chance to work with local growers, showcase local bounty, and always give back to local charities related to food and the education of chefs.

"I've been in Banff for over four years now and as my network grows I'm able to find more suppliers that can handle our needs. We bring in two to three whole carcasses of Benchmark Angus beef each week. Four K Farms supplies pork and Galimax Trading (see page 250) provides Mans Eggs. Poplar Bluff (see page 267) farmer Rosemary Wotske is planting specific potatoes for our menus now."

Foster churns butter from Vital Green Farms (see page 247) and uses oils from Highwood Crossing (see page 274). "We use all the local honey we can get from Galimax. I'm encouraging small producers to expand and grow for us."

The apprentices make artisanal bread to sell at the weekly Banff Farmers' Market. "It's entrepreneurial and they've used the money to buy greenhouses that will allow them to be even more local.

"Every Fairmont has the mandate to give our guests an authentically local experience, wherever the property is located. The way I look at it, if you can only come to Alberta for one night, I want to give you the most of Alberta as possible."

Darryl Huculak | Olive Bistro and Lounge | 401 Patricia Street, Jasper
780-852-5222 | olivebistro.ca

Chef Darryl Huculak. Photo by Karen Anderson.

Like a lot of flatlanders, Darryl Huculak, born and raised in Winnipeg, was curious about life in the Rocky Mountains. Huculak had started working in kitchens as a dishwasher at age 15. "I went to university but still worked in kitchens. When I decided to take a break from school and come out west to see what mountain life was all about, again, I worked in kitchens. In Jasper, I realized that cooking is what I truly loved and wanted to do with my life."

Huculak moved to gain more skills in the kitchens of Montreal for a few years but the lure of mountain life called him back. His experience meant that he now started running cafés and he soon ended up as head chef of a small tapas bar. Despite the long hours he met his wife Stephanie who'd been raised in Jasper. "Stephanie understands restaurant life. Her dad immigrated from Greece, worked as a miner but then met his wife in Jasper and in the 1970s they built and ran a restaurant called the Palisades, which Stephanie's brother took over."

The Huculaks knew they wanted their own place and after a brief stint in Winnipeg they took over the Palisades. Rebranding the restaurant as Olive Bistro, they pay homage to Stephanie's family's famous Greek recipes but have also broadened the menu to include Mediterranean foods done with Canadian flair. There is organic lamb, bison, elk, prime rib beef, wild boar, BC salmon, and vegetables as well as cheeses from Sylvan Star (see page 101). "I was vegan for a while so I love to create special dishes for vegetarians and vegans. Cooking this way strengthened my creativity. Michael Smith, Paul Rogalski (see page 174), and Thomas Keller are chefs that inspire me."

As if in testimony, a plate arrives with a sweet potato croquette shaped as a perfect pear. It's surrounded by yam purée, delicately grilled vegetables, and balsamic drizzled quinoa topped with freshly sliced scallions. "I'm always looking to grow as a chef." With ingredients so imaginatively but deliciously prepared, Huculak delivers.

Note: If you visit Jasper in winter, watch for special dinners where Huculak makes perogies from scratch to bring in the flavours of his own Ukrainian-Canadian heritage.

Hans Sauter | Post Hotel | 200 Pipestone Road, Lake Louise
403-522-3989 | posthotel.com

Executive chef Hans Sauter.
Photo by Karen Anderson.

"We lived by the seasons." Hans Sauter is talking about his childhood in eastern Switzerland but these are also the words that inform his cooking. "We ate cabbages and apples in winter and whole foods year-round. That's where nutrition comes from."

In 1976, Sauter watched the Olympics in Montreal on television and decided to immigrate to Canada. He'd apprenticed and worked in top hotels in Switzerland before landing a job at the Queen Elizabeth Hotel in Montreal. He worked for Hilton International in Geneva, Chicago, and Toronto and for CN at the Hotel Vancouver and the Palliser in Calgary. He gained Japanese sensibilities in food presentation working in Sapporo on Hokkaido. Banff's Rimrock, Budapest's Kempinski, and time in San Francisco led to Washington, D.C., where he was in charge of George W. Bush's inaugural ball for 55,000 people. "There's no other profession that lets you travel the world like this. But, for me, no other place is better than here."

Sauter arrived at the Post Hotel in June of 2005. He has a husky dog and gets up at five o'clock in the morning on his days off to prepare elaborate hiking lunches for the team members he treks with. "In the restaurant, everything is made from scratch with classic technique. It's my job to develop the abilities of our team so I must let them cook there. This chance to cook for them is a joy for me."

André and George Schwarz, who've owned the Post Hotel since 1978, give him the luxury of a budget that allows their guests to experience the very best ingredients. "That would be impossible if you only cared about the bottom line." His respect is sincere. "Our most popular dishes are Alberta wild game. I use as much local as I can find—Galimax Trading (see page 250), Valbella Gourmet Foods (see page 208), and Rocky Mountain Game Meats are my stalwarts. And with that, he leaves to get a late start on his hike. Up to now, he hasn't mentioned that this is his day off. That humility is what hospitality legends are made of.

Note: The Post Hotel has been a Relais & Châteaux member since 1990. In 2002, with over 27,000 bottles and 1,600 labels in its wine collection, it received the ultimate honour—the Grand Award from *Wine Spectator* magazine.

Michel Leblanc | Rocky Mountain Flatbread Co. | 838 10 Street, Canmore
403-609-5508 | rockymountainflatbread.ca

Owner Michel Leblanc (left) with executive chef and general manager Kyle Maier. Photo by Karen Anderson.

Suzanne and Dominic Fielden started Rocky Mountain Flatbread Co. after careers as British investment bankers. They wanted to create a family-friendly eatery serving healthy food that would also become an integral part of the community. In 2009, when they moved to Vancouver to open another location, they set up a franchise system and sold Canmore's Rocky Mountain Flatbread Co. (RMFco) to Michel Leblanc.

Leblanc was born in Saint-Eugène, Quebec, and came to Alberta to work in Medicine Hat on the oil rigs in the late '80s. He came west to forget a failed romance. On a ski trip to Banff, he spent a night in Canmore and loved it. He got a job as a dishwasher at a bar in Banff, and then in construction as Canmore prepared for the '88 Olympics. He met his wife Debra during this time and though they lived in Calgary for a few years, they moved back to Canmore in '91 to be close to her widowed mother and to raise their two daughters.

Leblanc's parents had owned a small grocery and he spent as much time as possible helping them as a child. He adored them. "They were kind and cared deeply about their community. People had accounts and when they couldn't pay, my parents helped them feed their families until they could." Leblanc had managed a national pizza chain restaurant but when the opportunity to buy RMFco came up, he saw it as the chance to realize the community values his parents had instilled in him.

RMFco uses organic locally milled flours, pasta made in Canmore, and meat toppings from Hoven Farms (see page 127) and Valbella Gourmet Foods (see page 208). They source greens from Canmore's Alpine Edible Schoolyards (see page 221)—a project that they helped launch and continue to fundraise for.

Monday evenings at RMFco are community nights. Groups can apply to host the night and receive 10 percent of all profits from the evening for their project. Each year five percent of the company's profits are put back into the community. Local heroes have been honoured with support for their initiatives like solar power, bike-friendly Canmore, and education programs to teach children how food is grown.

Le Chocolatier | 121-701 Benchlands Trail, Canmore | 403-679-3351
lechocolatier.ca

Belinda and John Spear. Photo courtesy of Le Chocolatier.

John and Belinda Spear are the couple behind this dynamic chocolate shop. John is the chief confectioner, affectionately known as Chocolate Dude. Belinda is quality and beauty control, responsible for artful hand-packaging and product display.

The Spears bought the three-year-old Le Chocolatier company in 2004 after a successful career owning a catering company in England. With John and Belinda's passion for chocolate, Le Chocolatier quickly grew beyond the Canmore basement where it was started, and they soon moved to a space in the town's industrial area.

In December 2008, Le Chocolatier finally moved into the customized chocolate-making factory and retail store that is their business hub today. They supply locals and visitors with chocolate treats from this retail location, and also sell wholesale to retail food chains and hotels in Alberta and across the country.

John continually stretches the boundaries of creative chocolate making. Brand-new inventive confections are added each year to Le Chocolatier's offering. "I don't want to think outside the box," John claims. "I want to recreate the box!"

Despite their phenomenal growth, you will find John and Belinda in the store if you pop in for a chocolate goody. John will be crafting chocolates or joking with customers, and Belinda will be packaging and filling custom orders. They always have time to talk or create a custom box of chocolates for you.

Paintbox Lodge and Cooking @ The Box | 629 10 Street, Canmore
403-609-0482 | paintboxlodge.com

Former Olympians Sara Renner and Thomas Grandi show their exuberance for life in Canmore. Photo by Chris Bolin.

Between them, Thomas Grandi and Sara Renner attended eight Olympic Games as members of Team Canada. During their careers as a downhill and cross-country skier respectively, they travelled extensively and learned a lot about excellence in hospitality. In 2010, they bought Paintbox Lodge from Renner's father, Sepp Renner, the legendary mountain guide of Assiniboine Lodge (where Renner spent her formative years), and now they are putting their own stamp on it with values centred around taking care of the earth and their guests, staff, and community.

Cycling with them during their annual foray as hosts of a progressive dinner on mountain bikes during the town's Canmore Uncorked food festival was a chance to learn about what motivates them. "We were so supported by this community as athletes, it's our turn to give back," says Grandi. Along with co-owning "the Box" he also runs Grandi Guiding backcountry skiing excursions and is certified with the Association of Canadian Mountain Guides.

"We love great quality food and we have this fabulous kitchen. It just seemed natural to offer it as a place where people can gather to learn about food and cooking, enjoy music together, or celebrate a special occasion," says Renner. Their Cooking @ The Box cooking school offers five classes per week fall through spring. Popular local chefs from the Bow Valley like George Bayne, Sue Shih, and Alessio Pontarollo instruct.

Renner and Grandi have also joined a movement of businesses worldwide who give one percent of their net profits to increase sustainability for the planet. Their recipient is Canmore's Alpine Edible Schoolyards (see page 221).

They strive to use local, organic ingredients and guests of the lodge wake up to baking made from scratch using the kitchen's very own sourdough. And, of course, if they need any tips on cycling, hiking, or ways to be active, Grandi and Renner are happy to share their local knowledge.

Mountain Mercato | 102-817 8 Street, Canmore | 403-609-6631
mountainmercato.com

Raegan Fodor. Photo by Karen Anderson.

Born and raised in Banff, Raegan Fodor was working her way through nursing school waiting tables and bartending when she decided to switch things up one summer to start her own landscaping company. That experience taught her that while she loved being an entrepreneur, she missed working with food. When she mentioned this to a friend in the industry, he told her that a small café in Canmore was for sale.

That was 2005 and the rest is history. With two weeks of barista training, Fodor changed the name to Mountain Mercato and over the next five years slowly built her business and her community so that she could expand from two tables and a few shelves of goods into the elegant café and local-meets-global market you enter today.

The contrast of crisp white walls against black café tables is softened with ornate mirrors reflecting the warm light of hurricane lantern pendants. While you might find expensive olive oils from Greece, Italy, and Spain and other quality ingredients that can't be sourced locally, you'll also find an abundance of regional produce. If you step into the back parking lot in summer you'll find raised beds where the cooks can clip fresh herbs and edible flowers. More produce comes from Alpine Edible Schoolyards (see page 221), Valbella Gourmet Foods (see page 208), Galimax Trading (see page 250), and bakeries like Sidewalk Citizen (see page 156), Le Fournil (see page 206), and Homestead Bakeshop (see page 239). A local woman makes all the cakes. The coffee beans and training for the baristas come from Phil & Sebastian (see page 154) in Calgary.

"I love the simplicity of our food program. We use things from our own deli. We find out what's available weekly from our local suppliers and develop soups, sandwiches, and baking to feature those fresh seasonal flavours." Many of the staff are Olympians in training at the Canmore Nordic Centre. The café is LEAF certified and a member of Bike Friendly Canmore.

"We are a one-stop shop. You can come for wine, beer, espresso, or food and then shop for a hostess gift or pick up some staples. Our clientele come from diverse backgrounds but they all appreciate quality in their food."

Park Distillery Restaurant and Bar | 219 Banff Avenue, Banff
403-762-5114 | parkdistillery.com

Matthew Hendriks foraging spruce tips.
Photo courtesy of Park Distillery.

There are not a lot of ingredients in spirits. Water is key. Park Distillery's water comes from six different Rocky Mountain glaciers. Travelling through limestone it is naturally filtered. "We filter it again before use in distillation to remove anything the town might've added. We like to say that we are 'glacier to glass.'" Matthew Hendriks is the master distiller.

A former mixologist who lived and worked in Banff for over a decade, Hendriks was well known for the amount of education he pursued about spirits and for the cocktails his well-informed palate created. "When I was given the opportunity to become the distiller I read every book I could get my hands on and then started practising in a 50-litre pot. Now my still is 600 litres."

Another element in fine distillation is the quality of the grain used. "We use only certified organic grains. Again, we're about purity. We know the Alberta family that grow our grains and we hand mill and mash everything."

Since opening in May of 2015, Park has released rye, numerous flavoured vodkas, and a few gins. The Park Alpine Spruce Gin is a favourite of Hendriks's. "We are not allowed to forage in a national park but we harvest Engelmann spruce tips in the foothills of the Rockies, vacu-seal them, and freeze them for freshness. It's like a Bombay or London Dry gin but the presence of the mountains is duly noted."

What about local juniper for that gin? "It takes six pounds of juniper berries for each batch. It's hard to forage that much here so we have to import them. If we ever do manage it, it would be a very limited release."

In Alberta distillations must be aged a minimum of three years before they can be called whisky. "Ours will turn three in September of 2018 but that doesn't mean we'll release it then. It will only get better so we might wait five, seven, or even ten years. You only get one chance to make a first impression." Park has a campfire theme for the restaurant's food and gives free tours daily.

Wild Life Distillery | 160-105 Bow Meadows Crescent, Canmore
403-678-2800 | wildlifedistillery.ca

Matt Widmer. Photo by Karen Anderson.

"I'm sorry, Matt and Keith are out foraging for botanicals today," said the voice on the phone. Of course they are. They aren't making spirits in downtown Toronto; they are in Canmore, the Gateway to the Rockies. Wild Life Distillery is a microdistillery and owners Matt Widmer and Keith Robinson have the freedom to be creative.

"Exactly," says Widmer when we finally meet. "There's a lot of hyperbole out there about local but we wanted to see if we could create a gin that *only* used locally foraged botanicals. We hired Julie Walker of Full Circle Adventures (see page 253) to help us gather—in a very responsible way—Rocky Mountain juniper, wild silver sage, Labrador tea, wild rose hips, and cow parsnip for starters. I don't want to give everything away. We only made 360 bottles but it's a chance for people to see what Alberta really tasted like on one hot summer's day in August of 2017."

We are in the distillery's tasting room on the edge of an industrial park that affords us a full-on view of the Three Sisters and the Rundle mountain ranges. Copper mugs line a rustic Douglas fir and smoky grey mirrored bar along with carefully arranged bottles of their spirits. But there's no smoke and mirrors when it comes to their ingredients or their craft. They use spring wheat from the Drumheller area and Alberta malted barley and hand mill and mash it before distilling it in stills they purchased in Spain and Holland.

Robinson was born and raised in Canmore and Widmer in Banff. Widmer's family owned a restaurant in Banff and Robinson, when not working in Northern Alberta's oil patch, trained his palate as a mixologist in the Bow Valley. Widmer took a distilling course in Chicago in 2011 and together they attended a whisky-making course in Scotland. They toured the country and surrounding isles to learn more about the traditions of the industry—including some trade secrets.

Robinson and Widmer opened Wild Life in January of 2017, and their spirits are already stocked at over 120 outlets in the province. Their home base is also a licensed bar for hosting events.

Alpine Edible Schoolyards | Canmore Collegiate High School and Lawrence Grassi Middle School, Canmore | facebook.com/alpineedible

Christian Wright. Photo by Karen Anderson.

"The problem *is* the solution. It's an old permaculture saying." Christian Wright is relaying how he became the school garden project manager for the Canadian Rockies Public Schools in Calgary. "I grew up in Ontario but tired of Toronto's size. I wanted to live in a small, pristine mountain town and came to Canmore and worked as a bartender for a few years."

The problem that led Wright to many solutions was his frustration with the town's lack of composting. He started worm composting his own food waste and began reading about healthy soils. Soon he was helping friends begin a company called Farm Box, which grew and sourced food for sale at the Canmore farmers' market. "We were surprised how much we could produce in a very small space and when we looked for more space we realized the high school had a green roof with just grasses. We approached the school with the idea of growing food instead and we got a lot of support right off the bat."

Rocky Mountain Flatbread Co. (see page 215) provided start-up funds to build the garden as the project dovetailed nicely with its own work to promote food literacy in children. The restaurant also buys a weekly allotment of greens all growing season. Mountain Mercato (see page 218) and Paintbox Lodge (see page 217) are other buyers and supporters of the program.

With a small greenhouse to grow microgreens and extend the season, plus a quarter-acre garden, Wright, who now holds a Permaculture Design Certificate, is able to produce over 2,000 pounds of produce in a season.

"I'm content for now but I know this is just the start. I would like to see the day when we can achieve food sovereignty for the community."

Note: Permaculture is a design system that mimics natural ecosystem patterns and features. The term was coined in 1978 and means both permanent agriculture and permanent culture as the social aspects of farming are just as important to its sustainability as the natural farming principles of Masanobu Fukuoka, the Japanese farmer whose philosophy and teachings inspired the movement.

Jasper Local Food Society and Jasper Community Garden
305 Connaught Drive, Jasper | facebook.com/jasperlocalfoodsociety

Janet Cooper and Karl Peetoom at the Jasper Community Garden. Photo by Karen Anderson.

"I think it is important for community members to have the opportunity to grow and to educate youth about where food comes from. While we grow our food here we are actually growing community at the same time," says Karl Peetoom. He's been the manager of the Jasper Local Food Society's (JLFS) community garden for several years now. The gift shop he owns and operates sits kitty-corner to this cheerful space between the Canadian Pacific Railway line and the town's main drag, Connaught Drive.

"Putting the garden in this location has been great," adds Janet Cooper, sustainability officer for the town. "So many people stop to talk to us to learn about the challenges of accessing locally grown food in our isolated national park location and to see what we can actually grow here. The garden has actually become a bit of a tourist attraction."

There are 56 four-by-eight-foot plots in the garden, which receives full sun and is surrounded by elk-proof fencing. All involved sign an agreement to grow without chemical fertilizers or pesticides. Mentoring just happens. Any excess food is donated to the local food bank.

"The garden is important because we are under rigid restrictions. It is illegal to farm or mine and sell goods for a profit in a national park. We are so isolated, we have a hard time getting growers to bring fresh vegetables and fruits to our weekly summer farmers' market (which JLFS is also in charge of). Our nearest farmers are from the Robson Valley in BC," Cooper laments. "Our third goal is to provide learning opportunities around sustainability. We organize a Seedy Saturday exchange each spring and are setting up a seed library. Native plants and pollinator talks and classes on preserving are also coming."

Instead of one or two food artisans supplying 56 people, it seems JLFS creates 56 food artisans for their town each year.

Summit Hill Farm | Bottrel | 587-709-7009 | summithillfarm.ca

Alberta and Corey Telfer. Photo by Karen Anderson.

"People tell us we can't grow here, but we are doing it. The soil is fertile and we've had a surprisingly good crop." Alberta and Corey Telfer and their daughter Una have moved to Cochrane from Edmonton to return to Alberta's farming roots.

Alberta can still work remotely with her government job. Corey is a linguist with great flexibility. They have plans for her family's half section of land. "We'd like to use regenerative methods with less inputs. We did a summer fallow this year on some fields and will plant cover crop for over winter to build nutrients," says Alberta.

With her background in economic development and trade, Alberta is good with numbers and stats. "We know that 50 percent of farmers work off the farm. The margins are so thin; my estimate is farmers make 20 cents per hour. People are used to supermarkets. They want maximal selection of perfect-looking vegetables. These things have become a priority over supporting local."

Still, on a day when their daughter won a ribbon at the Cochrane fair for a sunflower that was one foot in diameter, well, those are good days. "Health is another motivator for us. I feel so good. I know I have to get out here and I just do it." And the business?

"We only had five customers in our Community Supported Agriculture (CSA) this year. We are looking to have 20 customers and to be at the Cochrane Farmers' Market every other week next year," says Corey. "We'll grow different produce for the market—herbs seem to be popular."

"We'll also figure out ways to advertise the CSA more. We've engaged a succession planner. Dad wants the land to stay in the family and it was always our plan to return," says Alberta. The average age of the Alberta farmer just went down a notch.

LJ Ranch | Cochrane | 403-932-7777 | ljranch.ca

Joy and Lindsay Eklund. Photo by Karen Anderson.

"Raising cattle from birth to plate is much more satisfying for everyone involved," says Joy Eklund. She and her husband Lindsay should know. They've seen and done it all. After they married in 1996 they had about three and a half quarter sections of land on the ranch but leased another 3,000 acres for grazing on nearby Stoney Nakoda lands. Lindsay trained horses and taught team roping because those were important elements in being able to care for animals out where there were no corrals.

Joy moved her midwifery practice to their ranch and her clients started to ask if the Eklunds would grow beef for them without hormones or antibiotics. "We finish a few cattle at a time in our own yard on free choice of steam-rolled 85 percent barley and 15 percent oats plus hay for about a hundred days. Our animals are never crowded, stressed, or around strange animals. The morning of slaughter, we load and drive them to Balzac and within two hours they are hanging. They are dry-aged in a cooler for 21 days and delivered custom cut, wrapped in brown paper stamped with the customer's name," says Lindsay.

The Eklunds have about 150 customers but since Lindsay's son Travis Eklund took over neighbouring WineGlass Ranch (wineglassranchalberta.com) and they run their herds together, there's room for expansion. Much of their land is endowed with native fescue grasses and Jumpingpound Creek winds through the property. As you look out the windows of the ranch house, the Rocky Mountains stare you in the face.

"When people get to know you and they trust you, the beef sells itself," says Lindsay. "People are so happy. We've closed the circle for them. We raise the animals, they eat them, and they come back. We love this lifestyle and our connection with the community we sell to."

Uncle Bernie's All Natural Meats | Airdrie | 403-935-4907
uncleberniesallnaturalmeats.com ·

*Linda and Bernie Pagenkopf at the Banff
Farmers' Market. Photo by Karen Anderson.*

Bernie and Linda Pagenkopf's elk ranch is 320 acres of rolling hills and coulees east of Airdrie. They are in the Rocky Mountain section of this book because of their dedication to serving their loyal customers at the Cochrane, Canmore, and Banff farmers' markets. Though elk wander the Rockies and bison have been reintroduced to Banff National Park, without the Uncle Bernie's All Natural Meats stall at these markets, locals would not have access to these indigenous species.

The Pagenkopfs started ranching in 1987 to grow elk for the antler velvet market (it's used as a natural treatment for inflammatory conditions like arthritis). At one point, there were 400 elk ranchers in Alberta. When chronic wasting disease (CWD) was found in the province in 2001, most ranches went under. There are about 100 left. Now, every elk is tested for CWD at time of slaughter.

"Instead of getting out when CWD hit, we decided to diversify and to take the middleman out of the profit equation," says Linda. "We'd worked hard to establish our markets. We used to do seven in five days. Gradually we added bison, chicken, heritage breed turkeys, and a few beef cattle." Since 2010 they also keep bees and sell honey.

All-natural, grass-finished animals are important to the Pagenkopfs because Linda's mother had been ill with an inflammatory disease. Linda did a lot of research into the effects of diet. "We knew grain caused inflammation in the animals and that the inflammation could then be passed on to humans. Feeding and finishing our animals for 24 to 30 months on grass is a serious investment but we won't do it any other way."

Bernie has been able to work full-time on the ranch only for a decade. "We took a variety of routes to get where we are," he says. "People who shop at our market stalls value local goods. Face-to-face education about our products is crucial. We love farming and we love being entrepreneurs. We are happy to have found a way to make a living off a small piece of land."

FARMERS' MARKETS

Check the website for current hours prior to your visit.

BANFF FARMERS' MARKET

Banff Central Park | Wednesdays 10:00 A.M.–6:00 P.M., May to October
403-763-8772 | thebanfffarmersmarket.com

CANMORE MOUNTAIN MARKET

Next to the Canmore Civic Centre Plaza, 902 7 Avenue | Thursdays 10:00 A.M.–
6:00 P.M., May to October | 1-888-678-1295 | canmore.ca/residents/mountain-market

COCHRANE FARMERS' MARKET

Cochrane Ranche Historic Site, northeast of intersection of Highways 1A and 22
Saturdays 9:30 A.M.–1:30 P.M., June to September | 403-851-0562
cochranefarmersmarket.ca

JASPER FARMERS' MARKET

400 Geikie Street | Wednesdays 11:00 A.M.–3:00 P.M., June to September
jasperlocalfood@gmail.com | facebook.com/jasperlocalfoodsociety

WATERING HOLES

Check the website for current hours prior to your visit.

BANFF AVE. BREWING CO.

2nd floor 110 Banff Avenue, Banff | 403-762-1003 | banffavebrewingco.ca
⇒ **Tours: By special request for large group bookings.**
Favourite beer here: Banff Ave. Blonde Ale—great in summer.
Banff Ave. Brewing Co. is sister to Jasper Brewing Co.

THE GRIZZLY PAW PUB & BREWING COMPANY

310 Canmore Road, Canmore | 403-678-2487 | thegrizzlypaw.com
⇒ **Tours: Run daily.**
Favourite beer here: Grumpy Bear Honey Wheat.

HALF HITCH BREWING COMPANY

1-10 Griffin Industrial Point, Cochrane | 403-988-4214 | halfhitchbrewing.ca
⇒ **Tours: By appointment.**
Favourite beer here: Fire N' Fury.
Love their Bend and Brew Yoga followed by a session ale.

JASPER BREWING CO.

624 Connaught Drive, Jasper | 780-852-4111 | jasperbrewingco.ca
⇒ **Tours: No tours but lots of events like cask nite and brewmaster's dinners.**
Favourite beer here: Sutter-Hill Pil, because we love a great Pilsner.
First brewery in a national park.

KRANG SPIRITS INC.

315 1 Street East, Cochrane | 403-630-2431 | krang.com
⇒ **Tours: By appointment.**
Favourite drink here: The award-winning black currant liqueur.

PARK DISTILLERY RESTAURANT AND BAR (SEE PAGE 219)

219 Banff Avenue, Banff | 403-762-5114 | parkdistillery.com
⇒ **Tours: Run daily.**
Favourite drink here: Alpine Dry Gin.
Food in the restaurant has a campfire theme.

WILD LIFE DISTILLERY (SEE PAGE 220)

160-105 Bow Meadows Crescent, Canmore | 403-678-2800 | wildlifedistillery.ca
⇒ **Tours: Daily at 3:00 P.M. (during operating hours).**
Favourite drink here: Wild Life Gin.

SOUTHERN ALBERTA

- BLACKIE
- CLARESHOLM
- COALDALE
- COALHURST
- DALEMEAD
- DE WINTON
- DRUMHELLER
- ETZIKOM
- FOREMOST
- FORT MACLEOD

- HIGH RIVER
- IRVINE
- LETHBRIDGE
- MEDICINE HAT
- MILLARVILLE
- MOUNTAIN VIEW—
  WATERTON
- NANTON
- NOBLEFORD
- OKOTOKS

- PICTURE BUTTE
- PINCHER CREEK
- RAYMOND
- REDCLIFF
- ROSEMARY
- STRATHMORE
- TABER
- TURNER VALLEY
- VULCAN

Heading south of Calgary, as you hit Okotoks you face a fork in the road in terms of how to proceed. You can drive straight down the four-lane Queen Elizabeth II Highway (QE2) to Fort Macleod and beyond or turn west and dally your way along the Cowboy Trail (Alberta Secondary Highway 22) that runs parallel.

On the 22 it is easy to explore the cool little towns of Turner Valley and Black Diamond and pop back out at High River and carry on down the QE2 for a chance to hunt for antiques in Nanton. While the highway cuts through the prairies like a straight-edge sword and cars flow endlessly along it, Head-Smashed-In Buffalo Jump is another worthy detour. Here is a chance to connect with the wisdom of our indigenous people and their intertwined culinary and cultural history with the North American plains bison.

Meanwhile, if you choose to stay on the 22, after those cool little towns and Longview (famous for Ian Tyson, jerky, and the Longview Steakhouse) you come to Bar U Ranch and a chance to learn about our ranching history. Bar U, once 160,000 acres, had 30,000 cattle and 1,000 Percheron horses. It is a national historic site. Still further along, you can enjoy spotting cattle as they graze the rolling foothills of the Rockies towering to the west. This highway ends by running smack dab into the Crowsnest Pass (Highway 3) and its colourful history of coal mining and bootlegging in towns like Frank, Blairmore and Coleman.

Nearby Pincher Creek is the gateway to the Waterton-Glacier International Peace Park where Canada meets the United States in the state of Montana. In each small town here in Southern Alberta (and in most of Alberta for that matter), you'll find an important piece of our culinary history—the Chinese-Western restaurants that helped our Chinese immigrants establish themselves and their families.

Southern Alberta's Rockies to the west and south are matched in strength only by the winds that sweep through the area. This weather phenomenon is known as a chinook, an indigenous word that means "snow eater." Though the chinook can be fierce and at times unrelenting, Southern Albertans are used to these warm winds bringing periodic relief while our Northern Albertan friends often stay in the deep-freeze for the whole winter. The winds do, however, create a challenging environment for growing food.

They leave the southeastern corner of the province, part of Palliser's Triangle, arid to semi-arid. It is only with the damming of mighty rivers like the Oldman, widespread irrigation, and a booming hothouse industry that the area has become an abundant source of produce for the province.

East, at the border between Saskatchewan and Alberta, nestled along the banks of the South Saskatchewan River, is Medicine Hat, which is famous for its Medalta clay works factory. Now a museum, it was once a vital centre of industry supplying household crockery, building bricks, and tiles for our early pioneers. Cypress Hills Interprovincial Park lies to the south.

From Brooks to Drumheller along the Trans-Canada Highway, cottonwood poplars mark river valleys that have carved their escarpments over millennia. The windswept hoodoos here are home to Dinosaur Provincial Park and the Royal Tyrrell paleontological museum.

Travel Tips

➤ Explore southeastern Alberta with Prairie Sprinter (prairiesprinterinc.ca). They specialize in multi-day guided tours to ranches, museums, provincial and national parks, and fun food tours and farm experiences.

➤ Looking for a complete western ranching immersion? Jim and Carol Hern of Bar Diamond Guest Ranch (bardiamondguestranch.ca) offer the real deal.

➤ No trip to Lethbridge would be complete without a visit to Nikka Yuko Japanese Garden (nikkayuko.com), which is rated one of Canada's top 10 botanical gardens.

➤ Fuel up with a quick coffee and cinnamon bun at the Cinnamon Bear in Coleman or spend a leisurely evening savouring both local cuisine and music at the Holy Ghost Café and Music Hall, also in Coleman.

Facing page: photo courtesy of Neil Zeller Photography

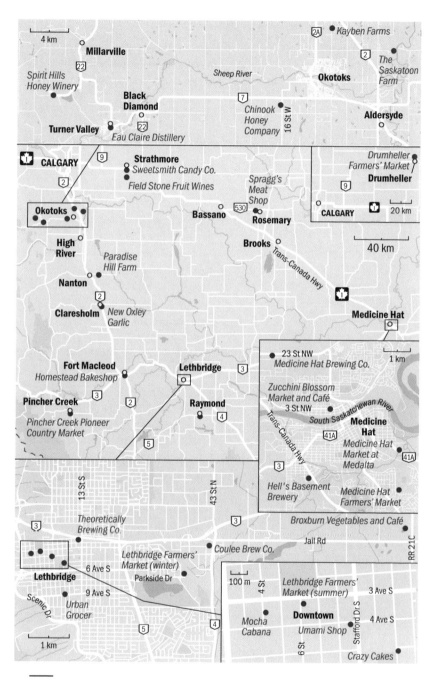

4 km

Millarville

Spirit Hills
Honey Winery

Sheep River

Kayben Farms

Okotoks

The
Saskatoon
Farm

Black
Diamond

Chinook
Honey
Company

Aldersyde

Turner Valley

Eau Claire Distillery

CALGARY

Strathmore

Sweetsmith Candy Co.

Field Stone Fruit Wines

Spragg's
Meat
Shop

Drumheller
Farmers' Market

Drumheller

Okotoks

Bassano

Rosemary

CALGARY

20 km

High
River

Paradise
Hill Farm

Brooks

Trans-Canada Hwy

40 km

Nanton

Claresholm

New Oxley
Garlic

Medicine Hat

Fort Macleod

Homestead Bakeshop

Lethbridge

23 St NW
Medicine Hat Brewing Co.

1 km

Pincher Creek

Pincher Creek Pioneer
Country Market

Raymond

Zucchini Blossom
Market and Café

3 St NW

Medicine
Hat

South Saskatchewan River

Medicine Hat
Market at
Medalta

Trans-Canada Hwy

Hell's Basement
Brewery

Medicine Hat
Farmers' Market

13 St S

43 St N

Theoretically
Brewing Co.

Broxburn Vegetables and Café

Jail Rd

RR 21C

Lethbridge

Coulee Brew Co.

Lethbridge Farmers'
Market (winter)

Parkside Dr

100 m

4 St

Lethbridge Farmers'
Market (summer)

3 Ave S

6 Ave S

9 Ave S

Scenic Dr

Urban
Grocer

Mocha
Cabana

Downtown

Umami Shop

Stafford Dr S

4 Ave S

6 St

Crazy Cakes

1 km

Note: Only artisans and producers who welcome visitors on site are shown on this map.

FOOD ARTISANS OF SOUTHERN ALBERTA

Luco Farms | Lethbridge | 403-892-6533 | lucofarms.com

Ben Luco and his father, Robert, make stone-ground mustard from local seed. Photo by Matilde Sanchez-Turri.

The 1,000 acres that comprise Luco Farms has been in Robert Luco's family since 1937. Situated just outside of Lethbridge near the river valley, the Lucos had a mixed farm and grew grains and legume crops until 1964. That year, Robert's father was given five pounds of oriental mustard seed and he became a pedigreed seed grower. This meant the Luco family couldn't grow other varieties due to the risk of cross-pollination, which would ruin the pedigree of their seed.

By the mid-'70s, the Luco family had a tough choice to make. They could either expand, diversify their crops, and integrate processing into their operation or withdraw from the life they'd known and lease out their land. Since oriental mustard is more of an acquired taste due to its spicy, pungent flavour, and was not in huge demand, the family decided to lease the land. Robert's parents continued to live on the farm and Robert and his family lived abroad.

While working in California in 2009, Robert and his son Ben were surprised to find some Alberta mustard seed at a local farmers' market. The irony and timing weren't lost on them. "We had been talking about making mustard for 30 years. With my mom ready to move off the farm and Ben and I looking for an opportunity to work together...things fell into place for us to move back to the farm and we went for it."

Robert and Ben began making small batches of their artisanal mustards in 2013 using brown, yellow and some oriental mustard seeds from local growers. They sold out their first weekend. "We had three cases of our five different mustards and we sold them all, which was wonderful."

If you ask Ben and Robert what makes their mustard so special, they'll hand you a sample. "You really have to taste it to know. We use a slow, natural process free of additives and preservatives and with minimal amounts of salt. Using stone instead of metal to grind the mustard seeds helps keep all the nutrition and flavour intact and it gives us more control over the texture."

Home cooks, chefs, and mustard connoisseurs can find Luco Farms' mustards at the Lethbridge Exhibition Park Farmers' Market year-round, at specialty food and health food stores in Lethbridge and Calgary, and on the menus of Coulee Brew Co. and Mocha Cabana restaurant in Lethbridge.

Saucy Ladies | 1254 3 Avenue, Lethbridge | 403-329-8719
saucyladies.com

Barbara Whitelaw, the original Saucy Lady.
Photo by Matilde Sanchez-Turri.

Looking for something productive to do while her kids were in school, Barbara Whitelaw dug up some of her grandmother's recipes and started canning. She still remembers falling asleep to a lullaby of "pings" as jars of pickled beets, carrots, and asparagus sealed in her kitchen. "That sound is still as gratifying to me now, after 30 years, as it was back then."

Showering her friends and family with her canned creations, Whitelaw kept hearing them say her preserves were too good to give away. Requests for more kept pouring in so in 1990, she moved her operation to a commercial kitchen and began selling three signature items at farmers' markets and Christmas shows, and to local retailers. "I always had samples so people can taste things and that's all it took. I would test new product at the shows because I was coming up with new recipes all the time. I really enjoy that part of it."

Now the Saucy Ladies brand has 18 items and counting as part of its catalogue including pickles, chutneys and jellies, cabbage rolls, and handmade perogies. People rarely leave with just one thing. "We don't use preservatives or additives and process all of our seasonal vegetables less than 48 hours after they're picked."

With demand still exceeding supply, Whitelaw leans on her two full-time staff and four apprentices during high season to help prep, hand pack, and preserve as many fresh local vegetables in every jar as she can. They literally process tons of pickling cucumbers, carrots, beets, peppers, and herbs delivered to them from local Hutterite colonies.

Their pickled asparagus, which come from Tamminga Farms, is their bestseller. Whitelaw's award-winning seafood antipasto is a close second along with her gourmet salsa containing 21 different types of peppers. "People say my salsa is the best thing since Mexico." Place your orders online for delivery to the closest city centre near you or find Saucy Ladies preserves at select retailers throughout Alberta.

237

Crazy Cakes | 1102 5 Avenue South, Lethbridge | 403-327-4990
crazycakes.ca

The Crazy Cakes team (left to right): Heather Farough, Amanda Kawchuk, Roberta Clemis, Bill Sokol, Wolfgang Otto, Matt Tuttle, Denise Hammon, Becky Baunton, Jessica Leong. Photo by Matilde Sanchez-Turri.

Denise Hammon promised to open a cake shop with her daughters Rebecca and Jessica if they both moved back to Lethbridge one day. When that day came, she kept her promise and in January 2007, Crazy Cakes opened its doors. How the city's first and only specialty cake shop ended up in the historic Spudnut building is another story.

"We had a vision for Crazy Cakes and the Spudnuts space was the only one we felt would work." In 1997, when daughter Rebecca and her now husband Craig were travelling through Germany, they stopped in at a wine store and the salesman told the couple that he had an uncle in Lethbridge and asked them to say hello. The uncle turned out to be Wolfgang Otto, the city's legendary Spudnut man.

Wolfgang had retired but the building hadn't been sold because he was looking for a family who would run a bakery or resurrect the Spudnut tradition in the space. In 2006, Wolfgang sold the building to Denise. Now, Wolfgang is part of the family and every Thursday, the Crazy Cakes team wakes up at 3:00 A.M. to make Spudnuts, the potato-flour doughnuts that Wolfgang made in that same building for 50 years.

"If you come by on a Thursday morning, don't be alarmed if there's a lineup around the block. If you come to the northeast door at the front of the building around 7:00 A.M., you can get a hot, freshly glazed Spudnut. There's never been a doughnut that tastes as good as a hot Spudnut does."

Denise has three Red Seal pastry chefs on staff and one apprentice. Her daughters and staff have been trained in cake decorating at Bonnie Gordon College of Confectionary Arts and Ron Ben-Israel in New York City. They've also taken courses in chocolate work from Sarah Bell of Bobbette and Belle bakery in Toronto. Their freshly made cupcakes, custom cakes, cheesecakes, French macarons, homemade ice cream, and seasonal treats are all made with real ingredients and look as amazing as they taste.

Homestead Bakeshop | 228 24 Street, Fort Macleod | 403-553-4328
homesteadbakeshop.ca

Kim Vanden Broek, co-owner and operator of Homestead Bakeshop. Photo by Matilde Sanchez-Turri.

When you walk into Homestead Bakeshop, you won't want to leave. Kim Vanden Broek and Julena Schipper opened their bakery in February 2017. The pair are both alumnae of the Southern Alberta Institute of Technology's Baking and Pastry Arts program and between them have gained valuable experience at numerous fine restaurants and bakeries throughout Alberta, including the Beltliner, Charcut Roast House, the Fairmont Banff Springs Hotel, Corbeaux Bakery, and Alforno Bakery.

Everything in the bakery is made from scratch, by hand. Schipper focuses on 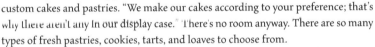 custom cakes and pastries. "We make our cakes according to your preference; that's why there aren't any in our display case." There's no room anyway. There are so many types of fresh pastries, cookies, tarts, and loaves to choose from.

Vanden Broek oversees the bread-making program including their artisanal sourdough loaves made with their own starter, La Fontaine. "It's ironic in a way, because as a kid I hated bread. I came up with all kinds of ways to hide it so I didn't have to eat it!" Now, Vanden Broek "listens to her fingers" and reads the dough so she doesn't rip the gluten or shape the loaves too tight.

Both Schipper and Vanden Broek grew up near Fort Macleod and are thrilled to have their bakery on Main Street. Schipper is from Monarch and Vanden Broek grew up on Broek Pork Acres (see page 275), her parents' pasture-fed Berkshire pig farm near Coalhurst. Using local produce and supporting other small businesses and producers is a priority for them. "We believe quality ingredients produce a quality product. We source our flours from a mill in Lethbridge, our organic flour comes from Highwood Crossing Foods (see page 274), and we use Mans Eggs from Galimax Trading (see page 250)—lots of them."

Every day, half a dozen locals come in and enjoy a pastry and some coffee. "We didn't expect it but it sure makes us happy. They feel they belong here and because of their support, so do we."

Zucchini Blossom Market and Café | 50-3 Street NE, Medicine Hat
403-526-1630 | zucchiniblossom.com

Kristine Dalzell. Photo by Rose Sanchez.

Kristine and James Dalzell had just started a family. "We were talking about opening a business; little did I know he had already leased a space a block from our house. He told me three months after he did it. We cashed in all of our savings to renovate the space."

The Zucchini Blossom Market and Café opened in March 2004. It started as an organic produce market and grocery with a small café. "We'd get most of the organic produce from California and it had a short shelf life so we used it in the café." Pretty soon, the café took off and with challenges getting produce certain times of year and another vegetable market opening up nearby, the Dalzells stopped selling produce in 2007 to focus on the café and grocery store.

When her husband passed away in 2014, Kristine continued to run the Zucchini Blossom and raise her sons with support from her family and community. "I have very loyal customers and am so grateful to be a part of this neighbourhood." Her customers feel exactly the same way.

In 2015, the Zucchini Blossom was voted one of most loved small businesses in Canada by her customers. She and three others co-won the Canadian Federation of Independent Business and Interac contest in recognition of their contributions to their community. That same year, the Zucchini Blossom moved into the space next door as they needed a bigger kitchen and better cooking equipment.

Everything from quiche to muffins to salads to pie are homemade from scratch in the café. Kristine still lives a block away and uses and features as many local producers and artisans on her menu as she can. The bread comes from Redcliff Bakery, Creekside Coffee Roasting provides their java, and Grainworks (see page 272) delivers right to their door. "If there's one thing I don't get tired of, it's hearing how much people love my baking. People really love our food and you can see it in their eyes and hear it in their voice . . . . That's why I can't imagine doing anything else."

Chinook Honey Company and Chinook Arch Meadery | 386087 16 Street West, Okotoks | 403-995-0830 | chinookhoney.com

Cherie and Art Andrews. Photo by Leah Hennel.

Art and Cherie Andrews may have silver hair but they seem to have tapped into a golden fountain of youth working with bees, honey, and mead. While still a commercial pilot, Art began beekeeping as a hobby with two hives in 1995. He had 10 in year two and 50 the following year. Now, in their retirement, the Andrewses care for 150 hives and run a thriving retail store, bee education centre, and honey-wine meadery. They also add value to their honey by making their own pickles and chutneys and by collaborating with local businesses like Evelyn's Memory Lane to make ice creams and Fiasco Gelato for unique gelato flavours.

When Cherie retired in 2004 she started a retail outlet with just 150 square feet. Now, they have 25,000 square feet on their property south of Okotoks, which sits high on a knoll, facing due west toward the Rockies. They work like the bees they admire, attending to visiting school groups, families stopping in for ice cream, and wine connoisseurs tasting their award-winning meads. With over 25,000 visitors a year they've won awards from Travel Alberta as the Rural Tourism Champion and from Alberta Agriculture for Farm Direct Marketer of the Year in 2015.

Twice they've represented Canada's beekeepers at Slow Food International's Terra Madre in Italy. We joke about their failure as retirees and when pressed on what keeps them going Cherie says, "It's people's curiosity about bees. I love being able to satisfy that." For Art, it's the fact that "only bees can make honey—humans have tried to recreate it, but they cannot get the humidity right. In nature, only bees were given the ability to achieve the perfect humidity to keep honey from fermenting and to produce a substance that will never spoil." That will keep Art and Cherie Andrews going for some time to come and our lives are sweeter for it.

Medicine Hat Meat Traders | 5016 Township Road 132, Cypress County
403-488-1344 | mhmt.ca

Left to right: Ben, Jackson, Joanne, and Greg Pahl; Robin and Hudson Pahl (seated). Photo by Rose Sanchez.

Greg Pahl's grandfather came from the United States in 1934 and bought a tract of land outside of Medicine Hat. For 70 years, generations of the Pahl family ranched there. Greg and Joanne were bringing up their family and raising cattle and hogs until 2003, when bovine spongiform encephalopathy (BSE), or mad cow disease, was discovered in Alberta. "When the BSE crisis hit, we knew we had to move up the value chain in order to survive."

That led Greg to Olds College where he enrolled in the Meat Processing program. After earning his certification, Greg built a small butcher shop and smokehouse on their land. On January 1, 2006, Medicine Hat Meat Traders (MHMT) opened its doors, selling a range of products including steaks, roasts, sausage, stuffed peppers, and beef jerky.

There were a lot of new things for Greg to get used to. "I had ranched my whole life. In one day at the farmers' market, I'd see and talk to more people than I would in a year when I had cattle." Still, he welcomed the opportunity to connect with his customers and get feedback on his products.

Over time, Greg noticed sales of his soft beef jerky steadily increasing. "We are very passionate about making a high-quality product with Alberta beef. We grind up a mixture of muscle groups to make our jerky. Then we add seasonings, forming the meat into strips before smoking and drying them."

As demand grew, Greg and his family decided to focus exclusively on producing their craft beef jerky. In 2013, they added a second smokehouse to keep up with demand and Greg's son, Jackson, took over production after completing the Meat Processing program at Olds (like his dad). "My favourite thing is working with my family and watching the next generation make the business their own. We are very blessed to have this life."

MHMT's jerky is available in seven flavours and they're always working on new ones. Order online at their jerky shop or look out for them at one of the 15 farmers' markets and 40 retailers in Alberta that carry their products.

Old Country Sausage Shop | Golf Course Road, Raymond | 403-752-3006
oldcountrysausages.com

Chris Bragg, owner of Old Country Sausage Shop.
Photo by Matilde Sanchez-Turri.

When you walk into the Old Country Sausage Shop, it's like you are stepping back in time. The walls are as seasoned with cherry wood smoke as the sausages in the deli case.

Chris Bragg, the new owner of Old Country Sausage Shop, has eaten his fair share of cured meats travelling throughout North America and Europe. He moved to Calgary from Northern Ontario in 2010 to set up a business. Living a busy lifestyle, Bragg relied on snacks and ready-made foods to keep going. Finding food he could eat on the go that was made from pure ingredients was a challenge.

"I came across Old Country Sausage pepperoni at Community Natural Foods and was struck by how good it tasted. It was local and had a clean ingredient list, which I really liked." After a few years of eating different products that they made, Bragg called the owners, Klaus and Mary Lee Schurmann.

"Originally, I wanted to help them build and grow their business by leveraging technology, which is something I specialize in." But, the Schurmanns were looking to slow down and they ended up selling the business to Bragg in March of 2017. Bragg and his team at Old Country Sausage Shop continue making all the same products using the Schurmanns' tried-and-true recipes.

Slow Food principles, like using sustainably raised meat from local producers such as Rangeland Bison and Top Grass Cattle (see page 283), are vital. All the products are naturally smoked and do not contain binders, fillers, MSG, artificial colouring, or added nitrites. The sausages are still made the same way the Schurmanns made them, with just meat, herbs, spices, and sea salt. And that won't change.

"We are merging technology with tradition to preserve the authenticity and artisanal quality of our products while we scale up. Making high-quality sausage and cured meats is essential but so is getting it into more people's hands at an affordable price."

Check the website for retailers throughout Alberta carrying Old Country Sausage Shop bacon, ham, and sausages or stop by their store.

Fairwinds Farm | Fort Macleod | 403-553-0127 | fairwindsfarm.ca

Anita and Ben Oudshoorn with their milking goats. Photo by Karen Anderson.

Just off the QE2 highway, close to Fort Macleod, Fairwinds Farm lies nestled at the base of a hill, which protects it from the strong western winds the area is known for. A lone tree marks the turn for the driveway. A gravel lane cuts through the pastures leading up to the farmyard where a shelterbelt of trees and a broad expanse of lawn separate Ben and Anita Oudshoorn's family home from the gabled roof of their goat barn and cheese processing facility.

The Oudshoorns started keeping a few goats in 1994 after discovering their youngest daughter had an intolerance to cow's milk. The family drank their fill of milk and Anita and Ben made soft cheese and yogurt with the surplus.

Stock cattle and farrow-to-finish hogs were the base of their operation then, but when the hog market crashed in 1998 things changed dramatically. "We had to sell our cattle and I found a job in order to keep the farm," says Ben. A year later they bought 20 goats and began selling milk.

By 2003, the Oudshoorns had a plan for going organic and scaling up to commercial cheese production. But, they needed more land so they bought Fairwinds, enabling them to grow their own organic forage for winters and give the herd access to organic pastures in summer. Fairwinds achieved its organic certification in 2007. Their goats are bred once per year, each fall. They do not use synthetic methods or hormones to induce breeding outside of their natural cycle. The mothers receive an organic whole-grain treat twice daily during milking. "Goats don't eat garbage. That's a total myth. They are smart, very social, and love attention."

While chèvre (soft cheese) and feta were their first cheese products, they've added hard aged cheddars and Goudas and now have a line of fine French-inspired goat's cheeses in delicate pyramid, cylinder, and wheel shapes. Some are coated in vegetable ash, others have washed rinds. "Our artisanal products allow us to overcome the challenges of competing in the open market. We are proud that our products are made locally, sustainably, and are of the highest quality." Look for them in organic markets and fine dining establishments throughout Alberta.

Noble Meadows Farm | noblemeadowfarms.com

Carolyn Van Driesten.
Photo by Matilde Sanchez-Turri.

Noble Meadows Farm began as a goat milk supplier to a local cheesemaker in 2005. Finding it difficult to generate income from selling a commodity, Harvey and Carolyn Van Driesten and their family built a provincially licensed and inspected processing plant on their farm in 2010.

The decision to start making value-added products was a natural progression for the family. "We had always been interested in making cheese and yogurt and wanted to work together to create something as a family. We do everything from start to finish ourselves, so it's hard work—but very rewarding." The Van Driestens were recognized in 2014 when they won Best Farmstead Cheese at the Canadian Cheese Awards for their Plain Soft Goat Cheese.

Noble Meadows has 350 goats (mostly Saanen and Alpine breeds) that are milked twice a day. The milk is piped underground to the plant where it is processed the same day. Carolyn pasteurizes the milk and bottles some, then turns the rest into yogurt, cheese, and ice cream. "I make all of our products by hand using small-batch recipes we've developed."

Harvey grew up on a dairy farm, so overseeing the milking, feeding, and care of the herd is second nature to him. The goats get access to the pasture as soon as the grass is green in mid-April. They spend winter in the barn with lots of room to eat, exercise, and explore. They are fed locally grown alfalfa as well as a special grain ration.

If you aren't sure whether you like goat cheese, Noble Meadows products have a high conversion rate because their milk is milder and not as "goaty" as many others. "Our goats are never given synthetic hormones. We feed them prebiotics and probiotics to keep them healthy and remove animals we've had to treat from the milking herd." Pinpointing why their cheese is so delicious is difficult, but we're pretty sure their happy goats are a big part of it.

Old West Ranch | Mountain View | 403-653-2331 | farm@oldwestranch.ca

James Meservy with Hannah and Brody.
Photo by Karen Anderson.

The year 2018 marks a major milestone in the cheesemaking career of James Meservy. After 18 years of investment in Alberta's first water buffalo herd—and many false starts in producing his famous *mozzarella di bufala*—he will finally have his own federally inspected cheese processing facility.

Meservy was living in Texas when the call came from his in-laws needing to retire from their ranch near Waterton. Meservy and his wife Debra decided taking over as the fifth generation would offer their family a life closer to their values. They moved from Houston in 2000 and vowed to find a way to make farming sustainable for their children's future. Enter the water buffalo.

Meservy reasoned that if he could find a greatly desired niche food product (that incredible cheese) and make it in Alberta, then he might have the missing link in farming sustainability. While teaching at the University of Lethbridge, he researched water buffalo herds in North America and visited herds in British Columbia, Vermont, Michigan, and Quebec before finally finding a willing seller in central California in 2009. Chefs in Calgary couldn't get enough of his product and it was featured at all the best places.

"It's been a roller coaster ever since. The animals are great and we have 36 cows and two bulls now. The challenge was always to find a place to process." After his third strikeout at borrowing time in others' facilities, he vowed not to start up again until he had a place of his own.

"I had to sell land to buy the building. My banker wouldn't lend me money. We decided to do it on our own. The entire family went to Italy this summer to the Tenuta Vannulo factory to see where this cheese comes from. We want to show that we can do the same thing here."

We walk out to meet these docile and curious creatures and, seeing and hearing Meservy, they come to meet us halfway. Hopefully, the lineup for Old West Ranch cheese will be all the way from here in Waterton to Wood Buffalo National Park in the north.

Vital Green Farms | Picture Butte | 403-634-1197 | vitalgreen.ca

Left to right, back: Dimo the dog, Levi, Coralee, and Mitchell Mans; front: Remy, Caleb, Caroline, and Joe Mans. Photo by Matilde Sanchez-Turri.

Joe and Caroline Mans and their family started Vital Green Farms in 2004. They are a certified organic dairy and have their own processing plant on site. They started milking their own cows when they couldn't find any organic, natural milk for their family. As Mans says, "milk is not just milk."

If you ask him what he means, he says, "I'm a forage farmer more than a dairy farmer. I feed the soil so the plants my cows graze on have all the vitamins and minerals they need to be healthy and produce nutritious milk." Mans regularly tests his soil and amends it to keep everyone in the food chain healthy.

They pasture their herd during the summer and supplement their diet with vitamins and minerals to make sure their animals are in optimal condition. Mans grows all of his own winter feed including alfalfa, prairie grasses, clover, barley salad, hay, and grain. If a cow in their herd becomes sick, Mans uses organic approved methods to treat the animal.

Organic producers like Vital Green Farms don't use herbicides, pesticides, or fungicides on their land, because they kill important micro-organisms in the soil. They also don't use genetically modified organisms or synthetic hormones.

Vital Green Farms is the only organic dairy in Alberta that doesn't homogenize its milk and pasteurizes at a low temperature for a longer period (64 degrees Celsius for half an hour instead of 76 degrees for 30 seconds) to preserve as much of its nutrients as possible. For most, all of this extra effort is too much, but for Mans and his family it's the only way. "I love working with nature, tending to the soil, the plants, and cows to influence the process and produce milk and products we feel good about sharing."

Look for Vital Green products including milk, yogurt, heavy cream, crème fraîche, sour cream, kefir, buttermilk, and cheese at more than 30 grocery and health food stores in the province or buy direct at the farm.

Angel Harper and Jaclyn Geddes | Mocha Cabana | 317 4 Street South, Lethbridge | 403-329-6243 | mochacabana.ca

Jaclyn Geddes (left) and Angel Harper.
Photo by Matilde Sanchez-Turri.

Distinguished by its Spanish colonial facade and barrel-vault roof, the historic Bell Building once housed a thriving welding shop. Now, it's the home of Mocha Cabana, Lethbridge locals' favourite farm-to-table restaurant.

Angel Harper and Jaclyn Geddes were co-workers and friends long before they opened Mocha Cabana. Both are trained chefs and met while working in the food service supply industry. Sharing an unwavering commitment to their community and all things local, Harper and Geddes source all of their ingredients from producers in the region. If they run out of local products before their next delivery, they stop serving the menu item. For Harper and Geddes it's not just about freshness and flavour; they see every partnership as a commitment. "Around here we always say, 'Do the right thing,' which isn't always the easiest thing. For us, our values guide us and are the foundation of our success."

Beyond the plate, Harper and Geddes source craft beer, mead, and spirits from Alberta brewers and distillers for their beverage list. They regularly hire musicians from the area for fundraisers and to entertain guests during special events. They even commission florists, and local artists to paint eye-catching murals throughout the restaurant.

Upholding their pledge to nourish and sustain their community extends to their hiring practices too. The pair supports the Lethbridge College culinary program in many ways. They hire apprentices and Red Seal chefs so the next wave gains exposure to local ingredients and develops a deeper awareness of Alberta's signature foods.

To ensure both front of house and kitchen staff understand how different ingredients are grown and why they're so special, Harper and Geddes close the restaurant to the public one evening each spring. They host a dinner for their employees and invite all of the farmers and ranchers to attend so everyone can meet, break bread together and learn from one another. "We're proud of what's grown locally and of our producers and think it's important to bring things full circle so our servers can share their story with our guests."

Sweetsmith Candy Co. | 214E Canal Court, Strathmore | 587-889-2567
sweetsmithcandyco.com

Dannah Davies, owner and confectioner at Sweetsmith Candy Co. Photo by Matilde Sanchez-Turri.

Dannah Davies's initiation into the world of candy making didn't start off so sweet. Her family had moved to Arizona. Davies was 15 years old and her father, a computer teacher, had just started a tutoring company when the recession hit. To make enough money for rent, the family got creative.

They looked at what they had, which happened to be some peanuts, and pulled some money together for sugar. Using a four-generations-old family recipe, Davies, her mom, and her younger brother made peanut brittle. Davies's father sold the brittle in parking lots and at car washes. Over time, sales grew and Davies helped her mom with production until she turned 18 and moved back to Alberta to go to school.

Enrolled in the entrepreneurship program at Mount Royal University, she worked two jobs to pay her way. During her first semester, she was struck by the fact that many of her professors had never run a business, let alone owned one. Her thought was, "You don't know what you haven't experienced." So, she made a bold move.

Already familiar with the ins and outs of starting and running a candy manufacturing company, she took a break from the program and started Sweetsmith Candy Co. in 2012 with the $6,000 she had saved for university. She began selling her handcrafted brittle once a week at farmers' markets in and around Calgary and demand for her candy soared.

"I have several dietary sensitivities and know there isn't a lot that's safe to enjoy or that tastes good for people with certain restrictions." Every flavour of Sweetsmith Candy Co. brittle is gluten-free and egg-free. There is also vegan, vegetarian, soy-free and nut-free and even sugar-free brittle for diabetics.

As much as Davies loves making and eating candy, her ultimate goal is to create happiness for her staff through their work environment and for her customers through the treats she creates. Visit the Sweetsmith Candy Co. store and factory in person or check online for a full selection of flavours and allergy information.

Galimax Trading Inc. | Nobleford | 403-715-8470 or 403-315-1093
galimaxtrading.com

*Left to right: Rudy Knitel with partner
Corne Mans and his brother Joshua Mans.
Photo by Matilde Sanchez-Turri.*

After farming for 25 years, Rudy Knitel moved into the export business, selling hay to countries in Europe, the Middle East, and Asia. He often travelled to Italy and was really impressed by the food. "I wouldn't consider myself a foodie but after eating there, I couldn't believe how delicious everything tasted."

In 2001, he established Galimax Trading Inc. with his wife Faye and an Italian partner and began importing fine Italian foods to sell to hotel and restaurant clients throughout Alberta. After an issue with a shipment, Faye suggested they source and distribute locally grown foods instead. By 2005, they had stopped importing Italian goods altogether to focus on marketing and distributing locally grown products of the highest quality.

"Most producers run smaller operations and are already putting everything they have into their farm and families. It's too much extra work for them to do the marketing and deliver all on their own without the time, skills, contacts, and equipment." With Rudy's network, persistence, and 13,000-square-foot Canadian Food Inspection Agency–approved warehouse, Galimax fills a major gap in the marketplace by putting high-quality artisanal foods into the hands of chefs, restaurants, hotels, and retailers who value it.

While visiting the organic dairy Vital Green Farms (see page 247) in 2010, Rudy met Corne Mans. Impressed by his work ethic, understanding of the business, and great sense of humour, he invited Corne to become his partner at Galimax Trading.

Together, they sell locally grown vegetables, fruit, dairy products, and eggs along with some specialty items such as honey and maple syrup, delivering twice a week to clients throughout Alberta. "We have a very close relationship with the farmers we work with and represent. They are the stars of this show and we're proud to help them get a fair price for their products so they continue to grow our food in sustainable ways."

Umami Shop | 814 4 Avenue South, Lethbridge | 403-328-8899
umamishop.ca

Patricia Luu and Sven Roeder.
Photo by Matilde Sanchez-Turri.

Nothing makes Patricia Luu and Sven Roeder happier than giving people the opportunity to live their life philosophy: "Eat and laugh. Together." After travelling the world, they launched their first (and still successful) Umami Shop in Chalon-sur-Saône, France, with Luu's sister in 2009. Returning to Luu's hometown, Lethbridge, they opened their own version of this world grocery boutique and cooking school concept in 2013.

Umami is recognized as the fifth taste after sweet, sour, bitter, and salty. Naturally occurring in many foods, the umami taste was discovered by Kikunae Ikeda, a Japanese chemistry professor. The word means "savouriness," but on the tongue it's what makes a food taste delicious. It leaves us wanting more and is an inspiring name for a food business.

The Umami Shop brings together Luu and Roeder's love of food and travel and represents a natural progression for Luu, who grew up in the food industry working alongside her Vietnamese parents at their Asian supermarket. "One of the first connections we make with a culture is with their food and we wanted to eliminate the frustration many people have when trying to recreate exotic dishes they've eaten on a trip or seen in a cookbook," she says.

Prioritizing quality, freshness, and authenticity, the grocery boutique helps cooks by stocking ingredients from near and far in one convenient place. On-site cooking lessons in the bright, open kitchen are an invitation to play and discover those ingredients plus culinary techniques, delicious new flavours, and recipes from around the globe—without having to venture far from home.

The Umami Shop also features a bakery, deli, kombucha taps, catering, and eat-in lunch or to-go dining options in their café. They regularly host food tastings to showcase local food artisans. Luu and Roeder have made it their mission to elevate people's quality of life in their community and beyond, by enabling them to explore food together.

Urban Grocer | 1016 9 Avenue South, Lethbridge | 403-942-6922
urbangrocer.ca

Julia Mitchell. Photo by Matilde Sanchez-Turri.

Julia Mitchell wanted to start an environmentally and ethically conscious business that aligned with her values. She bought the Urban Grocer in October of 2014 from Cheryl Meheden, who had converted a convenience store into a local food market, sourcing artisanal foods and gluten-free, organic products.

Mitchell embraced Meheden's original vision for the Urban Grocer and expanded upon it. Now, the store is teeming with local delicacies from bakers, ranchers, farmers, and crafters. There are fresh, specialty, and staple items including bread, organic produce, ice cream, soup and sandwiches, gluten-free choices, ready-made foods, preserves, fresh coffee from Red Engine Coffee Roasters, and ethically sourced meats including beef, chicken, pork, and bison. "Our goal is to keep the distance our products travel to a minimum. We primarily source locally made and homegrown products, year-round. This way, we can provide healthy and sustainable food to our customers."

For Mitchell, filling the shelves and coolers with food from artisans she knows not only tastes better, but also feels right. Prioritizing social and environmental factors with economic ones is part of the value-based business model Mitchell uses to run the Urban Grocer.

Before Mitchell became a business owner, she earned her permaculture certification from Verge Permaculture (see page 186) and had her own hobby farm with a passive solar greenhouse. She raised chickens and grew her own vegetables. She has a keen understanding of what producers face and is very mindful of how she lives, always looking for ways to prevent waste. Synergy Urban Farms (a local Small Plot INtensive farmer) collects the store's spent coffee grounds for composting and a local chicken farmer receives produce that can no longer be sold.

"We really care about the producers we work with, the products they create, and the community we serve." Managing inventory from more than 70 local suppliers has its challenges but Mitchell sees it as her way of giving families access to unique, healthy foods and helping the local economy thrive with as small an environmental footprint as possible.

Full Circle Adventures | Turner Valley | 403-933-4432
fullcircleadventures.com

Julie Walker. Photo by Karen Anderson.

"I took the summer of 2017 to go deeper into nature." Julie Walker's connection with nature is already fathoms deeper than most humans'. Born and raised in Calgary, she took photojournalism at the Southern Alberta Institute of Technology (SAIT) before finding the path that led her to her happy place, a degree in outdoor pursuits at the University of Calgary.

Working as a guide, she was familiar with plant names but when she picked up Terry Willard's *Edible and Medicinal Plants of the Rocky Mountains and Neighbouring Territories* she began to see the connections between each plant in nature and with human preservation as well. "I fell in love with the earth."

Since founding Full Circle Adventures in 1998, her focus has been on helping others deepen their connection with nature. On her foraging expeditions edibles might include pennycress, dandelion leaves and roots, burdock root, lamb's quarters, strawberry blite, sheep sorrel, curly dock, stinging nettle, plantain, horseradish, wild asparagus, and mushrooms like morels, shaggymane, and puffballs. Leading annual wild-food day retreats with the SAIT chefs has increased Walker's knowledge of ways to prepare nature's bounty, and colleagues like *The Boreal Herbal* author Beverley Gray have helped her learn to process wild herbs and seeds for taste-based or medicinal teas.

Wanting to take things still further, Walker studied for four years to attain elder status with the Institute for Contemporary Shamanic Studies. Lessons were based on the ancient teachings of Deer Tribe Métis Medicine Society in Arizona. The elders of that tribe realized that their knowledge had to be shared with more than their own people for it to be carried forth. Each expedition with Walker starts with asking for permission to be on the land and a smudge and gift of tobacco. She also acknowledges the people of Treaty 7, the first people of the land where she usually roams.

Check the website for current offerings. "Harvesting is the easy part. From now on we'll do more gathering and I'll also focus on processing workshops. It's much more fun to do with a group."

Note: Did you know Alberta has a mushroom enthusiasts' club with annual forays all over our province? Check out the Alberta Mycological Society at wildmushrooms.ws.

Eau Claire Distillery | 113 Sunset Boulevard NW, Turner Valley
403-933-5408 | eauclairedistillery.ca

David Farran with a wee dram of Eau Claire's first whisky release. Photo by Karen Anderson.

David Farran was born and raised in Millarville. At age 20 he was the first employee hired by Ed McNally for his Big Rock Brewery. Farran did whatever was needed. Attracting master brewer and distiller Larry Kerwin to put the craft into their brewing was key to their success.

"Ed encouraged me to get an education." Farran earned an economics degree in two years, worked in the British diplomatic corps, got an M.B.A., and ran successful travel and veterinarian companies. He returned to Big Rock in the '90s as senior management.

In 2005, he bought a Turner Valley ranch and fulfilled a dream of growing and harvesting grains using only horse and plow. "We didn't grow enough barley to sell to the wheat pool but I wanted to do something with it. I found out that a lot of Scottish whisky is made with Alberta barley and that Alberta did not have a single malt whisky maker. I had witnessed what craft had done for beer so I called up Larry and asked if he'd like to start fine distillation in Alberta."

After three years of hurdles they got legislation changed to allow their micro facility to open. Kerwin's abilities are complemented by Scottish master distiller Caitlyn Quinn. Kerwin thinks it's unlikely he'll see their first whisky barrels reach their 25-year status, but Quinn will.

A tour group enters the distillery. They watch as some of the 20,000 tons of Alberta barley—all produced at Farran's ranch or nearby national historic site Bar U Ranch—is shovelled into the mash. They admire the giant copper kettles and peek into the barrel room to check out the oloroso sherry and French oak casks purchased to age the whisky.

Gins and vodka have been sold for a few years now. The whisky will be released in December of 2017. Farran pulls a wee bottle from a drawer and pours a dram. The buttery kiss of those sherry casks has left its lipstick on the cheek of this whisky. A love affair has begun.

Field Stone Fruit Wines | 251073A Township Road 232, Strathmore
403-934-2749 | fieldstonefruitwines.com

Elaine and Marvin Gill.
Photo by Matilde Sanchez-Turri.

Elaine and Marvin Gill both come from a long line of homesteaders. "We love being on the land," says Marvin.

In 1998, they bought a quarter section (160 acres) of flat prairie just south of Strathmore, and over a two-year period, they planted more than 50 acres of saskatoon, raspberry, strawberry, and chokecherry bushes. Once the plants matured, they opened a U-pick operation called Bumbleberry Orchard and fruit lovers flocked to the farm to pick as many berries as their pails would hold.

The Gills follow biological farming practices. They regularly test and amend their soil with life-promoting organic matter rich with nutrients. "This is why our berries are so juicy and full of flavour." They do not use pesticides or fungicides and use tillage to control weeds, aerate the soil, and allow for proper drainage.

Eventually their fruit yields were so bountiful the U-pickers couldn't keep up and the Gills had to come up with a way to use the fruit that would otherwise be wasted. Alberta Agriculture approached them with the idea of making fruit wine and in 2005, Field Stone Fruit Wines became Alberta's first estate winery.

Working with Dominic Rivard, a world-renowned fruit wine maker, they bottled their first wine made with their fruit. At first, they found people reluctant to "drink outside the grape wine category" but after enticing them with tastings and winning countless awards, they amassed a loyal following both locally and internationally.

The wines are made using Alberta-grown fruit exclusively, with 75 percent of it grown on site in their own orchard. They freeze the berries to extract as much juice as possible, then each small batch is made separately and blended into the different wines just before bottling. Fruit wines don't need to be aged, though the Gills have two oaked varieties that are.

"There's one pound of fruit in every bottle of Field Stone Fruit wine." The wines can be purchased online, at 100 different retailers and farmers' markets throughout Alberta, and—where it all began—at the winery.

Spirit Hills Honey Winery | 240183 2380 Drive West, Millarville
403-933-3913 | spirithillswinery.com

Left to right: Hugo, Ilse, and Bjorn Bonjean.
Photo by Matilde Sanchez-Turri.

The creation of Spirit Hills Honey Winery "was the culmination of many factors colliding," says Hugo Bonjean, who, along with his wife Ilse, daughter Amber, and sons Bjorn and Fabian, opened Spirit Hills' doors in December of 2012. A major contributing factor was the family's lifestyle.

The Bonjeans have lived entirely off the land for over a decade. They have chickens for eggs, buy organic grain to make their bread, and hunt game with bow and arrow for meat. "We eat fruit and vegetables from our garden in season, then freeze, can, and dry the rest." They only buy staples like spices, grains, salt, and oil.

In 2011, they brought two beehives onto the farm and saw their vegetable yield increase by 50 percent with the bonus of a wildflower honey harvest too. Coming from a long line of French winemakers, Bonjean came up with the idea to turn their excess honey into wine. The honey winery also evolved from their desire to work with their adult children and to make something they all enjoyed consuming.

They now have 300 hives and ferment their honey using traditional techniques, adding locally grown fruits, flowers, and spices to create their unique food-friendly honey wines. "Most people don't realize that the flavour profile of mead is as diverse as wine and beer put together." Since 2013, their honey wines have won awards year after year from the Alberta Beverage Awards as well as the North-West Wine Summit.

The Bonjeans have big plans for 2018 and beyond. They will be starting their own black currant orchard and Alberta's first grape vineyard. They'll follow the same organic and biodynamic practices that make their honey wines so special. "The local food scene is a key building block for a sustainable society." The Bonjean family prove that every day by the way they live and make their honey wine.

Winery tours and tastings are available from April to October. You'll also find Spirit Hills honey wines in more than 200 liquor stores, restaurants, bars, and farmers' markets in Alberta and Saskatchewan. Check their website for details.

Broxburn Vegetables and Café | 90008 Range Road 210, Lethbridge
403-327-0909 | broxburn-vegetables.com

Hilda and Paul de Jonge.
Photo by Matilde Sanchez-Turri.

Born and raised on an onion farm in Holland, Paul de Jonge always knew he'd have his own piece of land and make a living from it one day. "Farming is in my blood and it's a lifestyle we wanted our children to experience."

Paul's family immigrated to Canada when he was in high school. After graduating, he worked as a farmhand at the neighbour's where he met Hilda, now his wife.

In 1994, Paul and Hilda got their dream of raising their children on the farm. Broxburn Vegetables and Café started as a U-pick strawberry operation with a house just big enough for their growing family. In 1996, they built a greenhouse to grow peppers. By 2000, Paul decided it was time to leave his role as controller at a software company and work on the farm full-time.

By 2001, a larger greenhouse was added to grow tomatoes, cucumbers, and other vegetables including eggplant, lettuce, and beans. With a three-acre greenhouse teeming with produce, Paul and Hilda remodelled the barn the following year to set up a retail space to sell their extra vegetables. Before long, a café was added to welcome guests year-round looking to experience "plant-to-plate" cuisine, the de Jonges' specialty.

"Our focus is on producing fresh, flavourful vegetables in the most natural way and with the smallest environmental footprint possible." To prevent damage to their crops without using harmful chemicals, they release insects into the greenhouse that naturally prey on pests and use only organic-grade sprays such as biological bacteria sparingly, when needed.

Whether you're after fresh produce or craving a piece of pie, Broxburn Vegetables and Café is worth the trip any time of year. Their ever-bearing strawberry patch starts producing fruit in early summer and continues sporadically in flushes through to the fall. "Our strawberries are exclusively for U-pickers and the best berries are in October. The cool nights make them unbelievably sweet and flavourful. Come pick some...you can thank us later."

Busy Bea's Market Garden | Lethbridge | 403-553-2343
busybeasmarketgarden.com

Certified Organic Produce

Trevor Aleman and his children sell certified organic produce at the Exhibition Park Farmers' Market in Lethbridge. Photo by Matilde Sanchez-Turri.

You won't hear too many people say they farm organically for stress relief, but Trevor and Cindy Aleman and their six kids do. As tough as organic farming is, taking care of the earth and the next generation are values the couple live by and instill in their children every day.

While Trevor enjoys being a full-time teacher he says, "I always look forward to getting my hands in the dirt whenever I have the chance." The oldest of seven siblings, he and his family took over Busy Bea's Market Garden in 1999 from his parents, John and Bea Aleman, who were looking to slow down.

Finding him at the bustling Lethbridge Farmers' Market was easy. He said, "You'll be able to smell my herbs from 10 feet away, they're so fragrant." And he wasn't kidding.

Busy Bea's Market Garden offers only certified organic produce, with most of it grown less than 50 kilometres from where it's sold. "We harvest the night before to maximize freshness and nutrition." Most of the vegetables and herbs sold at Busy Bea's, such as potatoes, onions, beans, and zucchini, are grown on the family farm in the Oldman River valley just outside of Fort Macleod.

Along with growing, Aleman also resells local fruit and vegetables including melons, corn, cucumbers, and nightshade vegetables (tomatoes, peppers, and eggplant) from Mans Organics (see page 262). He also sells organic root vegetables from the Leffer Brothers and an array of seasonal fruits from Blush Lane Organic Orchard in Keremeos, BC.

You can find Busy Bea's flavourful, organic produce at any of the Blush Lane Organic markets in Calgary and at the Lethbridge Farmers' Market every Saturday from May to October. During the winter months, customers can sign up for Busy Bea's Winter Box program.

Forage & Farm | Millarville | forageandfarm.com

Cheryl Greisinger. Photo by Marnie Bukhart.

After working 20 years in the energy sector, Cheryl Greisinger longed for a less complicated life and deeper connection with nature. "I was looking for humane and ethically raised foods but had troubles finding them." In 2009, Greisinger and her husband James (a blacksmith) bought a small farm west of Millarville. "I found growing our food very therapeutic because I knew where it was coming from. We knew we wanted to raise our family this way even though neither of us came from farms."

While on maternity leave with her first child in 2012, Greisinger got six beehives and began beekeeping. In 2014, while on her second maternity leave, Greisinger received certification from Verge

Permaculture (see page 186) and the following year established Forage & Farm, her regenerative homestead, based on permaculture design principles.

Her family's main crop is hard-neck garlic. They grow seven types on one-acre plots that they rotate every year. Greisinger and her husband seed the garlic by hand in the fall with worm castings as fertilizer. They use non-desiccated straw (straw that hasn't been sprayed with Roundup) and their own seed, which is acclimatized to their unique terrain.

Forage & Farm is at the edge of the Rockies (4,200 feet above sea level) and only gets 100 frost-free growing days a year. "Hard-neck garlic grows really well here and we produce high-quality seed.

"From cracking the bulb to curing, our garlic has been handled at least nine times." Growing soft-neck garlic is easier because seeding can be mechanized, but it doesn't grow in Alberta. Hard-neck garlic is more flavourful anyway, and it also produces garlic scapes. Greisinger harvests the scapes in July and sells them fresh, but she also makes garlic scape pesto and powder. Her other specialty is black garlic.

Full bulbs of garlic are slowly aged under special conditions of heat and humidity. There are no additives, preservatives, or burning of any kind but the garlic turns black and takes on a mild, sweet, caramelized flavour. Look for Forage & Farm products at Mountain Mercato (see page 218) in Canmore or order direct on their website.

Jensen's Taber Corn | Taber | 403-223-8385 | jensenstabercorn.ca

David and Susan Jensen. Photo by Arica Jensen.

David Jensen is the third generation to farm the land he calls home. Married for over 46 years, David started growing corn when his wife Susan suggested it as a way for their children to earn some spending money. They started with three acres and planted two varieties. They harvested the corn by hand and trucked it to Calgary and the Crowsnest Pass and sold out. That was more than 35 years ago. Now, David and his son Jeremy grow and harvest 12 varieties of gourmet corn on 250 acres to sell at certified Taber Corn stands throughout Alberta.

If you want to know how to select the best cobs of corn, David will tell you his secret. "Pull the husk back and taste a few kernels. If it's good raw, I guarantee it'll be fantastic cooked." David inspects and tastes every variety in the field and before it's shipped. "It's important . . . . I'm looking at how flavourful it is, the texture, how full the cobs are, and how well the corn holds after picking."

According to David, what makes his corn so special is a combination of the soil, sun, water, and seed he uses. Corn grows best in well-irrigated, sandy loam soil with lots of sunshine. "Our land is well suited for corn and we use certified seeds from the USA; none are genetically modified organisms."

While David loves farming, when he looks out at his cornfield he can't help but be a bit worried about the future. "Getting food to the table is a lot more in-depth than most people realize. There are so many pressures and production costs are rising so fast it'd be next to impossible to get into farming now unless you inherit the land. Otherwise, it's a million-dollar investment, minimum."

Jensen's Taber Corn operates all of its own retail locations throughout the province. Ask to see the certificate of authenticity to be sure you're buying the real thing. You can also get your fill at the legendary Taber Cornfest, which takes place on the last weekend of August each year.

Kayben Farms | 316034 32 Street East, Okotoks | 403-995-5509
kayben.com

Judy and Claude Kolk, owners of Kayben Farms.
Photo by Matilde Sanchez-Turri.

Claude and Judy Kolk bought a quarter section (160 acres) of land outside of Okotoks in 1997. They had a lot of different business ideas for the property, but none took root until 2002, when they planted 25,000 black currant bushes and Kayben Farms was born.

They recruited their three daughters and niece to help weed the 20-acre orchard and were set for their first commercial crop in 2004, but a hard frost hit the orchard at blossom time. The following year, when the Kolks finally opened their U-pick, the price of black currants dropped—to 30 cents a pound. To help recover some of their investment, they starting processing their berries, increasing their value in the marketplace. They made pure unsweetened black currant juice and black currant punch base along with other farmstead creations like jams, jellies, and barbecue sauce. "We chose black currants for a few reasons, mostly because they're healthy, but also because no one else in the area had them at the time, and they thrive in marginal soil."

Once the U-pick was ticking along, the couple opened JoJo's Café in 2010 with their daughter Stephanie, a trained chef from the Southern Alberta Institute of Technology. The menu at JoJo's Café features fresh and healthy choices for the whole family as well as specialty coffees, beer, and wine. Claude even built a massive outdoor pizza oven at Stephanie's request.

While Judy oversees the ag tourism arm of the business, Claude runs the landscaping construction part of the operation. Their latest collaboration is the 12-acre Sunshine Adventure Park complete with a climbing wall, duck pond, picnic area, and pedal cart track. They add new attractions to the park every year and are excited to share the wonders of nature and farm life with the next generation. "We raised our daughters here and now we get to give our grandchildren and families a place to come and learn and have fun."

Kayben Farms hosts team-building events, birthday parties, school field trips, and their own seasonal festivals from May to October. "We are trying to recreate our childhood and build a place where kids can be kids."

Mans Organics | Coaldale | mansorganics.ca

Three generations of the Mans family.
Photo by Matilde Sanchez-Turri.

Mans Organics is "bringing greenhouse growing back to the soil." In 2007, Rita and Henk Mans converted their conventional farm to a certified organic operation. In 2012, their son Andrew and his wife Denise (and their five children) joined the farm as partners.

Putting his engineering background to work, Andrew built the greenhouse, but there was a condition: the facility would have to fit within the farm's organic model. "Hydroponic greenhouses cannot be certified organic. Only vegetables grown in soil can be."

Andrew visited numerous greenhouses throughout the province to gather information and best practices. He found some greenhouse operators still planting their crops in soil, but their produce wasn't organic. Most relied on conventional chemical fertilizers and pesticides. "Growing in soil (conventionally) is more costly and labour-intensive compared to hydroponic operations." Growing plants in soil organically requires even greater effort and knowledge. "They wished me luck."

In 2013, the Manses grew peppers, tomatoes, and cucumbers organically in their acre-wide greenhouse. In their fields, they produced organic onions, garlic, shallots, squash, and melons. "We feed the biology in the soil—the bacteria, fungi, and plant roots—with different amendments like alfalfa pellets and fish fertilizer. As a race, we grossly underestimate the complexity of nature's systems."

The Manses work with nature by planting non-GMO seeds and use natural predators within the greenhouse for pest control. "Soil is so full of life. Science doesn't understand it fully yet, but we're learning more and more all the time...and our soil gets better and better every year," says Henk. The more nutrient-dense the soil, the more flavourful the produce, and the Manses produce some of the most mouthwatering fruits and vegetables we've ever tasted.

While proving it can be done has been gratifying for the entire Mans family, Andrew is also extremely grateful. "We wanted our kids to be able to go into the greenhouse and eat anything they wanted without having to worry. Growing up this way is a privilege not many families have anymore." For a taste of Mans Organics produce, visit Busy Bea's Market Garden (see page 258) at the Lethbridge Farmers' Market or check the Mans Organics website for other retail partners.

Neubauer Farms | 6416 Township Road 122, Cypress County
403-580-9654 | neubauerfarms.ca

Mark and Nichole Neubauer. Photo by Heather Hart.

The Neubauer Family Century Farm was established north of Irvine, Alberta, in 1910. Knowing that only members of their family have owned and worked the land they live on gives Mark and Nichole Neubauer a great deal of pride. "We honour and respect this land and believe agriculture is the fundamental connection to life."

The Neubauers grew up in the country, so it was surprising for them to learn that most of the people they knew had never set foot on a farm or seen how food was grown. In fact, most of the students Nichole worked with as a special education teacher, and later in early interventions for Alberta Health Services, were many generations removed from rural life.

When Nichole decided to be on the farm full-time, she knew she wanted to continue working with children, use her skills as an educator, and share her passion for agriculture. She made her wish come true in 2005 when she launched the Growing Minds education program in partnership with Ag for Life. Through hands-on learning opportunities on their farm, children and adults from Medicine Hat and the surrounding areas get to experience farm life and see first-hand how their food is grown.

Since 2013, the Neubauers have also offered a Community Supported Agriculture program. Their all-natural one-acre market garden provides 30 families in the area with fresh, homegrown vegetables each week during the summer. Beyond that, it gives participating families the opportunity to reconnect with the land and shoulder some of the risk most farmers are left to bear on their own.

Over the years, the Neubauers have been in touch with more than 60,000 people through their agriculture-based outreach programs. In 2016, the Neubauers received the BMO Farm Family of the Year Award in recognition of the positive influence they've had in both agriculture and their community.

New Oxley Garlic | Claresholm | 403-625-5270 | newoxleygarlic.com

Jackie Chalmers at New Oxley Garlic Ranch.
Photo by Matilde Sanchez-Turri.

Jacqueline Chalmers, the Queen of Garlic, grew up on a century-old farm near Millarville. She and her husband bought part of the historic New Oxley Ranch west of Claresholm in 2006.

Formed in 1886, New Oxley Ranch was one of the largest cattle operations in Alberta. Willow Creek runs through the property and while Chalmers enjoyed seeing the wildlife passing through to drink from the creek, she was frustrated by the deer who would help themselves to whatever she grew. She asked an aunt for advice. "Turns out they don't like garlic and I wanted to plant something they wouldn't bother with but would grow well here." Chalmers got started by seeding 50 plants in 2008.

After a successful harvest, Chalmers planted thousands of cloves the following year, harvesting her first commercial crop of hard neck-garlic in 2010. "I do everything by hand. Planting, weeding, and harvesting." She plants in the fall so the roots set before the ground freezes. Each clove has to be placed the right way, whereas soft-neck garlic can be sown with machines. Hard-neck varieties are the most common type of garlic grown in Alberta because they are better suited to our climate.

The first thing Chalmers harvests are garlic scapes in early July. They are the soft, bright green flower stems and are highly sought after by chefs and home-cooks. Harvesting them also encourages the plant to send more energy into developing the bulb.

While chinook winds and drought affected her 2017 crop, Chalmers gets a lot of joy from growing garlic and enjoys the unique terroir of her plants every day. "I love all aspects of growing garlic, especially harvesting. I plan to do this as long as I physically can."

As the driving force behind the Slow Food International chapter in Southern Alberta, she is proud to produce "good, clean, fair" food free of pesticides, herbicides, and chemical fertilizers. Buy direct or check the website for a retailer near you.

Noble Gardens | Nobleford | 403-393-2059 | noblegardenscsa.com

Brenda and Tim Vrieselaar.
Photo by Matilde Sanchez-Turri.

Tim and Brenda Vrieselaar both grew up on farms and both valued the lifestyle so much they couldn't see themselves raising their nine children anywhere else. They started Noble Gardens, a Community Shared Agriculture (CSA) garden, in 2010, just outside of Nobleford, near Lethbridge.

The Vrieselaars prefer Community Shared Agriculture over the traditional term Community Supported Agriculture because, they say, members buy a *share* and for that share they receive a portion of the harvest for 16 weeks of the growing season starting in June. They also have winter shares available from November to March. Share types can be customized according to size (light, half, and full) and the type of produce they receive each week through a voucher program.

Nobles Gardens added two greenhouses in 2015 but most of their produce and fruit are grown in open fields on their 35 acres. "In summer, our share boxes contain about seven different types of vegetables. We seed our gardens according to the number of families who sign up and add some extra, to accommodate newcomers." While they have over 400 members, Noble Gardens can feed twice that and welcome new members from Calgary to Lethbridge. "All of our fruit and vegetables are harvested a maximum of two days before they are delivered so they are fresh and flavourful."

While they haven't pursued certification, Noble Gardens follows organic principles including crop rotation and use of fish fertilizers and green manure to feed their soil. All of their produce is grown chemical-free. "Soil health is very important; cover crops provide nutrients and smother weeds. We want our kids and anyone who comes here to be able to eat from the plant without worrying that there's anything on it that shouldn't be."

Noble Gardens also offers their CSA members opportunities for BC fruit shares, free-run egg shares from their own hens, and pasture-raised fresh chicken shares. Unlike many CSAs, Noble Gardens does not have a minimum work requirement for their members. However, members have an open invitation to visit the farm at any time, which we think is the nicest share option of all.

Paradise Hill Farm | 280011 Township Road 162, Nanton | 403-646-3276
paradisehillfarm.ca

Karen and Tony Legault.
Photo by Matilde Sanchez-Turri.

As you enter Paradise Hill's farm store, you'll see a sign with owners Tony and Karen Legault's mission statement on it: "To create great tasting tomatoes and basil as naturally as possible." The placard also thanks their customers for the important role they play in supporting their family-run operation and for choosing to shop locally.

Located less than 10 minutes east of Nanton, Paradise Hill started as a sheep farm and while the Legaults still have a small herd, since 2000, their focus has been on growing produce. Paradise Hill supplies all of the Calgary Co-op grocery stores with vine-ripened Big Dena beefsteak tomatoes and live basil. "It has been a great relationship and every year it's renewed with a handshake."

Over time, that relationship has only gotten stronger. "When we had a fire blaze through our property days before we were supposed to plant in January 2012, they said, 'You are our family, how can we help?' A couple weeks later, the Calgary Co-op VPs, members of the board and the produce managers from all the stores were out here helping us plant. It was amazing. Now, it's a tradition."

If you ask Tony what makes his tomatoes so special he'll tell you, but he prefers to show you. "Our tomatoes are ripened on the vine, picked, packaged, and delivered to Calgary Co-op stores the next day. My special nutrient mix is carried to the plants in Nanton water, which is some of the best in the world. Also, the cool air from the Porcupine Hills sweeps in here each night, causing the sugars in the tomatoes to concentrate, and that's a home run for taste."

Using water wisely is extremely important to the Legaults. "It's our most precious natural resource. I'm working on being a zero-waste water emitter. We already use the water from our tomatoes to grow the basil. Now, I'm working on using the basil water to grow fodder for the animals." That's just one more reason to find them at the farm gate or any Calgary Co-op.

Poplar Bluff Organics | Strathmore | 403-324-3259
poplarblufforganics.com

Rosemary Wotske. Photo by Matilde Sanchez-Turri.

Rosemary Wotske's farming philosophy mirrors her approach to life and is deeply rooted in the belief that "eating is one of the most important things we do each day...not sending people to the moon."

Wotske knew she was meant to be a farmer after visiting family friends at the age of 12. "My parents had to physically carry me to the car because I didn't want to leave their farm. That's when I knew." However, figuring out how to acquire the land and know-how took some time.

Wotske earned a degree in biochemistry from the University of Calgary and a master's in genetics from the University of Manitoba. She lived abroad and saved. When she returned to Alberta in 1985, she bought her farm near Strathmore.

Until 2002, Wotske grew every vegetable from asparagus to zucchini. She made jams, pickles, and other products to sell at farmers' markets. "I got burnt out growing and processing so many things, so I decided to focus on potatoes. Customers loved the taste of mine."

Poplar Bluff Organics now grows a wide variety of North America's favourite vegetable in many colours, flavours, and textures. Wotske says, "Every vegetable has terroir, not just (wine) grapes." Poplar Bluff is located in the middle of the Palliser Triangle, an area deemed unfit for most agriculture (desert-like conditions, low yields, and extremes in weather), but it couldn't be better for cultivating root vegetables. The long sunny days and cool nights are key to having sweet root vegetables, according to Wotske and her neighbour Cam Beard, who runs Carrots by Cam.

Beard grows heritage varieties of carrots, parsnips, beets, and turnips, following the same rigorous organic protocols as Wotske. The two partner in the business. Beard fixes and runs most of the machinery while Wotske markets his crop to her network of chefs and retailers. "Doing this makes me whole," says Wotske. If love of the land is part of terroir, then it's no wonder Poplar Bluff's vegetables taste so good.

Rafferty Farms | Okotoks | 403-710-5484 | raffertyfarms.ca

Left to right: Nick Hsu, James Rafferty, and Ben Hsu. Photo by Matilde Sanchez-Turri.

In 2015, after watching countless documentaries about how food is produced and distributed in North America, James Rafferty and Nick Hsu were fed up. Armed with the idea "to create innovative solutions for a better future," they founded their parent company, EarthisLtd. Despite their lack of training, they built a 1,200-square-foot modular aquaponics greenhouse on a relative's acreage near Okotoks. They called their new venture Rafferty Farms.

Overhauling North America's food system was never their plan. Instead, they set their sights on developing a more ethical and sustainable way to grow food locally, with the long-term goal of equipping others to do the same. "We're currently developing an aquaponics greenhouse kit that brings together all we've learned and know, to make it easier for people who want to produce their food like we did."

Aquaponics is an integrated system of plants, fish, and micro-organisms in a closed-loop production cycle. "Our greenhouse basically mimics a pond like you'd find in nature, except we grow basil instead of cattails." Since aquaponic systems are very sensitive to environmental changes, Rafferty, a former aircraft maintenance engineer, integrated solar panels, a wind turbine, and a rainwater collection system into the design so the greenhouse can operate off-grid.

They primarily grow heirloom Genovese basil along with quick crops like microgreens and wheat grass for distribution by wholesaler Galimax Trading Inc. (see page 250).

"We do not use herbicides, pesticides, synthetic fertilizers, or chemical nutrients. All of our plants are non-GMO varieties, grown from certified organic seed. To keep pests at bay, we use predatory insects such as ladybugs in the greenhouse...that's it. All the nutrients the basil needs to grow are naturally occurring."

To try Rafferty Farms' wildly flavourful basil and microgreens visit Sobeys in Okotoks, Sunnyside Natural Market in Calgary, or Urban Grocer (see page 252) in Lethbridge, or find them on menus of restaurants specializing in regional cuisine throughout Southern Alberta.

Note: There is no soil in their greenhouse, which means they don't currently qualify for organic certification, but all of their seeds are non-GMO and certified organic.

RedHat Co-operative Ltd. | 809 Broadway Avenue East, Redcliff
403-548-6208 | redhatco-op.com

RedHat Co-op has 50 families growing fresh produce.
Photo by Jeremy Pollock of Dreadnaught Digital.

The RedHat Co-op is located in Redcliff with some members in Medicine Hat, hence the name. For over 50 years, RedHat growers have supplied Albertans with fresh produce. It used to be shipped in from as far away as Mexico, California, and South America. Now, there are more greenhouses in this corridor than anywhere else in Canada because of the low price of natural gas and the fact that it is one of the sunniest places in the country.

Founded in 1966 by 10 independent greenhouse operators, the RedHat Co-op currently has 50 experienced growers (some fifth generation) and 160 acres of cultivated greenhouse space in their network. Forty acres of that is equipped with lights so they can grow produce year-round. Tomatoes, cucumbers, and peppers are the mainstays with specialty crops like eggplant, microgreens, and lettuce rounding out their offering. "The co-op is owned by the growers and their families. They are very passionate about what they grow. When you buy from RedHat you're buying from local, family-driven businesses, not a faceless entity," says Mike Meinhardt, who oversees sales and marketing for RedHat.

The RedHat grading, packing, and shipping facility is 98,000 square feet with a 40,000-square-foot cooler. "To maximize freshness, quality, and taste, we pick, pack, and ship our produce overnight to retailers across Western Canada."

The RedHat facility and co-op members are certified under the Canadian Horticultural Council's food safety program to ensure packers know and follow the same food safety practices. Water and energy conservation, using natural pest control, natural pollinators, and non-GMO seeds, and preventing food waste through their Misfits Program are all top priorities of RedHat Co-op's members.

If you buy tomatoes, cucumbers, or peppers in a large grocery store in Alberta, chances are pretty high you're eating produce grown by a member of the RedHat Co-op.

The Saskatoon Farm | 80181 338 Avenue East, De Winton | 403-938-6245
saskatoonfarm.com

Karen and Paul Hamer own and operate the Saskatoon Farm. Photo by Matilde Sanchez-Turri.

Paul Hamer's affinity for saskatoon berries started when he was a kid. "We'd pick saskatoons by the river and my mom made jam with them. One of my favourite memories was sneaking a jar of that jam and eating it all."

Now, Hamer has around 50 acres of saskatoons to feast on. He doesn't have to sneak them anymore. Instead he's created a thriving working farm that celebrates all things saskatoon. U-pickers delight in fresh berries from mid-July to mid-August. Hamer harvests them for use in the farm's famous bakery and café, which is open almost 365 days each year. Visitors will also find a general store stuffed full of fresh or frozen berries, pies, tarts, breads, syrups, and, of course, his beloved jam.

Hamer attended Olds College. He is one of the few people to specialize in the cultivation of prairie-hardy fruits. Such work can take as long as 20 years. Hamer has patented several saskatoons and a pear tree, and is working on sea buckthorn varieties. He has also helped popularize sour cherries in Alberta.

His time at Olds was fruitful in more ways than one. He earned his degree and met his wife, Karen. He's grateful for her can-do attitude and that he "met other people who thought in a similar way." Despite being horticulturists, neither Karen nor Paul had any real farming experience when they bought their land in 1987. Fortunately, that didn't stop them.

Their many offerings have taken years of investment, hard work, and vision but now, their children, Austin, Shawn, and Johanna, also work on the farm with them. They host weddings, stage community events, teach cooking classes, and have a nursery, garden centre, and market garden in summer. Some days, the Hamers wonder how they managed their success amidst all the red tape, permits, and bureaucracy. "We are proof that great things are possible if you ask 'Why not?,' work hard, persevere, and plant a lot of trees."

Back 40 Organics | 92032 Township Road 42, Etzikom | 403-666-2157

Three generations of the Ehnes family.
Photo by Matilde Sanchez-Turri.

Back 40 Organics, near Etzikom in the deep southwestern corner of the province, has been in the Ehnes family for over 100 years. "I love farming, especially that smell in the air after the first till in spring," says Bernie Ehnes.

In 1988, Bernie's parents gave him and his twin brother, Brian, each a quarter section. At an ag expo in Lethbridge "a mustard contractor told us about organic farming. We didn't know what it was, so we researched it." Within three years they converted all of their land and practices to certified organic.

In 1995, they built a custom seed cleaning plant so they could have complete transparency with their product from

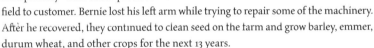

field to customer. Bernie lost his left arm while trying to repair some of the machinery. After he recovered, they continued to clean seed on the farm and grow barley, emmer, durum wheat, and other crops for the next 13 years.

In 2009, Sharon Rempel, the "Godmother of Red Fife wheat," reached out to see if they'd grow and help preserve the ancient grain. The brothers planted 15 bushels of her Faith Red Fife seed on 10 acres and harvested 260 bushels of wheat. The following year, Bernie lost his twin in a traffic accident, but continued planting the Red Fife. By 2011, he had a lot of it stored in bins and sought out buyers.

Now, Bernie is one of the main suppliers of Red Fife wheat to Vibrant Health, the parent company of One Degree Organics, Silver Hills Sprouted Bakery, and Northern Bakehouse. He uses only veganic farming practices, which means no animal-based fertilizers are used to grow his crops.

Instead, crop rotations and plow-downs of peas or clover help build a healthy soil. "There's been a steady increase in irreversible health issues from the overuse of chemicals. Knowing where your food comes from couldn't be more important."

Since 2013, Bernie has been passing on his knowledge of the land to his son Christopher who has joined him full-time.

Grainworks Organic Tillers & Millers | Vulcan | 1-800-563-3756
grainworks.com

*Dwayne and Doreen Smith.
Photo courtesy of Doreen Smith.*

Dwayne and Doreen Smith started Grainworks Organic Tillers & Millers on land that has been in Dwayne's family since 1912. Grainworks specializes in producing and distributing high-quality certified organic cereal grains, pulses, and oilseeds. They earned organic certification in 1988 in Canada and in the United States and Europe shortly after.

The Smiths were early adopters of organic farming in Alberta and continue to lead the way in producing quality food while caring for the planet. Farming, family, and environmental stewardship are inherently linked to the Smiths' commitment to grow their crops in harmony with nature. "We never forget that we are an integral part of the living earth."

They are transparent about their organic farming practices from "seed to spoon," and that starts with their soil. Using plow-downs, the Smiths seed sweet clover with their crops to fix nitrogen into the ground and choke out weeds. This technique is pivotal in producing nutritious food without using animal fertilizers, while promoting biodiversity and protecting watersheds. Crop rotation and crop diversity disrupt the life cycles of pests and weeds and help balance ecosystems and increase yields. The Smiths only plant seed without GMOs and grow all their crops without synthetic chemicals, municipal sewage, or exposure to ionizing radiation.

To preserve the organic integrity of their products from the ground up, Grainworks cleans, mills, processes, packages, and distributes over 130 products at their facility in Vulcan. They stone grind their grains, pulses, and seeds at low temperatures to preserve the valuable nutrients and produce flours rich in fibre, minerals, and vitamins. They do not put additives, blending agents, or preservatives into their milled products.

Murray Lambkin, general manager for the company, sums up Grainworks' market advantage. "For the last 50 years, there's been a steady rise in health issues that weren't as prevalent in the past. People want transparency. They want to know, not just believe, that their food was grown and handled in a healthy way through the whole process."

Heritage Harvest | Strathmore | 403-934-3457 | heritage-harvest.ca

Mark Gibeau in a field of Red Fife wheat.
Photo by Matilde Sanchez-Turri.

Mark Gibeau and Lorie Hedemark were professional glass-blowers for over 30 years. They showed and sold their work around the world but after the 9/11 terrorist attacks, their careers quickly came to an end. "The global economy shifted and it was extremely hard to sell anything abroad," says Gibeau. The couple "retired" and took up organic farming full-time.

They raise free-range chickens and turkeys, keep beehives, tend a massive organic garden, and have two small greenhouses full of heirloom tomatoes—for themselves. Commercially, they grow heritage grains on a quarter section and other small plots from Strathmore to Cluny including purple barley, emmer, and Red Fife wheat.

Heritage grains are more challenging to grow and produce smaller yields compared to modern varieties, but that doesn't bother Gibeau. From seed to table, he's in control of the product and focused on quality, not quantity. He loves growing tasty ingredients for other artisans—like Aviv Fried at Calgary's famous sourdough bakery Sidewalk Citizen (see page 156)—to create with. Gibeau sourced his Red Fife wheat seed from the Heritage Wheat Project.

Despite Red Fife wheat's exceptional flavour and desirable baking properties, it had not been grown commercially in Alberta for almost a century. In 1988, Jim Ternier, Dan Jason, and Sharon Rempel shared their saved seeds with their farmer friends and challenged them to grow it. If it weren't for the seed savers in the Heritage Wheat Project and farmers like Gibeau, we probably wouldn't be eating Red Fife wheat today.

Modern wheat is a hybrid derived from several varieties. The flour is not as tasty or as nutritious as those from heritage grains. Part of that has to do with how it's milled. Gibeau's company Heritage Harvest uses its own stone mill imported from Europe to provide customers with a traditional stone-ground product. More nutrition is preserved through the no-heat, slow, stone-to-stone milling process. "We grow our grains for their taste first and foremost. To get the best flavour we spend a lot of time and energy putting more nutrients back into the soil than we take out."

Highwood Crossing Foods | 403-652-1910 | highwoodcrossing.com

Penny and Tony Marshall by the Highwood River. Photo by Karen Anderson.

Standing at the kitchen sink window watching the Highwood River flow by, it's easy to understand why Tony Marshall's family chose this stretch of rich black soil atop the river's ever-curving banks as the place to settle 120 years ago. Tony and his wife Penny's turn to steward the land came when they married in 1981. Two daughters later, they began to question the use of chemical fertilizers and pesticides on the farm and the impact on their young family's health.

In 1989, they turned to farming practices much like the ones Tony's great-grandfather had employed by default. Instead of pesticides, they use crop rotation to control weeds and pests. Instead of chemical fertilizers, they grow legumes and then plow them under as "green manure" to fix nitrogen and increase the health of the organic matter in the soil. "You don't have to choose between local and organic with us—we've got both covered."

Though farming is a busy life, it was still only a part-time job for Tony until 1996. He was a custom clothing manufacturer and on a trip to Germany to sell the now highly sought after vintage Caravan cowboy shirts, he found a small-scale expeller machine that created cold-pressed edible oils from seeds. Tony came home with one and built a press house on the farm. The Marshalls added processing, marketing, and distributing to their role as producers. They began at the Millarville Farmers' Market and slowly gained restaurant business and space on grocery shelves.

On New Year's Eve in 1998, Tony had enjoyed such a great holiday with his family on the ranch, he decided he could not return to his city job. The couple put Penny's home economics degree to work to develop a wider product line, basing it on the wish list of their early customers. Along with their certified organic, non-GMO cold-pressed canola and flax oils, they make granola, hot breakfast cereals, baking mixes, specialty flours, and whole grains. The website has a gold mine of Penny's tried-and-true recipes.

Broek Pork Acres | Coalhurst | 403-381-4753 | broekporkacres.com

Allan and Joanne Vanden Broek.
Photo by Matilde Sanchez-Turri.

A fine mist sprays from a sprinkler while a few dozen black Berkshire pigs, in an array of sizes, take turns wallowing in the mud bath. Others rest on mounds of dirt nearby, curing their muddy bodies in the sun. Still more graze and root in the paddocks closer to the quiet country road.

Until 2005, Allan and Joanne Vanden Broek and their family had a conventional weaner pig operation and grain farm. Things changed when they decided to hold back some of their piglets that year and raise them for meat. After hearing about Berkshire hogs, a hardy heritage breed that could withstand Alberta's winters, Allan and Joanne were intrigued.

In January of 2007, they bought a couple and launched a "Berkshire pilot project" to learn more about raising them. Since 2009, they've focused exclusively on raising Berkshires because they keep their fat cap through winter, are good foragers, and do well outside, no matter the weather.

"From breeding to rearing to feeding and slaughter we are hands-on at every stage. This gives us control over the animals' quality of life and ensures our pigs are humanely treated, from start to finish." The Vanden Broeks' animals are free-range and have access to pasture, sunshine, and fresh water year-round. They don't receive antibiotics, artificial growth hormones, or feed that contains any animal by-products. "The more time we take to raise them, the better they do. There's no substitute for time with this breed. They're not meant for intensive commercial production."

The Vanden Broeks process their animals in their provincially inspected facility on the farm and sell fresh cuts, bacon, hams, sausages, and other specialty products. Meat from Berkshire pigs is darker and has more marbling than other varieties, and many find it more flavourful and juicy. With the animals being grass fed, it also has a healthier ratio of omega-3 to omega-6 essential fatty acids. Look for Broek Pork Acres products at their farm retail store and at fine restaurants and butcher shops.

Calico Farms | Blackie | 403-601-1613 | facebook.com/CalicoFarmsPoultry

Krista Ball at Hillhurst Sunnyside Farmers' Market. Photo by Karen Anderson.

Krista Ball is a fourth-generation farmer and owner of Calico Farms outside of Blackie. She comes by her love of chickens honestly. "My grandma raised 1,500 hens on this land and now I'm doing the same."

Ball has a bachelor of science in agriculture—animal sciences—from the University of Guelph. She specialized in poultry production and genetics. After earning her degree, she returned to the family farm to work with her parents, Grant and Sharon Cooke. With Cooke Livestock, they raised pedigreed Black Angus breeding stock and miniature donkeys.

Around 2006, the sale of their Black Angus bulls took off. When her parents started talking about retirement, Ball realized she couldn't manage the cattle operation on her own, so they sold all their stock in 2016. At that point, Ball wasn't sure what to do. "You can't be afraid of change if you're a farmer. You have to roll with it."

Back in 2013, Ball had bought 30 Barred Rock laying hens for her own use. She sold the excess eggs and got great feedback. "People really loved the taste of them so I thought, I'm going to increase my flock and give that a try."

Now, Ball has 300 ISA Brown laying hens, which is all she's permitted to have until she receives quota from the Egg Farmers of Alberta. "I manage the flock on my own and sell my eggs at farmers' markets and through YYC Growers and Distributors. It's gratifying. I can't imagine doing anything else." Ball works with a poultry nutritionist to ensure her hens have a rich, varied diet so they stay healthy and produce strong, flavourful eggs. She is passionate about educating her customers on her practices and the impact their support has on local producers.

"I am a farmer and my family is generations deep in the ag industry but most of my customers are so removed from farm life they don't understand how it all works. They get a skewed perspective from the news and documentaries. I help them fall in love with what we do. Our survival depends on it."

Deerview Meats | Irvine | 403-527-2221 | deerviewmeats.com

Chris and Perry Deering. Photo by Sheenism.

Walking into Deerview Meats' country retail store is heaven on earth for carnivores. The facility is owned and operated by Chris and Perry Deering and their family. Both grew up in the ag industry.

Chris was raised on an orchard in Ontario and Perry was a third-generation cattle rancher. After they married, the couple raised beef cattle but Perry had his heart set on starting a deer ranch. So, they sold their cattle herd and in 2004 opened Double D Ranch, the largest whitetail deer farm in Western Canada. "We raised them for meat and took them to an abattoir in Duchess for slaughter. Two local meat shops butchered and processed the meat for us." The Deerings sold their processed venison meat products to customers throughout Southern Alberta at the farm gate and through a few local retail locations.

Over time, the cost and difficulty of maintaining quality control and consistency of their products led the Deerings to research opening their own processing facility. By late 2009, they broke ground and were ready to open their doors in June 2010, when a flood hit. It took them months to rebuild, but they opened Deerview Meats—a 9,300-square-foot provincially inspected abattoir and meat processing facility—in February of 2011. With the facility in high-gear, they sold their deer herd to concentrate solely on processing.

Deerview harvests and processes locally raised meats such as beef, pork, lamb, bison, and venison in their facility and offer mobile processing services for ranchers looking to harvest for their own use. For hunters, they provide custom curing, cutting, and wrapping of game meats including deer, antelope, elk, and moose. They'll even make custom sausage, pepperoni, and jerky using their customers' family recipes.

In their retail store, they sell fresh cuts and frozen meats, from beef roasts and steaks to whole chickens, legs of lamb, and ground bison. They also sell an extensive variety of hot sauces as well as jerky, salami, pepperoni, and sausages. "We make 35 types of sausage in-house and they're all gluten-free with no added preservatives. We're known for our sausage and host an annual tasting event at the end of September every year so people can try all the different flavours."

Driview Farms | Fort Macleod | 403-553-2178 | driviewfarms.com

Gerrit and Janet Van Hierden.
Photo by Karen Anderson.

For over 40 years, Gerrit and Janet Van Hierden have been raising sheep on their family farm near Fort Macleod. "Farming is either in your blood or it isn't. With the hours farmers put in that they never get paid for, you really have to love it as much we do."

The Van Hierdens crossbreed Suffolk sheep for wool, meat production, and breeding stock. Their crossbreeding program improves meat quality, bone structure, and the resiliency of their flock. When asked why Driview Farms lamb tastes so good, Gerrit is quick to reply, "You are what you eat and drink."

Driview sheep eat a nutritionally balanced diet of homegrown hay, silage, and grain, but Gerrit says it's the natural spring water that the sheep have access to that makes the flavour of their meat so special. "The spring water is high in minerals, contains no bacteria, and is pure and clean. It creates a signature taste and people love it."

They harvest their lambs between five and six months of age when they are 120 pounds and use a provincially inspected facility close by. They do not use artificial hormones, steroids, or unnecessary antibiotics on their herd. You can order their lamb meat fresh or frozen, as well as merguez sausage, kebabs, or lamb burgers, online or at their booth at the Millarville Farmers' Market.

The Van Hierdens are happy they could raise their children in the country and grow their own food but are concerned the next generation won't be able to make a living farming. They've seen how much pressure the rate of commercialization in ag is putting on small operations. "We have seen native grassland and tame fields torn up for cereal crops because there's a better return. We're grateful for every one of our customers. We have some who save up to buy meat from us and we appreciate that loyalty and support."

Highwood Valley Ranch | High River | 403-601-3891
highwoodvalleyranch.com

Jaimie and Wade Nelson with daughter Jayden and son Tristan. Photo by Matilde Sanchez-Turri.

Jaimie and Wade Nelson are the fourth generation of Nelsons to run Highwood Valley Ranch (HVR) along the cottonwood-shaded banks of the Highwood River. Looking out at his pasture Wade says, "This land has never been tilled. It's exactly how God left it." But making his living at HVR wasn't a sure thing, so his mom, Jacqueline, encouraged him to leave and go to school.

Wade got a cooking diploma from the Southern Alberta Institute of Technology, an agriculture business diploma from Olds College, and then a business degree from the University of Lethbridge. An avid traveller, he spent a year in Australia and was travelling in Greece when he saw a man harvesting hay. "In that moment, I instantly got homesick."

When he returned to the farm, his mom's sale of homemade products at local farmers' markets inspired the idea to direct market their beef. They calculated that eliminating the middleman would allow a sustainable income without having to work off the farm.

The Nelsons invest 30 months to raise each cow for market, which can be up to a year longer than cattle raised conventionally. Once calves are weaned, they graze on native grasslands west of Longview at HVR's summer range. The herd winter on pasture near the ranch where they're supplemented with homegrown hay and free-choice oats. "Our forage and grain crops are grown without chemicals of any kind. Cattle in our 'feed program' never see a feedlot. They have oats available so we can offer beef year-round and a more consistent flavour." After slaughter, the animals are dry-aged for 21 days to allow for the connective tissues to break down. The result is tender, tasty meat. Animals needing treatment are removed from this program, so they sell only beef free of added hormones, antibiotics, and steroids to their client base.

"We care deeply for the land because we know they're not making more of it and we want our kids to have the chance to farm here too. It brings us a lot of pride to have grown up in this community and to be able to feed our family and our customers with our beef." Contact the Nelson family to purchase HVR beef or to arrange a tour of their ranch (they love visitors).

Mitchell Bros. Beef | Pincher Creek | 403-874-2719
mitchellbrosbeef.com

The Mitchell family (left to right): Kevin, Bennett, Ian, Bette, Phil, and Patrick. Photo by Karen Anderson.

Since the 1950s, three generations of the Mitchell family have called Flint Rock Ranch home. Nestled into the southern tip of the Porcupine Hills, the property is named after the creek that flows through it. Scanning the front porch vista, there are two bunkhouses (now comfortable Airbnb rental units) below a stand of jagged pines on the hill to the east and grazing cattle that dot an unobstructed view to the Oldman River a few miles straight south.

Phil and Bette Mitchell and their sons bought the original homestead of 1,000 acres from his parents, Lorne and Agnes, when the elder Mitchells were ready to leave the ranch in 2007. "We weren't prepared to lose it. At one point my father and uncles owned 11,000 acres here," says Phil.

While his parents had a conventional cattle operation where they sold their calves at auction, Phil and Bette and their sons have taken a different approach. Bette is a certified holistic nutritionist and the family have established holistic management practices to create a low-stress environment for their animals and the land. It's something they are all very passionate about.

"Our pasture is all native fescue grasslands. It has never been tilled and there are natural springs and shelterbelts all over the property. Our cattle graze on grass that hits their knees and we move them off it when it's down to their ankles. This ensures they're getting the maximum nutrition and there's no overgrazing," says Bette.

Their grass-finished beef is a seasonal product. They harvest in late summer and early fall. The cattle live a whole year longer than those finished on grain in feedlots. That extra year on the land takes lots of resources because the animals are not given any grains or oats. Just grass, as nature intended.

The Mitchells encourage visits to the ranch to see how they balance the health of the animal, consumer, and planet in equal measure. Check out the website to order beef or book your stay in one of their cozy on-site cabins.

Spragg's Meat Shop | 438 Centre Street, Rosemary | 403-378-3800
spraggsmeatshop.com

Greg and Bonnie Spragg on their farm in Rosemary.
Photo by Karen Anderson.

When Greg and Bonnie Spragg bought a rundown old dairy farm in Rosemary (population 342) with the idea of converting it to a conventional hog farm operation, they never dreamed their plan would literally be put out to pasture. "Greg is a pig whisperer. He's wonderful with these animals and always dreamed of having his own pig barn," says Bonnie. "We couldn't afford to do that so I bought him three little pigs for his birthday just for fun. We had to raise them on pasture and what we learned is that the pigs thrive this way."

While pigs in conventional barns spend their life in small pens and have their tails docked, the Spraggs' pigs are free to root, wallow, and play. Conventional hog farms have foul-smelling sloughs. Pastured pigs contribute to soil health. After those first three little piggies went to market, the next year they bought 50 pigs.

The Spraggs realized they needed to create their own demand and differentiate their product. Their experience with growing antibiotic- and hormone-free, pasture-raised animals fed protein-rich faba beans and non-sprayed grains gave them the confidence to begin a "birth-to-plate" operation.

They contract a farm to do their farrowing (nursing piglets stay with their sow until eight weeks) and raise the weaned pigs in groups of about 50 per pasture to maturity. They hire other farmers to grow feed, have an independent abattoir near Brooks for their slaughter needs, and their own processing facility. They now raise and process over 2,000 hogs a year.

In 2012, Bonnie was the recipient of the Farm Credit Canada Rosemary Davis Award, which honours women who are active leaders in Canadian agriculture. She won a trip to a women leaders' conference at Simmons College in Boston, Massachusetts. In 2017, the Spraggs won an environmental stewardship award for their farming and processing practices. They are now Alberta's largest free-range pork supplier and are changing the face of their industry. Check their website for retail locations.

Sweetgrass Bison | Foremost | 403-360-4572 | sweetgrassbison.ca

Cody Spencer. Photo by Matilde Sanchez-Turri.

After seeing portraits of North American plains bison in a coffee table book, Cody Spencer was intrigued by everything about them. Prior to European contact, there were between 30–60 million bison on our continent. By the end of the 19th century, only a few hundred remained.

History credits Samuel Walking Coyote with saving the North American plains bison from extinction. He came to Alberta to be with a Blackfoot woman. When he returned to his ranch south of Flathead Lake in Montana he gathered two male and two female calves from the Sweetgrass Hills in Alberta and started his own herd.

The more Spencer learned about bison and their 120,000-year history in Alberta, the more he wanted to know. He searched for a local ranch and through friends, in the fall of 2013, was invited to Rick MacKenzie's bison ranch near Foremost to help round up the herd. He was hooked. Before long, he was working on the ranch and on his own business plan.

Spencer started Sweetgrass Bison in 2014 and began by marketing local grass-fed bison meat direct to consumers. "I buy finished animals from Rick. I also bought 15 heifer calves from him to start my first herd. I am so appreciative of his help and guidance."

Spencer keeps his heifers with MacKenzie's on the ranch and uses holistic management practices to keep the grasslands and herd in top form. In 2015, he bought a bigger herd from a couple who wanted to get out of bison ranching, bringing his herd count to 60 animals.

Sweetgrass Bison produces and sells meat from animals that are free range and entirely grass fed. With native grasslands disappearing, managing and preserving the wild prairie that is left is a top priority for Spencer. "Bison ranching is an act of conservation, not just of a species but of an entire ecosystem. The intrinsic value of having bison on the land cannot be measured. They shape the land by the way they graze."

Order through the website or find the prime cuts, ground, jerky, and soup bones at Urban Grocer (see page 252) in Lethbridge.

Top Grass Cattle Co. | Drumheller | 1-888-856-5873 | topgrass.ca

Calvin Raessler. Photo courtesy of Top Grass Cattle Co.

Calvin Raessler grew up on a mixed farm near Delia at a time when hail, drought, and high interest rates spawned more than a few country music songs. In 1990, he moved to Calgary to work for a large multinational company. On weekends, he tended his herd of cattle grazing on rented pasture. Longing to have his own ranch, Raessler kept looking for land.

In 2004, he found a 1,300-acre parcel of wild prairie with 140 acres of cropland. He bought it. For the next few years he raised his cattle there, feeding them grass and grain, with no added hormones or antibiotics. He sold the beef to friends and family.

Having read studies from the United States and Australia about the benefits of grass fed beef, he began a pilot project in 2006. In 2009, he declined a promotion that involved a move to the United States and spent a year learning Canada's grass fed beef model instead. "I had the opportunity to pursue what I love and put all the knowledge I had on agriculture and marketing to use."

In 2012, Raessler launched Top Grass Cattle Co. His cattle are reared on some of the rarest land in Alberta, wild prairie. Top Grass offers certified free-range Alberta beef raised completely on grass. His cattle are never confined in a feedlot. They receive no hormones, steroids, or antibiotics, or grain or grass treated with pesticides or herbicides.

"We've lost 70 percent of our native grassland in North America and, with it, much of our wildlife and biodiversity." Raessler is trying to change that using a rotational grazing method that mimics the way wild bison grazed on the prairies. Every week, his herd is moved to a new paddock, so the grass they've grazed on can regenerate without stressing the environment. This method sequesters 1.2 tonnes of carbon dioxide per acre each year, which adds up to a lot of carbon going back into the ground where it belongs.

"I feel a sense of peace when I'm out walking with the herd and see them content. I love having that contact with nature."

Trail's End Beef | Nanton | 403-601-5467 | trailsendbeef.com

The Herbert family. Photo by Paula Fuchs.

Tyler and Rachel Herbert operate Trail's End Beef and are the fourth generation of Rachel's family to live on this historic ranch near Nanton. Rachel's great-great-grandfather Fred Ings ran cattle on the open range in 1881, starting OH Ranch near Longview. He moved to Nanton to start Trail's End and Midway Ranch in 1903. Both are still in the family.

In the early 2000s, Rachel's mom, Linda Loree, inherited part of the family ranch around the same time Rachel met and married Tyler Herbert, a working cowboy. Linda had tried raising conventional beef for one year, but was too distressed to continue. From then on, she decided to raise cattle entirely on grass and sell the meat direct to customers, instead of at auction.

In 2007, when Rachel finished her master's degree, they purchased their Parkland property, which had untouched native prairie grass pasture. There, they built the facilities to handle the calves in spring and keep the herd over winter with hay from her uncle's organic farm. In summer the herd grazes on native shortgrass and fescue in the Porcupine Hills.

With Tyler, they carried on the family tradition and raised cattle even though both Linda and Rachel had been vegetarians most of their lives. "We got into this very consciously and believe we're making a difference by ranching sustainably."

Linda passed in 2014, but her connection to the land, commitment to animal welfare, and love of family live on. The Herberts continue to raise their Angus cattle on 100 percent grass. They use low-stress animal-handling techniques and are Animal Welfare Approved. Their animals are not given growth hormones or subtherapeutic antibiotics. Their pasture is holistically managed without the use of chemical fertilizers, pesticides, or herbicides. They do bale and rotational grazing to restore and rest the land.

Demand for Trail's End grass-fed beef exceeds supply. "They spend every day of their lives in a familiar herd, drinking spring water with the comfort of poplar and willow groves for shelter and lots of fresh air and prime forage. This is exactly how it should be."

Winter's Turkeys | Dalemead | 403-936-5586 | wintersturkeys.ca

Laurel and Darrel Winter. Photo by Karen Anderson.

A visit to Winter's Turkeys usually ends with someone in tears—but not for reasons you might think. For several years, Matilde and I took Calgarians on pre-Thanksgiving "shop at the source" bus trips. Despite the fact that the Winter family were in the midst of "catching" turkeys to load them up for the trip to the processing facility, they graciously found a way to smoke a couple of turkeys for sandwiches and allow us to arrive with about 50 people for lunch.

Darrel Winter raises turkeys the same way his grandfather who started the farm in 1918 did. The birds get clean straw every day and their barns are open to sprawling south-facing yards where they can gobble in all their glory. They have constant access to fresh water and feed for the 17–20 weeks of their life while most commercial turkey farms feed for about 13 weeks. Winter's birds get to hang out a bit longer and they have a good life at what our guests dubbed "Winter's turkey spa."

Corrine Dahm, Darrel's wife of 44 years, grows an organic vegetable garden for the organic birds. Bronze Beauty heritage breeds, with their dramatic black and brown plumage, stand out and remind us of the wild turkey breeds that populated North American forests when the Pilgrims landed. That someone thought to give thanks for the bounty of the harvest season by including these plumped up and most meaty of woodland fowl is a joyful thing.

When our guests learned about the love and devoted care the Winters take in raising food for their table, someone would inevitably be overwhelmed to the point of tears. When Darrel saw the gratitude in our guest's eyes, he'd usually break down too. Our visits were always a bit of a cathartic love fest.

Now, Darrel and Corrine's daughter Laurel has returned to the farm as manager and she is the fourth generation on these 480 acres of prairie just a little east and south of Calgary. The Winters will produce about 25,000 birds to sell at the farm gate, at all 26 Calgary Co-op stores, and throughout Alberta at fine meat shops.

It's minus 20 Celsius the day I show up to take Darrel and Laurel's photo. The late-afternoon sun paints them in a warm golden hue. Maybe it's that or maybe it's a reflection off those bronze beauties softly gathering around them or the glow that comes from their love of what they do.

FARMERS' MARKETS

Check the website for current hours prior to your visit.

DRUMHELLER FARMERS' MARKET

Co-op Mall, 555 Highway 10 East | Saturdays 10:00 A.M.–3:00 P.M.,
May to October | 403-334-0477 or 403-436-0494 | facebook.com/pages/
Alberta-Approved-Drumheller-Farmers-Market/358563711013565

LETHBRIDGE FARMERS' MARKET

Downtown: 309 6 Street South | Wednesdays 10:00 A.M.–3:00 P.M., July to
September | 403-328-4491
Exhibition Park: 3401 Parkside Drive sw, West Pavilion | Saturdays 8:00 A.M.–
1:00 P.M., May to October | 403-328-4491 | exhibitionpark.ca/farmers-market

MEDICINE HAT FARMERS' MARKET

Cypress Centre, 2055 21 Avenue SE | Saturdays 9:00 A.M.–1:00 P.M., May to
October | 403-527-1234 | facebook.com/MedicineHatFarmersMarket

MEDICINE HAT MARKET AT MEDALTA

713 Medalta Ave SE | Thursdays, monthly from October to May and weekly from
June to August | 403-504-4653 | medalta.org/market

PINCHER CREEK PIONEER COUNTRY MARKET

Memorial Community Centre Arena Lobby, 867 Main Street | Fridays 11:00 A.M.–
2:00 P.M., June to October | 403-627-0830 | facebook.com/pioneercountrymarket

WATERING HOLES

Check the website for current hours prior to your visit.

CHINOOK ARCH MEADERY (SEE PAGE 241)

386087 16 Street West, RR1, Okotoks | 403-995-0830 | chinookhoney.com
⇒ Tours: Groups of fewer than 10 can drop in.
Favourite drink here: King Arthur's Dry.

COULEE BREW CO.

4085 2 Avenue South, Lethbridge | 403-394-2337 | couleebrew.co
⇒ Tours: By appointment.
Favourite beer here: Bears Hump Nut Brown goes well with a sunset.
All of the tables and many fixtures are made of repurposed farm machinery,
barnwood, and local railway ties.

EAU CLAIRE DISTILLERY (SEE PAGE 254)

113 Sunset Boulevard NW, Turner Valley | 403-933-5408 | eauclairedistillery.ca
⇒ Tours: Varies by season; check website for tour details.
Favourite drink here: Single Malt Whisky—the first to be released in Alberta.
Join the cask club to get notice of barrel releases.

FIELD STONE FRUIT WINES (SEE PAGE 255)

251073A Township Road 232, Strathmore | 403-934-2749 | fieldstonefruitwines.com
⇒ Tours: By appointment September to May. June 3 to August 27 on-site store is
  open 11:00 A.M.–5:00 P.M. for tastings.
Favourite drink here: Award-winning Raspberry Fruit Wine.

HELL'S BASEMENT BREWERY

102-552 18 Street SW, Medicine Hat | 403-487-0489 | hellsbasement.com
⇒ Tours: Check the website and book ahead.
Favourite beer here: All Hops for a Basement and Polly's Ale.

MEDICINE HAT BREWING CO.

1366 Brier Park Drive NW, Medicine Hat | 403-525-1260 | mhbrewco.ca
⇒ Tours: By request.
Favourite beer here: Brick and Mortar Porter, with chocolate, coffee, and caramel notes.

SPIRIT HILLS HONEY WINERY (SEE PAGE 256)

240183 2380 Drive West, Millarville | 403-933-3913 | spirithillswinery.com
⇒ Tours: Book online.
Favourite drink here: Alberta's Red and their award-winning Wild Rosy.

THEORETICALLY BREWING CO.

1263 2 Avenue South, Lethbridge | 403-715-5140 | theorybrew.ca

⇒ **Tours: By appointment.**

Favourite beer here: Study Buddy Hefeweizen or any seasonal brew.

The first brewery in Lethbridge, in business for over 25 years. Makes German-style beers.

Facing page: photo courtesy of Neil Zeller Photography

CONCLUSION

Though I am not a farmer, I was raised in a family that knew where every morsel of our food came from. My paternal grandfather was a fisherman, as was my father. My maternal grandfather was a professional gardener with an acre of vegetables that sustained his family. He never used a chemical—ever. I grew up with my father's organic vegetable gardens as my snack bowl. Uncles had dairy cows for milk and hogs that they fattened, slaughtered, and butchered on the farm. When local farmers came peddling their vegetables to our back door each fall, we filled our root cellar, knowing that this would in turn feed their families.

I had three generations of great cooks in my family. We gathered on Sundays to eat humble but homemade food at my great-grandparents' table. We cooked from scratch, baked, pickled, and preserved and took joy in sharing our modest bounty with each other.

I attribute my great health to my deep connections to eating and preparing food in this way. In my 20-plus-year career as a registered nurse and nurse practitioner, I observed that the further people got from healthfully grown and prepared food, the sicker humanity was becoming. When I retired from nursing, I dreamed of one day having the opportunity to help people connect with their food and the health of the land again. This book is the fruition of that dream and I'm grateful to have had this chance. But, there was so much more to the story than I even realized.

Facing page: photo courtesy of Edmonton Tourism

During the summer of 2017 while Matilde and I were researching this book, we learned a lot about farming and ranching in Alberta. The rural-urban gap narrowed for us as we toured the province to meet the people that work this land. We've recorded a lot of very encouraging stories here and are grateful to each and every person that allowed us into their lives.

Observant and inquisitive by nature, we would often ask our subjects not only about their agricultural practices but also about things we observed while travelling the province. We noticed many fields of perfect commodity crops with nary a weed to be found and we learned they are often sprayed with synthetic fertilizers and pesticides.

Synthetic fertilizers change the pH of the soil, halting critical microbial life. Microbial life is needed for plants to absorb nutrients, vitamins, and minerals via something known as the plant-microbial bridge. Organic or non-sprayed soils have trillions of microbes in each teaspoon of soil. The microbial life is there to work with the plants during photosynthesis to sequester carbon and release vitamins and nutrients into the roots of plants. Healthy soil leads to nutrient-dense, naturally disease-resistant plants.

Plants sprayed with synthetic fertilizers become weak because of the lack of access to nutrients in the soil. They are more easily affected by pests and therefore often need to be sprayed with pesticides like glyphosate (Roundup) and—as pests have become resistant to that substance—dicamba and the herbicide 2,4-D. The weeds die when sprayed with these chemicals. The crops are "okay" because they are often genetically modified plants with genes spliced into their seeds that allow them to survive being sprayed with these chemicals.

To me, it seems like the cycle of spraying synthetic chemicals on soil as either fertilizer or pesticides makes a junkie of the land and enslaves our farmers to the companies that sell these products. The farmers are just trying to make a living. The peer pressure they face is enormous. They are, after all, paid by the volume of crops they produce. It is so hard, doing what they do, who can blame them for wanting to make money to feed their families and stay on the land?

Chemical companies spend millions on marketing the possible increase in yields their products might help farmers attain. The yields might be real for a generation but knowing what those chemicals are really doing to the soils, I couldn't help asking as I travelled the province, then what? Depleted soils cause soil aggregates to break down. When that happens, water cannot infiltrate and the soil is more prone to erosion and runoff. Most of the world has no topsoil left. Will Alberta and Canada be next? How will we feed the world then?

In this book, we chose to focus on farmers who are building soil and regenerating the plant-microbial bridge. It's not enough to grow a large quantity of food; it is vital that quality—in the form of nutrients—is present in our food as well. Tim Hofer of Pine Haven Colony (see page 130) said it best: "If food producers got paid by the quantity and quality of nutrients in the food they produce, and not just on volume alone, farming would look very different."

We get the food system we vote for with each dollar we spend. More of us shopping locally and choosing to support farmers with regenerative practices will expedite the return of healthy soil and the future of life on the planet.

Organizations like Alberta Food Matters are working to secure healthy food for all Albertans. Grassroots organizations like the Food Water Wellness Foundation are finding fun ways to educate and involve Albertans in recreating how food is grown. The Young Agrarians are providing much-needed internship opportunities and community support for young farmers making their way back to the land. Technology and sites like farmon.com are making education more accessible so farmers can learn best practices in the comfort of their own homes, at their convenience. Technology is also producing new methodologies to grow food sustainably—like aquaponics and vertical food growing. Farmers' market sales have doubled in Canada and farm direct sales are also on the rise. Tourism is another vehicle to create value for Alberta's food producers.

When a pendulum swings, it goes to extremes on both sides before finally settling on middle ground. It is our hope that the pendulum that marks the treatment of soil will come to rest in a place where scientific breakthroughs in detecting and understanding the microbial life hidden within soil will change farming practices so that all life can be sustained on our planet for millennia to come.

If the plants we (and the animals we eat) consume are nutrient dense, they'll be better able to ward off diseases and so will we. The stronger we are, the stronger our nation and world will be. The next food revolution will be the realization that soil—literally the health of our earth—is all that matters.

This is a time for personal action. I believe we can create great transformation. Enjoy and support the food artisans in this book. When you choose them, you choose wisely.

May you and your family be blessed with the joy that comes from generations of connectivity to healthy food, soil, and life as I have been.

— *Karen Anderson*

ACKNOWLEDGEMENTS

Thank you to my dear friend Jennifer Cockrall-King for suggesting to Taryn Boyd at TouchWood Editions that I would be the perfect person to write this book. At first, it was meant to be a book about Southern Alberta food artisans only. I asked Taryn if Matilde could join me as my co-author so that we could write one cohesive and unifying story for Alberta. Thank you for agreeing, Taryn. And thank you, Matilde. I would never have tackled this project without you.

We are both truly grateful to the entire team at TouchWood. We thank Colin Parks for his magic with our photos and layout and Renée Layberry, our in-house editor, who made sense of this huge body of information. Also, thanks to Kate Kennedy for her "in-the-trenches" editing skills and enthusiasm, and to proofreader Meg Yamamoto— she's a star in our books. Thank you all for guiding us through this process and for your patience and compassion after Matilde was in a car accident driving home from one of her farm visits.

When we started this book, we did not really know how vast a project it would be. Alberta is big—really big. We both put thousands of kilometres on our cars but we loved every minute of the time we spent on the land, in bakeries, cafés, cheeseries, meat shops, and dairies.

We are indebted to the farmers who took time out of their busy lives to talk to us and host us. Some even let us stay overnight. Jerry Kitt in Goodfare—for as long as I live I'll never forget you greeting me at the door with a cold local draft beer and then cooking up huge slabs of bison over a wood fire. Ian Griebel and Dana Blume, thank you for putting me up for a night when you had a three-week-old infant and busy toddler to care for.

Thank you to my team at Alberta Food Tours Inc. for carrying more of the load than usual and for caring for me so well while I wrote this book. Callandra Caufield, my operations manager, has proven herself to be one of the most thoroughly competent human beings I know. She not only kept our business growing but also came up with a few of our Rocky Mountain farms and food artisans. Liane Faulder and Deborah Anzinger, thank you for giving me a home away from home in Edmonton, any time I needed one.

Thank you also to my nephew Bryn Smith who came out from Toronto to drive me around the province for a week in July. I know the people you met will forever transform you and I am happy we had that time of discovery together.

Thank you to our friends Paul Gremell, Alyssa Berry, Donna McElligott, and Pauli-Ann Carriere who lent their ears and eyes to the project.

Thank you to our friends in tourism who helped us access photos. Thank you to Neil Zeller of Neil Zeller Photography for so generously sharing so many of his stunning photos of this land with us. You chipped in thousands of words with your work, Neil, and we are forever your fans.

Thank you to my husband, Todd, and son, Cole. I know I was MIA in the summer of 2017 and most of that year, actually. Thank you for standing by. I'm looking forward to a lovely reunion with you and all of our friends.

I offer *Food Artisans of Alberta* as a loving tribute to my father, Reg Robicheau, who died just as we were finishing this manuscript. I'm grateful to have had a father who gardened almost until the day he died. He mentored and taught me respect for the earth and when the time came for me to grow my own gardens he got a shovel and helped whenever he was able. The insights from time spent growing my own food taught me to value our food producers even more than I already did. Thank you, Dad. I love you always. —Karen

*

I am exceedingly grateful to those already mentioned, but am especially thankful to Karen for this opportunity. Few know how hard she works and how much she poured into this manuscript when I was injured in a car accident at a critical point. Despite her increased workload on this project, she has been a tremendous support to me. Thank you for your loving, caring ways, my dear friend.

Thank you to my family, close friends and medical team who helped me recover, especially Dr. Sandy Macleod. A big thank you to Ashley Tyler for the photography pointers, my amazing sister-in-law Rose Sanchez and talented friend Darcy Sochoron for their photography skills and help on this project. Special thanks to my sidekick Polly and dear friends Jenni Neidhart, Chelsea Barlow, Christiaan van Blommenstein, Binh Tran, Matt Young, Sara Berry, Domenic Tudda, Megan Pangilinan, Rob Mackin, Robin Nellen, Gary Young, and Anders J. Svensson who were a tremendous help to me during my recovery and throughout the writing process.

This book has been written in honour of my mother, Vanda Sanchez-Turri. I think of her every day. Like most Italians, she was very passionate about her food. From the age of five, my brothers and I helped her cultivate several gardens and, in the fall, worked feverishly to help preserve our bounty. To this day, I am in awe of all she knew and taught us. I don't know how she knew what the soil needed just by running her hands through it, but she did. Thank you, Mama, for showing us how to take care of each other and the earth by growing our own food. By sowing seeds of wonder, respect, and gratitude you also made it possible for me to be a part of this project. *Il mio cuore e tuo. Ti amo.* —Matilde

*

Most of all, we thank all the Alberta food artisans we had the privilege to get to know. We did this for you in the hopes that new connections will be made and that people will appreciate what you do and how you do it. We also did this work for the missing generation of farmers. Wherever you are, we hope some of the great models of success we write about here might inspire you to farm again. We need you and we hope this book helps create value for what you do.

RECOMMENDED RESOURCES

BOOKS

Animal, Vegetable, Miracle: A Year of Food Life by Barbara Kingsolver (HarperCollins, 2007; 2017)

Food and the City: Urban Agriculture and the New Food Revolution by Jennifer Cockrall-King (Prometheus Books, 2012)

Foodshed: An Edible Alberta Alphabet by Dee Hobsbawn-Smith (TouchWood Editions, 2012)

The New Farm: Our Ten Years on the Front Lines of the Good Food Revolution by Brent Preston (Random House Canada, 2017)

The Practical Beekeeper: Beekeeping Naturally by Michael Bush (X-Star Publishing, 2012)

The Soil Will Save Us: How Scientists, Farmers, and Foodies Are Healing the Soil to Save the Planet by Kristin Ohlson (Rodale, 2014)

MAGAZINES

Avenue Magazine in Calgary and Edmonton—Watch for their annual Best Restaurants issues and Best Things to Eat issue as well.

City Palate—Since 1993 this magazine has helped shape Calgary's food scene.

Culinaire—This glossy magazine is available in Canmore, Calgary, and Edmonton. They are a key sponsor of the Alberta Beverage Awards.

The Tomato—Edmonton's Mary Bailey has had her finger on the pulse of the city's food scene for decades. Look for this free journal every other month at your favourite food businesses.

FOOD AND TRAVEL WEBSITES

albertaculinary.com—The Alberta Culinary Tourism Alliance was founded in 2012. It is a great resource for finding local producers and has begun to publish guides to regional food trails, craft beverages, and heritage buildings that offer food in the province. Check out its events calendar for a full listing of festivals and food happenings in the province.

albertafarmdays.com—Each August about 100 farms open their gates and invite Alberta to spend a day on their farm. Many host dinners and fun for the whole family.

albertafarmersmarket.com—We've listed our favourite markets in this book, but this is where to find the one closest to you.

albertafarmfresh.com—Home of the Alberta Farm Fresh Producers Association, it's a resource for its members who direct market and for their customers.

organicalberta.org—Your connection to organic growers and their events in the province.

travelalberta.com/ca/plan-your-trip/vacation-guides—Everything you need to know about planning a trip to or in Alberta. We've planned our regions to coincide closely with Travel Alberta's so that you might visit some of the great food artisans as you explore Alberta.

FARMING AND FOOD EDUCATION WEBSITES

amazingcarbon.com—Dr. Christine Jones's website disseminates breakthroughs in the science of soil and regenerative farming.

brownsranch.us—Surrounded by conventional agriculture, Gabe Brown is outproducing his neighbours with his regenerative soil-building methodologies.

ecofarmingdaily.com—Daily releases from *Acres U.S.A.* magazine, which is the world's leading forum on sustainable farming methods.

farmon.com—Sharing best practices in farming and ranching through videos and workshops.

foodsecurityalberta.org—Also known as Alberta Food Matters, this group works to create leadership, relationships, and actions to reconnect people, land, and food in Alberta, and to secure healthy food for all.

foodwaterwellness.org—Advancing the practice of regenerative agriculture.

holisticmanagement.ca—Empowering farmers and ranchers to make socially, ecologically, and financially sound decisions. Some of the most successful food artisans in this book are using these principles.

polyfacefarms.com—Joel Salatin, the world's most famous farmer, has a goal: "To develop environmentally, economically, and emotionally enhancing agricultural prototypes and facilitate their duplication throughout the world." He's always worth listening to.

slowfood.com—Since 1986, founder Carlo Petrini has led the charge to increase biodiversity, preserve heritage food skills, and bring back the joy in food by connecting us to local sustainable sources of food and enjoyment of it. Alberta has Slow Food convivia in Edmonton and Calgary and both organizations have sent dozens of farmers, ranchers, and chefs to the Terra Madre conference in Italy.

spinfarming.com—Wally Satzewich is a Saskatoon market gardener who along with Roxanne Christensen founded SPIN, or Small Plot INtensive farming, "to make agriculture accessible to anyone, anywhere."

youngagrarians.org—Resources and community for the next generation of farmers in Canada.

A QUINTESSENTIAL ALBERTA MENU

Alberta has seven signature foods, designated by the Alberta Culinary Tourism Alliance in 2015. They are: beef, bison, canola, honey, Red Fife wheat, root vegetables, and saskatoon berries. The menu that follows features all of these inspiring ingredients. We hope you'll enjoy making it for family or visitors, so they're left with an unforgettable taste of this place.

All-Star Alberta Appetizer Platter
PAGE 304

....

FOR SUMMER
Garden Greens with an Alberta Vinaigrette & Cedar-Planked Prime Rib Roast of Alberta Beef
PAGE 305

FOR WINTER
Roasted Root Vegetables & Alberta Bison Slow-Cooked with Silk Road Spicing
PAGE 307

....

Saskatoon Berry Squares
PAGE 309

Facing page: photo courtesy of Edmonton Tourism.

All-Star Alberta Appetizer Platter

Welcome your guests with a platter of Alberta charcuterie and cheeses. Choose Valbella Gourmet Foods' smoked bison slices, elk salami, and wild boar pâté, Sylvan Star Grizzly Gouda, assorted pickled vegetables from Innisfail Growers, Fairwinds Farm soft herbed chèvre, Fuge Fine Meat's Lazarenko Kielbasa, Chinook Honey's honeycomb, and some fresh baguettes from bakeries like Boulangerie Bonjour or Bon Ton Bakery in Edmonton or Sidewalk Citizen in Calgary. Or make your own crackers with the recipe that follows.

RED FIFE SEED CRACKERS

ADAPTED FROM *CANADIAN FAMILY* MAGAZINE

Time: 50 minutes
Yield: 30 large crackers

¾ cup Red Fife flour
¾ cup semolina flour
½ teaspoon salt
½ cup warm water
3 Tablespoons canola oil
1 egg white
Black poppy seeds, sesame seeds, pepper, and salt

Mix the flours, salt, water, and oil and then knead them together on a floured surface for about 5 minutes. Cover with oiled plastic wrap and let rest for 30–40 minutes.

Preheat the oven to 450°F.

Cut the dough into 8 even portions and roll them out one at a time to a 1/8-inch thickness.

Brush each piece of dough with egg white and sprinkle them with seeds, pepper, and salt.

Bake on a baking sheet for 7 minutes or until golden brown. Cool on a wire rack.

For Summer

GARDEN GREENS WITH AN ALBERTA VINAIGRETTE

Time: 5 minutes
Yield: 2 portions—may be multiplied as needed

Pinch salt
1 Tablespoon vinegar (champagne, apple cider, or rice wine)
1 teaspoon Alberta honey
1 teaspoon Alberta mustard—grainy or paste
3 Tablespoons organic Alberta canola oil
Pepper to taste
2–3 cups washed and dried mesclun greens, butter lettuce leaves or other lettuce
1 cup chopped cucumbers, tomatoes, and peppers

Dissolve the salt in the vinegar in a medium bowl.

Add the honey and mustard to the bowl and whisk it to a smooth paste.

Drizzle the canola oil in slowly while still whisking.

Taste the dressing and season with pepper. Add more salt if necessary.

Pour the dressing onto mesclun greens or butter lettuce leaves in another bowl and using your hands gradually toss them to coat evenly with the dressing.

Arrange the lettuce on a plate and top with the chopped cucumbers, tomatoes, and peppers.

Dressing variations: To make an herb dressing add a Tablespoon of mixed chopped herbs like dill, parsley, tarragon, mint, basil, chives, or chervil.

CEDAR-PLANKED PRIME RIB ROAST OF ALBERTA BEEF

Time: 3 hours (including resting before and after cooking)
Yield: 8 servings

An instant-read meat thermometer guarantees you'll get this right. And, when using the cedar plank, you may need to turn it halfway through cooking so that the roast cooks evenly.

For the roast

1–5 lbs prime rib roast with bones attached
1 large cedar plank, soaked overnight in water
4–5 (5-inch) whole rosemary branches

For the coating

½ cup grainy mustard (Brassica Mustard)
1 Tablespoon canola oil
1 Tablespoon finely diced shallots
1 teaspoon finely cut fresh rosemary
1 teaspoon finely cut fresh dill
1 teaspoon minced garlic
1 teaspoon freshly ground black pepper
½ teaspoon coarsely ground salt

Remove the roast from the refrigerator and bring it to room temperature (this takes about an hour and results in more even cooking).

Preheat your gas grill on medium-high until the temperature is about 500°F.

Remove the cedar plank from the water and pat it dry with a cloth.

Lay the rosemary branches across the cedar plank and set the roast on them.

Mix the coating ingredients in a bowl and then apply mixture to the surface of the roast.

Place the plank on one side of your gas grill and turn the burner off on that side. Cook the roast with the indirect heat of the other burner for about 1½–2 hours or until the internal temperature reads 125–135°F.

Remove the roast and place on a rack. Tent it loosely with foil and let it rest for 20–30 minutes before carving.

For Winter

ROASTED ROOT VEGETABLES

Time: 60 minutes
Yield: 8 servings

You'll get the best results by using parchment paper with your baking sheets.

2 lbs rainbow carrots, peeled and cut on the diagonal in 2-inch segments
2 lbs parsnips, peeled and cut on the diagonal in 2-inch segments
2 lbs fingerling potatoes, washed, dried, and cut in half lengthwise
½ lb red shallots, peeled and cut in quarters
2–3 Tablespoons olive oil
2–3 Tablespoons birch syrup (can substitute maple syrup)
1 Tablespoon chopped rosemary
1 Tablespoon chopped sage
Salt and pepper to taste

Spread the vegetables on one or two parchment paper-lined baking sheets and drizzle them with the olive oil.

Bake at 375°F for 45 minutes or until golden brown.

Drizzle with the birch syrup and sprinkle with the herbs and salt and pepper before serving.

ALBERTA BISON SLOW-COOKED WITH SILK ROAD SPICING

Time: 8 hours on slow cooker low setting
Yield: 6–8 servings

This recipe makes good use of a slow cooker.

2–3 Tablespoons olive oil
3½–4 lbs bison round or cross rib roast
1 finely chopped onion
2 finely chopped celery ribs
3 finely chopped carrots
2 cups mushrooms, stemmed and cut in half
4 cloves finely chopped garlic
1 teaspoon ground cinnamon
½ teaspoon ground cloves
½ teaspoon ground allspice
1 flower of star anise

1 teaspoon freshly ground black pepper
2 cups bold red wine (Cabernet, Merlot, Malbec, Zinfandel)
1 (28 ounce/796 mL) can diced tomatoes
Salt and pepper to taste
1 Tablespoon chopped parsley

Heat a large frying pan over medium heat and add the oil.

Add the meat and cook, turning until all sides are browned, for about 10–15 minutes.

Transfer the meat to a slow cooker.

Add the onions, carrots, celery, and mushrooms to the frying pan and cook until lightly browned (you may need a bit more olive oil).

Add the garlic and cook until fragrant, then add the cinnamon, cloves, allspice, star anise, and pepper and stir to distribute evenly.

Pour the red wine into the pan, stirring until all the brown bits on the bottom come loose (this is known as deglazing the pan—it's how you get ALL the flavour).

Add the tomatoes and bring to a boil, then transfer the liquids from the fry pan over the meat in the slow cooker.

Refrigerate overnight at this point or begin cooking on low for about 8 hours.

Season with salt and pepper to taste once the meat falls apart easily when tested with a fork.

Transfer to a serving dish and sprinkle with parsley.

Serve over polenta, mashed potatoes or roasted root vegetables.

Saskatoon Berry Squares

Time: 40 minutes
Yield: 24 slices

2 cups flour
Pinch of salt
½ cup sugar
½ cup butter
2 cups (fresh or frozen) saskatoon berries
1 cup sugar
1 Tablespoon flour
2 eggs (beaten)
2 Tablespoons melted butter
1 cup unsweetened, shredded coconut

Mix the 2 cups of flour, salt, ½ cup sugar, and butter together. Spread the mixture evenly in the bottom of a 13 × 9-inch pan, pressing down to form a crust.

Cover the crust with the saskatoon berries, arranging them in a single layer.

Mix the remaining cup of sugar, 1 Tablespoon of flour, eggs, butter, and coconut and pour over the berries and crust.

Bake at 350°F for 30 minutes or until golden brown.

Let cool, cut, and serve with vanilla, honey ripple or saskatoon berry ice cream.

INDEX

Karen Anderson is a Taste Canada award-winning cookbook author and owner of Alberta Food Tours, Inc. Having grown up in St. Andrews-by-the-Sea, New Brunswick, she admits she didn't feel at home in Alberta until she spent time on its farms with the wind blowing waves into the wheat fields and an endless sea of blue sky overhead. When not writing or leading tours, she loves to hike, and she is on a mission to stay at a different Alberta backcountry lodge each summer. *Photo by Danielle Paetz.*

Matilde Sanchez-Turri was born in Calgary and was raised in Southern Alberta in Claresholm and on a farm near Nanton. With parents from Italy and Spain, Tilly's cultural identity is entwined with good food, and she loves to cook and bake fine Italian delicacies from recipes passed on to her by her mother. She also indulges her love of all things culinary by working for Alberta Food Tours, Inc. *Photo by Danielle Paetz.*